D1712294

This Is Home Now

This Is Home Now

FLOYD A. ROBINSON

The Iowa State University Press

A M E S,   I O W A

Composed and printed by
The Iowa State University Press
Ames, Iowa 50010

First edition, 1983

Library of Congress Cataloging in Publication Data

Robinson, Floyd A., 1909–
   This is home now.

   1. Farm life—Middle West—History—20th century. I. Title.
S521.5.M53R6   1983   977.7′009734   82-25524
ISBN 0-8138-1776-5

THIS STORY is dedicated to the men who farmed the Midwest during the second and third decades of the twentieth century, to their wives and children who helped them shape their destiny and shared in it with them, and to their patient servant, the horse.

CONTENTS

Preface

IN 1969 I visited an old acquaintance in the community where I had lived as a youth. As we discussed the farm life of our younger days my friend told how he had been amused while watching his high school-aged son attempt to harness and hitch up a team of horses. When he and I were young, any farm boy of twelve could do this. But his son, then in his upper teens, spent the better part of an hour in trial and error, with no help from his father, doing it.

I then realized that children and grandchildren of yesterday's farmers may have little understanding of how their immediate forebears had lived. It seemed to me that while we explore and dig to understand bygone civilizations we should also record what is known of our immediate past. After this decision I set about to write some of this down for posterity.

I used our family and our immediate friends and neighbors as the cast and the localities where we lived as the setting, though these all bear fictitious names here. For the most part, I have avoided the use of events that were personal to the family or to which families today would react in a like manner. If the event did not have historical value for that time I gave it limited emphasis or did not use it.

The story is not intended as a memoir but is presented as an accurate account of typical farm life in the Midwest during the second and third decades of the twentieth century.

I want to thank the following people who helped bring this book to publication: my wife Elizabeth, an able, critical, and patient partner in proofreading and editing; Mrs. J. Miles Acker for her enthusiasm about the story and for her invaluable aid in typing and retyping during the editing; Ms. Gail Brooks for producing the final typed copy; Edwin Varo,

Henry Christians, Sr., and Sam Barber for explanations about the operation of some of the machines described; William Davids, who became interested in the story at the right time and helped bring it to publication; and to many other people who read all or part of the manuscript and urged me to complete the project.

Introduction

A T the beginning of World War I there was little mechanical power on the farm in midwestern United States. Almost no farmers had electricity. The few steam tractors then seen served primarily as power for threshing and shelling corn. Occasionally one saw an internal combustion farm tractor, which was used for plowing. Almost every bit of farm fieldwork was done by horses, a few mules, and by human muscle.

Water was pumped by a windmill or a small-horsepower gasoline engine. Automobiles were becoming popular, but almost never was a truck seen as a part of the farm equipment. Farm hauling was done by team and wagon.

Gasoline was inferior by present standards and the ignition systems of internal combustion engines were unsophisticated, so these machines were hard to start and needed frequent repairs. The usefulness of this sort of power was further limited by the fact that the average farmer had little knowledge of this piece of equipment.

Following World War I, improved types of automobiles and tractors came onto the market. This prompted better fuels, improved highways, and other improved types of farm equipment. By 1925 the farm was becoming more power centered.

This Is Home Now

Home in a New Land

JEAN HARPER awoke with a start. Beside her, her husband, tense and quivering, muttered incoherently. In his terror he partially understood that the scene unfolding before him was a dream. But so vivid was it that he tried to shout, only to have the words choke in his throat.

"Tom!" Jean shouted. "Tom, wake up! Wake up, Tom! You're all right!" She shook him sharply.

His body slowly relaxed. He sat up in bed. "Oh!" he said. "Oh. Oh. I thought — I thought —"

"You're all right, Tom. Remember? That's all past now. You won't ever have to go down in that mine again. You had another bad dream, that's all."

Tom rubbed the top of his head slowly, then in the dimness of the moonlit bedroom he stared at his fingers.

Gently Jean ran her hand across the top of his head, feeling the old scar. Softly, she patted it. "See, it don't hurt an' it's not bleedin'."

"I could hear 'em yellin' that the cable'd broke. I could feel the wind whistlin' out through the door. I knowed the cage was fallin' an' I tried to get out, but I couldn't move. I knowed the cage was fallin' an' there I was reachin' into the sump to get my dinner bucket an' I couldn't move. I couldn't get out of the way."

It had happened eight years before and the nightmares had recurred ever since. Sometimes it would be his brother Ed, with a big slab of slate across his throat gradually shutting off his wind, while Tom and Hank Thompson crawled in beside him to pry it up enough so that he could breathe. Sometimes it was Elmer Offitt, with his leg broken by a falling rock, trying to drag himself away before more rocks fell. It was terribly real until he woke up.

Tom Harper and his wife Jean had been married in 1900.

3

Raised on small farms in the coal mining area of Indiana, they had spent their first married years on a farm, with Tom working as a miner. Short of stature, standing less than five feet six inches, he was well built for mining. His body was thick and his limbs were short and strong. His round head was set on a short, thick neck and his pleasant face was full and sober. There were few miners who could turn out their daily quota of coal more quickly than he.

Jean was a slender woman, taller than Tom. Her long neck and slim body made her look taller than she was. Gentle with the children and a good cook, she had proven to be a good farm wife. Their life was congenial, but they did find one decision hard to make. Every time a man was injured or killed in the mine, she insisted that they must plan for the day when he would no longer work there. But because they needed the money, they had put off the final reckoning until the summer of 1912, when another man was killed, leaving a wife and two children. Tom quit the mine at the next payday.

The Harpers with their five children arrived in northwestern Iowa in February of 1913. They moved into a small house near the farm where Tom's sister Marie and her husband lived, and the children enrolled in the nearby rural school. By mid-March the snow was mostly gone. From the back door a strip of ice snaked its way past the privy back to the barn. This was all that was left of the path that a few weeks before had cut through deep drifts across the backyard. In the front yard the ground had begun to dry, but back toward the barn several puddles and a small pond still survived the sun's effort to make spring a reality.

Early one Saturday morning Eddie came puffing in with a bucket of water from the well.

"What are you so out of breath about?" questioned Jean.

"I been slidin' on the ice by the barn. Boy is that ice slick! Hey, you kids, after breakfast le's go slidin' on the ice. Boy, it's fun! Can we go slidin' on the ice, Pop?"

Tom consented, but he cautioned that it was a warm morning and would thaw fast. If they got their feet wet they'd come down with colds.

After breakfast the children went shrieking out of the

4

back door toward the pond. Tom picked his teeth as Jean began to do the dishes. She was glad it was warm enough so the children could play outside. It seemed as if they had been underfoot for an eternity in the small house.

After a bit, when Tom was preparing to go to Hank's place to milk, he called Eddie to go with him to bring back the milk. As they approached the barn, Hank emerged with a pail of milk to announce that one of Tom's cows had had a calf. Together they entered the barn. The calf stood spraddle legged near its mother, moving uncertainly with wobbly steps. It was a nice heifer calf all right.

"Well, old gal," Tom said, patting the cow on the hip, "you couldn't have done better by us. Looks like you might give a gallon and a half of milk when you get goin' good."

"You goin' to milk her now, Pop?" asked Eddie. "I don't know whether I can carry all that milk home without sloshin' some out."

Tom explained that they could not use milk from the cow for ten days, and anyhow, the calf would need most of it for some time. When Eddie inquired why they couldn't use the milk for ten days, Tom could not answer this question. He had heard that some people did use the milk from a cow that had just calved, but he guessed it had something in it that was just right for calves but maybe not for people.

Jean was finishing the breakfast dishes as she saw Eddie streaking past the window toward the pond where the others were playing. There he proudly announced the arrival of the new calf. He assured them that it could stand up but that it wobbled a lot.

At about this time Marie arrived carrying a crock of butter. She had churned the night before and was bringing some of it to Jean. Marie reported that Hank wanted her to go to town on Monday. He needed some chain for the oats seeder and she had cream and eggs to sell. She invited Jean to go along.

SPRING THAW

At a little after twelve the two women set out for town, driving Tom's team to the buggy. Tom thought it would be all

5

right to trot the horses wherever they could, but the road was muddy and it did not look much like trotting so far as the women could see. They turned out of the driveway and started along the road toward the schoolhouse.

"I don't remember seein' mud quite so bad," said Marie. "It sure is a warm day. I bet we're goin' to see some mudholes before we get to Deep Creek."

When they crossed the dredge ditch the water was almost up to the bottom of the bridge because of the melting snow. Marie was right; there was hardly a dry spot on the road in the five and a half miles to town. In places the water was across the road so that the horses waded up to their knees. The buggy pulled easily where there was water to wash the wheels clean. At times, however, they sank almost up to the axles in the mire as if there was no bottom to the road.

Main Street was a morass of water and mud. Teams hitched to wagons or buggies moved slowly up and down its three-block length. Mud clung to the wheels, making them heavy and cumbersome. The horses sank halfway to their knees at each step and their feet made sucking noises as they extracted them from the mire. A pipe attached to a row of posts offered a place to tie the team. Together the women carried the cream pail into the cream station.

"Well, Mrs. Bristow," said the man as he took samples for testing the butterfat of the cream, "looks like a real muddy spring day. Everybody that's been in today says the bottom went right out of the frost last night. It'll be bad for a week or two, then it'll begin to dry up. Takes a while for the water to drain away from this flat land."

They took the cream check to the store, where they cashed it. The clerk counted the eggs and wrote a credit slip. They got their groceries, completed some other errands, and started for home. It had been a short stop in town, and both women would have liked to have had more time to shop. But coming into town had been slow and they knew it might be slower going home.

All went well for a time; then the mud began to ball up on the wheels and as they came into a low spot the going became more difficult. The horses strained in the harness until with a snap the evener (doubletree) broke. In desperation they looked at each other. At length Marie got out and strug-

6

gling through mud made her way to the sod by the roadside. "I see a man in the barnyard near that house. I'm goin' to see if he can help us," she said. Presently she returned, accompanied by a man with steel eveners and a spade.

"Hi!" he said. "I'm Tim Crosby. Looks like you're in a bad fix here."

"Yeh, I'll say we're in a bad fix," said Jean. "I never lived in this country before an' I sure never seen anything like this where I come from."

Mr. Crosby agreed. His gum boots sank deep into the mud as he made repairs. With the spade he dug the mud from the wheels and poked it out from between the spokes; then they continued on their way. After two more miles they reached the corner where they would turn.

"Only a little over a mile an' we'll be home, that is, if the water's not over the bridge by now," commented Marie.

Jean scanned the landscape. "That looks like a church steeple back that way. Is there a church over there?" she inquired.

"Yeh, I been aimin' to tell you. There's a Methodist church a mile up the road. Thought you might want to go. It's a real friendly church, they say."

"Well, without a carriage we couldn't all very well get there, but the kids could walk, I guess. Do they have Sunday school?"

It was late when they drove into the barnyard. Hank and Tom came out from the barn as the children raced from the house to greet their mothers.

"If there's any more goin' to town with roads like this, you men are goin' to be the ones to do it," stated Jean. "The roads are terrible. You ain't goin' to get us out there breakin' the doubletree an' wadin' the horses an' ourselves through water unless you at least go along."

Hank slapped his thigh. "Found some mudholes, did ya? Yow, I figured it'd be sticky. Bottom went right out 'er last night, I guess. Well, it'll be wet for another week or two, then it'll dry off."

Sunday school was out at three o'clock in the afternoon. When the children had not reached home by four, Tom walked out to the road to look for them. Presently he returned, driving the calf that had been eating grass along the fence. "Little rascal's growin', ain't she?"

"That's what we expected her to do, I guess," said Jean. "See anything of the kids?"

"Not a kid on the road so far as I could see. Did look like there was a car comin' way up there towards the schoolhouse, though."

"Who in the world would be way out here on these roads on a Sunday afternoon with a car?" asked Jean. "Bet there's still a mudhole up there by Schultz's where the ice was on the road so long. But I do believe I see a car comin'. Now, who in the world would that be?"

And it was a car. When still a distance away, someone stood up and began to wave. In disbelief they recognized Eddie, Bill, and Jane in the back seat. At the opening in the fence the car turned through the shallow ditch into the yard. By this time, all of the children were waving and screaming at the tops of their voices. "Hey, Mom! Hey, Pop! We came home in a car! We came home in a Buick!"

Behind the wheel, a slightly built graying man smiled as he opened the door. "I'm Jim Hammond," he said. "This is my wife, Edith."

"Howdie," said Tom putting out his hand. "I'm Tom Harper and this is my wife, Jean. Glad to meet you. Where did you pick up the kids?"

Mrs. Hammond explained that when the children had continued coming to Sunday school alone, she and Jim decided they would drive out after church some Sunday and get acquainted. Mrs. Hammond was not fat nor was she thin. She was of strong stature but carried it well. Her face was ruddy in a pleasant way. She had a full bosom and strong arms. In fact, everything about her reflected the feeling that she was able to cope with life and had done it well. She laughed often, gentle and easy from down in her chest, which made you feel that if things were not quite right just now they would be soon.

"From the looks of the wheels, I'd say you found mud somewhere," commented Tom. "Surprised that you got through up by the widow Schultz's."

"Yeh. Pretty bad down by the school house, too. Thought for a while we might have to walk it from there."

"You got a real nice family, Mrs. Harper. How many children have you?" asked Mrs. Hammond.

"Well, there's five."

"We have eight. The four oldest ones are through high school now. Seems like they grow up so fast." The women went inside.

"I think your boy said you was workin' with Hank Bristow. I suppose you have this piece of land here where the house is?" asked Mr. Hammond.

"Yeh, Hank's my brother-in-law. He rented this place, but it was more'n he could handle alone and he didn't want to hire no man. I was a coal miner an' farmer in Indiana. Land there's poor, an' we'd been wantin' to get away from there for two, three year. Hank suggested I take this eighty an' he take the quarter across the road. He's a little short on horses an' I ain't got no machinery, so we'll work together. My woman's been pushin' me to look for a bigger farm, though. This house is too small for us, really, an' it looks to me like it's pretty flat an' wet here. I think she's right about movin'. How do you go about locatin' another place to rent?"

Jim smiled. He explained that this part of the country was known as the flats, and that Tom had picked about the flattest part of it. He didn't know of a place to rent, but some of the men at the church would likely hear of one sooner or later. He hoped Tom and Jean could come to church. Tom agreed. They missed church, but without a carriage it would be difficult for them to go.

"Now I have an idea about a carriage," said Jim. "See here. Before I got the car I bought a new carriage. Then we got the car last summer, so even the new carriage don't get much use except in the winter. An' the old carriage, which is really in pretty good shape, just sits in the corncrib. Now we got three, four old buggies an' carriages rottin' out in the grove an' I know this one is goin' out there, too, pretty soon. We ain't goin' to use it. Tell you what. If you want to come an' get it, you can have it. Several years of good use in it yet."

9

"How about me buyin' it from you?" countered Tom. So, it was agreed that Tom would take the carriage and pay for it when he could. Jim thought two dollars would be a reasonable price.

In half an hour the women came out from the house.

"Jim," called Mrs. Hammond. "Maybe we better be goin'. If we have to get a horse to pull us through the mudhole at Schultz's, we'll be late for supper. Besides, the kids'll be worried about us."

"How about lettin' me twist her tail?" asked Tom, approaching the front of the car.

Jim adjusted the choke and retarded the spark so that the engine would not kick. If the motor kicked it went backward and would sometimes dislocate the wrist of the person cranking it, or even break his arm.

Tom took his stance in front of the radiator, pressed the crank into place, then with an upward lurch lifted the crank. Nothing happened. He tried again, still with no response. A third time, but still it did not start. He smiled at Jim. "Shall I go get the horse now?"

After a few more turns the motor fired and began to hum. Jim eased the spark into the operating position, moved the gas throttle up and down, and put it into gear.

"Thanks for bringin' the children," shouted Jean.

"Glad you came," called Tom.

"Now you come and get the carriage," reminded Jim in parting.

At half past one the next Sunday afternoon the Harpers arrived at Fairhaven Church. Two teams hitched to carriages already stood at the long hitching rack with its high wooden windbreak. As Tom and Jean approached the front door of the church a couple emerged and introduced themselves as Joe and Louise Henderson. Joe indicated that they lived across the field where a silo stood. Further discussion revealed that Tom and Joe has already met when Tom and Hank were at a sale a few weeks before.

At this point the Hammond's Buick glided to a stop on a grassy area near the hitchrack. Jim shut off the ignition, and he and Mrs. Hammond and several children emerged. With a series of toots, a brass-fronted Ford approached from the north road and slid to a stop beside the Hammond's

Buick. Jack Fitsimmons, aged about twenty-five, squeezed the rubber bulb of the horn, squawking it three or four times. Then with a big grin he thrust his left leg over the false door on the driver's side and catapulted himself out onto the running board.

"Found out one thing," he said. "I got to get started earlier if I'm gonna beat that Buick to church."

"Hello, Tom," said Jim, shaking hands. "Glad to see you got here today, an' glad you've already met Joe. I was tellin' him I'd palmed my old carriage off onto you. Hope it hasn't broke down yet."

"All it needed was a little axle grease," laughed Tom. "If I could pick up one like that every week for two dollars, I think I'd go into the buggy business."

"Well, from the way things are goin', looks like the buggy an' carriage days are on the way out," said Jim. "Joe, here, says he has a new Dodge on order. Dodge Brothers make an auto about like the Buick."

"Yeh, it's about like the Buick, only better," interrupted Joe. At any rate I was smart enough to not get a Ford," he added, planting his elbow in Jack Fitsimmons' ribs.

"That's not being smart," objected Jack, "an' I can back it up with scripture."

"Now what's scripture got to do with it, anyhow?"

"Very plain an' simple. Do you recall where it says in the Bible that Moses went up on high? Well, he must have had a Ford, because if it'd been either a Buick or a Dodge he would never have made it up in high gear."

They compared notes about the progress of planting. Tom was deeply concerned about the cold, wet weather, but they all assured him that they were late with their fieldwork, too. All agreed that this was a slow spring but that soon the weather would improve. It was hard for Tom to feel optimistic. It had been so cold he had felt as though he was freezing when he rode on the disc. It seemed as if he might have, too, if he hadn't been so busy digging the stalks and trash out of the disc frame where they had lodged. In one twenty-acre field the horses walked through water every day. He hung onto the seat with one hand and stabbed at the trash with a stick in the other. And even then it balled up until the disc choked up and dragged. Walking behind the harrow had been the most comfortable thing he had done. At least he kept warm following the harrow. It was certainly different from Indiana, where spring came earlier and the weather was warm.

BETTER PROSPECTS

From where she was cleaning in the front room, Jean heard Tom come into the kitchen. She expected that he would wander in to where she was, as he usually did. When this did not happen, she went to the kitchen. He sat at the table staring, depression written on his face. His cap was still on his head and he had not cleaned the mud from his shoes. She sat down opposite him. "Is it still wet?" she asked.

He nodded. Tomorrow would be the first of June. Most everybody said corn should be planted by June to avoid frost in the fall. Part of the field up near the house was fairly dry, but all along the far end it was still too wet.

Jean sighed. The time for sowing oats had been discouraging. Many times Tom had come in at night quite defeated. Often he had said or hinted that he wished they had never moved to Iowa. She had always been able to revive his hopes by reminding him that this was good land, that other farmers were having the same problems, and that all would be well when summer arrived. Now spring was practically gone, but the wet, cold weather hung on. Hank still had ten acres of corn to plant before Tom could use the planter. It was hard for Jean to be optimistic today.

She tapped an envelope that lay on the table. In it her cousin Nora related that another man had broken his leg in the mine at Cloverbend, that the mine where her husband worked would close down in the middle of June, and they didn't know when it would open again. "With the mine down, it'll be slim pickin's for them, too, you know that. It's hard to get started here, but it's for the best. We'll look back a few years from now an' be glad we came."

He still was glum. Anxious to get into the fields, he had gone daily to walk impatiently over them, examining the soil. With a shovel or even a stick, he had drained small ponds to speed the drying of the land. Hank was amused at his impatience with the weather. But on this year's effort hung success or failure for himself and his family, and if putting his last ounce of energy into it would insure success, then he would give as much as was required.

For two months he had been at the barn for morning chores before Hank was out of bed. As soon as they were able to get into the fields, he had had his team out and had put in a half hour's work before any of the neighbors appeared. He often came home with his overalls smeared with mud, sometimes up to his knees, and his feet wet from walking through water. But this did not bother him so much. Everyone had said that oats would grow if the ground was wet. And everyone was sure that in June it would warm up.

Well, now it was June. And the weather was still cold and his fields were too wet for planting corn. In addition, while wet weather would probably not damage the oat crop much, it would drown out the corn or retard its maturity so that the early frost would kill it. These were facts, and all of his energy, all of his hard work, and all of Jean's optimism would not alter this. They needed a corn crop for a little money. Without that their whole venture was in jeopardy.

He looked across the table at her, spreading his hands in a helpless gesture. "Well," he said despairingly, "I'm just sorry we decided to come. At least, we shouldn't have come this year. But we still have the place back home, an' if this deal goes to pieces I guess we can make it back somehow. Prob'ly have to sell all the livestock here to get money for the trip." His lip quivered and tears welled in his eyes. He looked away.

Jean took his calloused hand understandingly. Gently she reminded him of the injuries and deaths in the mines. She recalled for him the year he had walked seven miles to the nearest mine where he could get work, dug coal all day, and then walked seven miles home again at night. "We don't need to go back to that," she emphasized. "You've got your health, you got no broken bones, and you're still alive. Now all of that means a great deal to me an' the kids, an' I know it means a lot to you. Besides that, Nora says the mine will close next week. Well, of course, it's summer there an' the gardens will be good an' the blackberries will come toward autumn, but if the mine's shut for two or three months, you know what kind of a livin' Nora and Bill's goin' to have. It's goin' to be just as thin as ours is here. So I say it may not look good just now, but it will improve. So let's not talk about goin' back home. This is home now."

As he turned the team and planter at the far end of the field, Tom saw a tall man approaching along the road. When he reached the end, the man had crossed the ditch and climbed through the barbed wire fence.

"Howdie," said Tom as he turned the team for the next round.

The man waited for him to dismount, then introduced himself. He was Simon Oberly. A nearby farm he owned was for rent and he inquired whether Tom was interested in renting it.

Tom looked at him a moment in surprise. Then he realized what this meant. "Yeh!" he said. "Yeh! I'm interested!"

At Oberly's invitation to go and see the place, Tom put his team into the barn and they set out on foot. As they approached the farm Tom surveyed the landscape. Corn was visible on the nearby slopes. In the field across the pasture the oats looked green and fresh. This compared well with what he had seen as they had crossed the Schultz farm. He was pleased.

A barn was built on a side hill, with room for milk cows and other livestock in the dugout below and stalls for seven horses above. It had a bin for feed and a large hayloft. There was an apple orchard with a dozen trees. The corncrib was relatively new, but it was the house that interested him most. A nice porch ran across the front. Mrs. Hobson, the tenant's wife, invited them in when Mr. Oberly knocked. The kitchen was large enough for a big dining table, with room to spare. There was a suitable living room, one bedroom downstairs and two good sized ones upstairs, in addition to a storage room over the kitchen—a place for the seed corn, thought Tom. Jean would be happy with the house.

Making a short tour across nearby fields they came around the grove past the hog pasture to the barn. "Now, Mr. Harper, if you're interested, I think we can come to terms," said Oberly.

"Yeh, I want to rent the place," responded Tom with no hesitation.

From his inside coat pocket Oberly produced copies of the lease, which after some discussion both signed. Tom pocketed his copy and with a smile of satisfaction and a light step headed for home.

Food for the Family

THE GARDEN

ONE of the first things Tom did in the spring after moving was to fence a half acre of land near the house for the garden. Here, a rectangular wood frame as large as a storm window was built, and the inside excavated a few inches deep. Manure from the horse barn was placed into the bottom and covered with soil. A storm window was laid over the frame to provide a greenhouse effect. Cabbage and tomato seeds were planted in this hotbed and watered. During the warm part of the day the window would be removed. When the plants were a few inches high, they were taken up and set out in rows in the garden. As long as frost was a possibility, the young plants were covered with fruit jars during the night.

Sweet corn was drilled with the corn planter, which dropped the kernels three to four inches apart. As soon as the corn was up, pole beans were planted in the corn row. The corn grew faster than the beans and the beans climbed up the corn stalks, eliminating the need for bean poles. A half dozen rows of popcorn were also planted.

A substantial section of the garden was set aside for planting early potatoes. Seed for potatoes was obtained by slicing the potato, leaving the peel on, and having at least one eye for each cutting. In the garden, Tom laid off rows by using a corn plow with the rear shovels set to make trenches about three feet apart. Cuttings of potato were dropped into the trench about a foot apart and stepped on to press them down. These were then covered with soil. Along about July the potato bugs appeared. To combat these, a sprinkling can was filled with water to which a measure of Paris green was added. Then one walked along the row sprinkling the plants. The residue of poison left when the water evaporated killed the bugs when they ate the leaves.

When the vines died it was time to dig the potatoes. For this, Tom hitched a team to a walking plow and turned the tubers out with the dirt. With a team and wagon moving alongside the plowed-out rows, he and the boys crawled on hands and knees, gathering the potatoes and throwing them into a single-box wagon. At the house these were stored in the cellar or basement.

Vegetables such as tomatoes, cabbage, radishes, celery, and onions were taken from the garden as needed for the table. In the fall, turnips, carrots, and onions were dug and stored like potatoes. Cabbage for winter use was buried stem up in a straw-lined trench and covered with straw and earth. When cabbage was needed during the winter, one went to the trench and removed a head or two, replacing the straw and soil. The head would be frozen solid, but when thawed it would be succulent and good.

Cabbage not to be buried was made into kraut. In this process, cabbage was cut from the stalk, the outer leaves were trimmed off, and the heads were brought to the house. There were various sizes of kraut cutters ranging from the small metal kitchen grater to a larger wooden model, which was composed of a heavy maple board ten inches wide and two feet long having slots through it in which knives were set. A bottomless wooden box fit onto the cutter board.

With the ends of the kraut cutter placed on two chairs and a stone jar below it and with a person at one end to operate the slicing box and another at the other end to stabilize the cutter, all was ready. The sliding box had a special purpose. The knives in the board cut a substantial piece from the cabbage, and as the head became smaller the operator could slice his fingers. By steadying the head in the box with one hand and pushing the box with the other, this danger was largely removed. Salt was added in the jar from time to time and the kraut tamped with a blunt stick. When the jar was full, a clean cloth was laid over the kraut, a board placed on the cloth, and a rock laid on top. Within a few days, brine would rise over the board, sealing out the air. Then a period of fermentation took place, leaving the cabbage in a semipickled condition. When it was time to open the jar for table use, as much as was wanted was removed. With the jar closed again, the contents would keep indefinitely.

Tom generally planted pumpkin seeds along with the corn in one field. During the cultivating season the boys made note of the location of the pumpkin vines. Then in October they took a horse and wooden sled with a large box on it and gathered a load of pumpkins. On Friday night during corn-husking season they would cut up a pumpkin, and for dinner the following noon Jean would serve them hot pumpkin pie, a delicious treat after a morning of hard work.

One fall Jean read about a way to store celery for winter use. To do this she partially filled two apple boxes with dirt. Taking celery stalks, root and all, she wrapped them in paper and set them in the soil in the boxes. These she placed in the basement near a window and watered them. From this basement garden she had fresh celery occasionally during the winter.

"Eddie," said Jean one evening during late summer, "the garden's gettin' awful dry. If we don't water it, it's gonna burn up."

"You got connections with the only One I know that controls the weather," objected Eddie. "If you haven't been able to get some rain for the garden an' the corn, I don't know what more we can do. It'd take a lot of water to do any good."

"Well, now, here's something I read. Take a look at this an' see what you think."

Doubtfully Eddie looked at the magazine. It showed a five-gallon can submerged into the soil, holes punched in its sides. Water poured into the container supplied moisture to the plants. He was not impressed. They didn't have enough big cans, and the water would have to be pumped and carried all the way from the well. But he continued to think about it and the next day had a suggestion. At the dump in town there were many old, leaky pails. They could get the buckets all right. But it would be a lot of work to pump and carry that much water. Then he realized that he could dip water from the cattle tank, which was near the garden. So they secured the cans and followed the described procedure. After three weeks a good rain ended this project. Thus the garden was saved.

In September and October the bounty of the garden reached its peak. It was time for canning. Jean usually canned 125 quarts of tomatoes, after which corn and beans would also be ready. After breakfast on the day set for canning tomatoes, the kitchen table was set out on the porch along with two or three chairs. The dishpan full of water was set on the stove to heat; as soon as it began to boil, fruit jars, lids, and rubber rings were placed in it to sterilize.

Fruit jars came in half-pint, pint, quart, and two-quart sizes. Some jars were sealed by metal covers that screwed down upon rubber rings, while others had glass covers that also sealed against rubber rings and were held with wire clamps.

While the sterilizing was in progress, the tomatoes were scalded and the skins, stems, and unripe spots removed. The tomatoes then were boiled in a kettle or dishpan. Using a funnel, each jar was poured full of tomatoes and juice, the rubber rings slipped on, and the cover tightened. Finally they were rinsed, wiped dry, and turned upside down to cool.

Canning as discussed here was called the open-kettle method and most fruit was canned in this manner. However, beans and corn required longer cooking, so they were generally processed by the cold-pack method. In this system the raw vegetables were packed into the fruit jar, which was then filled with boiling water and sealed without sterilizing. The jars were placed in hot water in a wash boiler that had a frame of wood slats in the bottom, and here they boiled. This cooked the food and sterilized the jars and covers. Then the jars were lifted out and set upside down to cool. Thus inverted, defective seals could be detected. Canning was later simplified by the use of the pressure cooker, but at that time pressure cookers sometimes exploded and as a result were little used.

After frost had killed the tomato vines, the remaining green tomatoes were sliced for tomato pickles or mixed with other chopped vegetables such as cabbage, carrots, and peppers to make piccalilli, chowchow, and relish.

The sale of cream was an important source of cash, and to increase the milk supply Tom had bought more cows. However, processing the additional milk presented new problems, and to these Jean now addressed herself. As they sat on the porch one summer evening she thumbed through the mail-order catalog.

Tom was churning. He did this by pouring cream into a gallon syrup pail, putting the lid on tightly, and bouncing the pail on his knees. This caused the butterfat to collect, first in small clumps like cottage cheese, then into a solid mass. The bouncing action, however, developed gas in the churn, which, if not released, blew the top off the pail and threw cream all over. To prevent this, a hole was punched in the lid of the pail; then in order that cream not dribble out from the hole, a sharpened wooden matchstick was stuck into the hole. Every few minutes this was removed to release the built-up gas. As Jean examined the catalog, Tom removed the lid and peered inside. "It's beginnin' to gather," he said. He continued to bounce the bucket.

"I was skimmin' the cream from the milk pans this morning," began Jean, "an' you know the cream pail is almost full. That's two gallon of cream in about a week. I really haven't got a place to put two or three days' more of cream 'til we can get to town to sell it. I need all the crocks an' pans we've got just to put out the milk to let the cream rise so I can skim it off. I can churn some of it, I guess, an' sell the butter at the store, but bouncin' the churn on your knee ain't a very easy way to make butter to sell."

They needed more crocks and also another cream pail. But the cellar was not very big, and by the time Jean set out the equipment for letting the cream rise the space was about used up. The jars from canning would probably fill the shelves, and when they dug potatoes, those would have to be stored in the cellar. They were running out of cellar space.

"I want you to look at this," she said, holding up the picture in the fading light.

"I see it, but what is it?"

"Read what it says, right under the picture."

Slowly Tom read the three words: "Butterfly Cream

Separator. By doggies, looks like a long-necked gourd standin' up on end."

"I been thinkin'," said Jean. "Instead of gettin' more crocks an' pails, why not spend a little more an' get a cream separator? When Mrs. Henderson saw we was skimmin' the cream off by hand she thought we was losin' enough cream in a year by skimmin' it to pay for a separator."

The butter was done. Jean brought some glasses, and together in the cool evening they drank the new, sour buttermilk.

As Tom had suggested, the cream separator, when it arrived, did look something like a gourd with the long neck pointing upward. The large lower part contained most of the machinery, thereby keeping the center of gravity close to the floor. This counterbalanced the weight of the milk pan, which held some three gallons and rested on a bracket at the top. A long hand crank on one side, when turned, provided power. A faucet on the bottom of the milk pan released the milk into a cup from which a spout directed it into an opening in the center of the spinning bowl below. The bowl was surrounded by sheet-metal parts, which were leak proof when assembled. As the milk spun inside the closed bowl the lighter cream was thrown toward the inside and upward, while the heavier milk moved toward the outside. The cream escaped out through one spout into a pan and the milk passed out through another spout into a pail. Some of the skimmed milk was fed to the calves, some was used for cooking or drinking, and the rest went to the pigs. The cream separator was their first piece of new household equipment. They would not be without one as long as they lived on a farm.

The syrup pail was soon replaced by a more modern churn. This was of tinned sheet metal made in the form of a container about eight inches square and twelve to fifteen inches deep, open at the top and having two wooden pieces as the cover. The container rested in a cast-iron base. The operating mechanism consisted of an iron casting that fit onto the tops of two upright rods. It had a crank at one side and a cast-iron beveled gear about four inches in diameter directly over the center. When the crank was operated the gear turned a rod that extended down into the container. A paddle on the bottom of the rod rotated, beating the cream until butter was formed. The butter was then taken out and worked by hand to remove water and milk. Then it was salted, ready for use. Modifications of this churn are still in use today.

An older type churn, almost obsolete at that time, consisted of a ceramic jar eight or ten inches in diameter and fifteen or more inches high. This was closed by a round board having at its center a hole about the size of a broomstick. The agitator for this churn consisted of two crossed pieces of lumber short enough to pass down into the jar. To these was attached a piece of broomstick, which came up through the hole in the cover. With cream in the churn, the operator lifted and dropped this dasher until the butter came.

Still another type of churn used for large amounts of butter was a small wooden barrel, perhaps two feet high and fifteen inches in diameter. Located halfway up the barrel on opposite sides were short iron shafts. To one of these a crank was attached. The base consisted of a wooden stand having two uprights into which the steel shafts on the sides of the barrel fit. One head of the barrel was removable but could be closed watertight. To operate this churn, the cream was poured in and the open end sealed. Then someone turned the crank, tumbling the barrel on the stand until the butter was churned. Buttermilk remaining after the churning might be drunk, used in cooking, or fed to the pigs.

There were several kinds of cheese made from the milk, cottage cheese being the most common. To make this, one allowed the milk, usually skimmed, to sour and turn to clabber. This was set on a warm stove until the curds collected and the whey separated from it. The contents were poured into a cloth bag and hung up to drain, leaving the white cottage cheese ready to season and serve.

BUTCHERING

Upon reaching home one cold evening after Thanksgiving, the children saw that Tom had hung the large iron kettle full of water over a fire. "We're gonna butcher," he announced. "Bert, you come help me grind the knives."

The grindstone was a sandstone wheel about two inches thick and two feet in diameter, mounted on a sawhorselike stand. A crank was attached to a shaft running through the center. Bert began to turn it as Tom poured water onto the stone and pressed a knife against it. He reversed the sides of the knife and from time to time added water to the wheel.

When the knives were sharpened, Tom directed Eddie to bring a pail of slop from the kitchen and Bill to bring the ax. Approaching the pig trough he called, "Pigs, pigs, piiigs, whooooie," as he poured the swill into the trough. The hogs came hurrying to the trough, burying their noses into its contents. Taking the ax, he selected a shoat of about two hundred pounds, and moving alongside it from the rear he brought the blunt end of the ax down on the pig's head between the eyes. The animal's legs crumpled under him and he dropped to his belly. Tom and Eddie each seized a hind leg and dragged the stunned pig away. After a short distance they dropped it, and Tom took up the butcher knife. Turning the porker onto his back he thrust the knife deep into its throat, turned it to make a short crosswise cut, then withdrew the red-smeared blade. Great spurts of blood issued from the wound with each beat of the pig's heart until presently the pulsations stopped. The pig was dead. They dragged him to the kettle of hot water.

A wooden barrel had been laid on its side, with rocks placed under the open end to hold it off the ground a foot or so. Boiling water was dipped into the barrel from the kettle. They hoisted the animal head first into the barrel of scalding water; after sliding it in and out they turned it over onto the other side and repeated the operation. After a short period of this, Tom plucked at the hair in several places about the head. It came off from the skin. With the head end now properly scalded, they pulled the pig from the barrel, reversed the body, and scalded the hindquarters. Then they dragged the carcass out of the barrel, dumped the water, turned the barrel upside down, and swung the dead shoat up onto it. The hair came off easily when scraped with a knife.

Tom had cut a heavy stick about two feet long and sharpened it at each end. With the knife he slashed the rear legs on the back side just above the feet, penetrating only through the skin. He inserted his finger into the cut, pulled out the tendons, and thrust the sharpened point of the stick between the tendons and the pig's leg. The other end of the gambrel stick, as it was called, was similarly attached to the other leg. The two legs thus held far apart would not come off the stick. This done, the carcass was dragged to a nearby tree, where Tom threw the rope, attached to the center of the gambrel stick, over a limb. They hoisted the pig a foot or so off the ground and secured the rope.

With the knife, Tom slit the pig from near the tail to the throat along the belly so that the entrails bulged out from the cut. Placing a dishpan under the pig's head, he took the ax and severed first the pelvic bone and then the ribs down to the throat. Thus freed, the entrails fell rippling into the pan. He cut free the liver and heart and placed these in a milk bucket. Because the lungs were not used for food they were fed to the chickens.

Eddie and Bill took opposite sides of the dishpan, Bert and Ernie took the milk pail between them, and they proceeded to the kitchen where Jean and Jane waited. They placed the pan of entrails on the cabinet top and Jean went to work on them. The fat hung in thin, almost transparent sheets from the intestines. To remove it, Jean began adjacent to the colon and pulled the intestine slowly from the pan so that it fell into a pail. As the intestines passed through her hands she cut the lard free. This was leaf lard, the finest then available for cooking.

When the boys returned to the butchering scene Tom had cut all the way around the pig's neck so that it hung only by the vertebrae. "Hold his front feet, now, good an' solid," said Tom.

Bert and Bill complied, as Tom, seizing one ear in each hand, twisted the head as far as it would easily go, then gave it a hard jerk in the same direction. With a snap the vertebrae parted and the head swung loose in his hands. He set it nose down in a pail. He then lifted the carcass onto his shoulder and carried it into the driveway of the corncrib, where they hung it up to cool.

Supper was an hour late, but it was well worth waiting for. Boiled potatoes with fresh-fried pork heart and liver covered with milk gravy was a tasty treat. Plates were passed again and again until nothing was left.

"Well, every dish is empty," said Jean. "That's the way I like to see my family eat. Clear day tomorrow!"

The next morning when the children had gone to school, Tom split the carcass down the spine and carried it to the kitchen. After whetting the knives on the unglazed edge of a crock, he and Jean began. The hams and shoulders were cut from the sides. Instead of cutting the ribs into pork chops, the meat was trimmed off, leaving the spare ribs with the connecting tissue. The meat thus removed was called tenderloin and would be sliced and fried. The head was split open and the brains removed. These were usually minced and cooked with scrambled eggs to extend them. The head was cooked and the meat from it, along with the gelatin, was ground in a food chopper and pressed into loaves to be sliced and used for sandwiches in school lunches. This was known as head cheese.

From a neighbor, Tom borrowed a sausage grinder. This was mounted on a heavy board eight inches wide and some three feet long. It was placed between two chairs, and a child sat on each end to hold it down. One of them turned the crank of the grinder, the other fed the chunks of meat into the opening at the top. The meat fell onto an auger, which pressed it forward inside a six-inch-long tube. A many-bladed knife on the end of the auger rotated with its cutting edges pressed against a steel sievelike plate. Pressure from the auger squeezed the meat into the holes in the plate and the knives cut it off before it squeezed through. This is still the process used in making commercial sausage and hamburger. The ground meat was seasoned with salt, pepper, and sage.

Meat would not spoil if stored in a cold place and rubbed generously with salt. It would also keep indefinitely if submerged in brine, but when ready for cooking this had to be freshened by soaking in water. Still another method was to rub the meat with brown sugar along with other ingredients. There were also on the market liquids that were said to preserve meat if applied to the surface with a brush.

Still another method for preserving meat, especially for summer use, was to slice and fry it. If a good deal of it was to be prepared, baking pans were used and it was cooked in the oven as well as on top of the stove. The cooked slices were placed in stone jars or fruit jars and the grease and liquor from the frying poured over them until the meat was covered. When set in a cool place, it would keep indefinitely.

The young pig killed in the fall was lean, having little lard on it. Later in the year Tom slaughtered a large fat hog, usually a castrated boar weighing four or five hundred pounds. From this they secured much of the year's supply of lard for cooking.

Rendering lard was usually the last step of butchering. For this, the iron kettle was hung in place, cubes of fat from the hog were dumped in, the fire was started, and a clean stick was brought for stirring. After a time, liquid fat began to appear in the kettle. This was dipped out and strained through a cloth into syrup buckets, then set aside to cool. The dipping continued until the chunks of fat became brown and small, containing little lard. A small amount of heat was kept under the kettle to extract the last bit of lard from the cracklings, as the remaining lumps were called.

Then the lard press came into use. This device, somewhat larger than a gallon pail, was made of heavy sheet metal; it had a drain spout at the bottom and rested in a cast-iron frame. The press was mounted on a heavy board. A muslin sack was placed inside the container and the hot cracklings dipped into it. When full, the metal cover was closed. Extending up from the top of the cover was a screw an inch or so in diameter set in a cog that had threads inside of it. A crank turned this cog, forcing the screw and the top downward into the container. The lard squeezed out of the cracklings ran out from the spout into a bucket. When no more could be secured from the cracklings, the press was opened and the bag emptied. The pressed-out cracklings were later processed with lye to make yellow laundry soap.

This was not the end of lard making. The skin removed from the hog had a good deal of fat on it. This was cut into strips or small squares, placed in a baking pan, and heated in the oven. After the lard was poured off, the strips would be crisp and blistery. With a little salt they were very tasty. Similarly rendered-out skins, also called cracklings, can now be bought, salted and sealed in cellophane, at snack counters.

If the farmer wanted to make stuffed sausage, he attached a tube to the front of the sausage grinder. Onto the tube he slipped a two-foot section of sausage casing. Ground sausage was fed into the top of the grinder. As it was pressed out of the spout into the casing, the pressure of the oncoming sausage filled the casing and moved it forward. At intervals the casing was twisted to make a link. Casings could be bought at any butcher shop.

Beef was usually not slaughtered until solid freezing weather had come. It was skinned instead of being scalded, the entrails were removed, and the carcass was hung up to freeze in a safe place such as the granary. From the carcass meat was cut as needed.

The Rural School

THE OLDER CHILDREN COME

IN early fall, generally only the smaller children attended rural school, the older ones staying home to work. The Monday after Thanksgiving, however, often found the enrollment doubled, as the big boys and girls arrived for the winter term. When the bell rang that Monday morning they poured into the hallway, kicking off their overshoes and contesting for the nails and hooks on which to hang their coats. Inside the schoolroom a coal stove stood to one side of the entrance. Between the stove and the front of the room were several desks, each accommodating two pupils. Along the other side of the room and down the center were several more double desks.

When the room at last became quiet, Miss Peterson stood at her desk smiling. "It's good to see you all," she said. "I expect that when spring comes and it's time to work in the field, many of you will leave school to help at home. That's too bad, but I know how it is. So we have December, January, February, March, and maybe part of April left — that's about four months, with a week out for Christmas. That's just about half of the school year. With the time so short, we'll all have to work hard and pull together if you are to get what you ought to from the year's work."

"I want to get what I should, Miss Peterson," volunteered Pete from his seat in the back corner. "I aim to pull together. So do you, don't you?" he glanced at his seatmate. "Yes, Gilbert aims to pull together, too, Miss Peterson." Pete nodded knowingly.

"All right," said Miss Peterson, "I don't intend to make any rules just now, and if we don't need any later, then there won't be any. You can help decide about that. You may help each other at your seats so long as you work quietly. In that way maybe you can go faster than if you had to wait for me to help you."

Immediately in front of the teacher's desk was the recitation bench, which seated four or five students. In front of it and just higher than an adult's head hung a globe representing the earth. This was supported on a rope with pulleys so that it could be lowered or raised as needed. Below the blackboard three or four erasers and some chalk lay on the chalk tray. There were three windows on the south side and three on the north. The only exit was the door by which the children had entered.

The building sat toward the front of an acre of ground at the crossroads. Two miles in each direction there would be counterparts of this structure, each by law required to hold school if there were five children of school age within the district. If there were less than five children the school might not operate, the children being enrolled in a nearby school.

At noon the Schultz children went home for lunch, a quarter of a mile away. Those remaining opened lunch buckets, usually syrup pails, and ate at their desks. Sandwiches for school lunches were composed of pieces of cured ham, flat cakes of sausage, pieces of fat side meat, or perhaps slabs of beefsteak between slices of homemade bread. These were supplemented by thick chunks of cake, cookies, and perhaps an apple. Sometimes a small jar of canned fruit would be included, but putting up lunches for several children between a late winter rising and time to depart for school was often reduced to the bare essentials, with little thought of the niceties. A jar of milk was seldom seen in the lunch pail of the rural schoolchild at that time, though some ten or fifteen years later the use of milk became the custom.

Because rural schools seldom had wells on the school grounds, water for drinking and washing hands was carried from the nearest farmhouse. If one was close at hand, two younger children went for water at recess and were back in a few minutes. But if it was a quarter of a mile or more away, then two older children went, often during schooltime. Even so, two gallons of water brought at the first recess for twenty or more pupils would not be enough. Everybody, including the teacher, used the same water for washing hands. A bar of soap went from person to person as each child made passes at water and soap and then at the towel. This last article of toilet was usually a strip of coarse yardage supplied by the teacher, who took it home and laundered it.

As soon as it snowed, a pan of snow could be melted for washing hands. This left more water for drinking, so that after his dry lunch, each child could hope to enjoy a cup or two of water. At first all drank from a common dipper, but after about 1920, individual cups became the rule. The water was dipped from the bucket and poured into each cup. Later, schools used a closed crockery container that dispensed water through a faucet. This was a real sanitary improvement.

RECESS

During recess or after lunch in winter, the boys stormed out to the nearest pond to skate. No one at that time had shoe skates. Rather, the skates clamped onto the soles of the shoes, a skate key being required to attach or remove them. The more experienced boys would glide across the pond with long, easy strokes, hoping that the right girl was watching. The less experienced made short thrusts at the ice with the toes of their skates to gain momentum. After two or three stabs they would coast on wobbly ankles for a few yards, a satisfying reward for their efforts and a promise of better performance to come. Not many of the girls had skates. However, not to be left out of the fun, they slid on the ice or played tag to keep warm.

One morning following a bad storm, Bill was the first to approach the boys' outhouse, which stood toward the back of the schoolyard. He squeezed through the partly open door. During the storm the wind whistling in through cracks under the seat had carried snow into the building, piling it up on either side of the holes so that it was drifted almost to the roof in the corners and stood up to a peak between the holes. "Hey, do you need to go to the privy?" he called to Gilbert, who was approaching the backhouse.

Gilbert laughed. "Boy, the wind comin' up through that hole would freeze your tallywhacker off. Le's get the shovel an' scoop it out."

"Le's bank it up on the outside," suggested Eddie, who

had just arrived. With the coal scoop they piled snow against the outside until the broken boards were covered, thereby providing reasonable comfort to those within.

At this point Mavis Schultz and Grace Thornton reported to Miss Peterson that their outhouse door was stuck and they couldn't get in. Miss Peterson delegated Eddie and Gilbert to get it open so that the girls could clean it out. This completed, it was time for school to begin.

"Teacher, can we leave our overshoes on?" inquired Pete. "It's so cold back here I don't know whether I can get my fingers warmed up enough to do arithmetic today."

It was agreed that during the winter anyone who wanted to keep his overshoes on might do so and that they might wear sweaters or coats as they saw fit. These details settled, the session began.

At first recess Pete and Joe Schultz bounded out of the door. They began to walk in a large circle where the snow was not deep, curving around until they returned to the starting point.

"Fox and Geese," yelled someone as the others burst from the doorway.

Having completed the circle, Joe and Pete marked the circumference into six spaces. The other children then cut across from one point on the circle to its opposite, making paths that crossed at the center.

"I'll be It," called Gilbert, taking his place at the center, which was the base. The others spread out around the circle. One by one they began to dart about the circle, avoiding Gilbert but being careful to keep on the paths. The bigger ones, anxious to take a chance and give a dare, cut across through the center to tempt him. Soon the game became a running, screaming, pleasant exchange of banter and daring as the fox pursued the geese. It was good exercise and great fun. Each one caught also became It until all had been caught.

Soon after school resumed after recess, someone snickered. Children glancing up saw that Pete had attached a pair of jackrabbit ears to his own with some bits of wire. Soon everyone was admiring them, much to Pete's enjoyment. The jackrabbit of the Midwest was larger than the cottontail, and few dogs could overtake it. Since there were few foxes and no wolves, there was no predator to decimate the jackrabbit, and they became numerous. Early settlers, seeing the similarity between the rabbit's ears and those of the jackass, called them jackass rabbits. This had been shortened to jackrabbits, and they were often referred to simply as jacks.

Miss Peterson observed Pete and his rabbit ears. "All right, Pete," she said, "We've seen them. Take them off now."

"Yow," said Gilbert. "Tomorrow I'll bring my dog an' sic him onto you."

Everyone laughed, and Pete, having had his fun, removed the ears. "You should have seen the dog go when he scared him up," he said. "The jack zigzagged all over the pasture. The dog couldn't even get close, but finally the jack come too close to the strawstack where Chris was waitin' with the shotgun. He got him."

"Well, don't go out around the straw pile with those on when you get home tonight," rejoined Gilbert. "Chris might be out there again."

During the noon hour one warm day, the snow was melting enough to make snowballs. Immediately a friendly snowball fight ensued. Soon sides formed as friends closed ranks against the enemy. Everyone joined in, and by the time the bell rang, the school was divided into two camps and war was the watchword.

At recess, Joe Schultz took command. He urged that they not spend recess snowballing but rather in rolling up big snowballs to make a fort. Then on days when it was warm enough to make snowballs they would have a real fort to fight over. Joe designated a site, and soon a line of several large snowballs marked the base for the fort. When it was long enough they placed a row on top of the base and finally a third row on top of that. Presently Miss Peterson appeared on the porch, bell in hand, to signal the end of recess. For a moment she stood admiring the fort. Pete and Grace rushed to her.

"Please, Miss Peterson, we ain't done yet," remonstrated Pete. "Can we have 'bout five minutes more to finish it? If it's cold tomorrow we won't be able to finish it, so can you let us have some more time to get it done? Then we'll come in."

Miss Peterson agreed, and setting the bell down she

slipped on her overshoes and came out to help finish it. Fifteen minutes passed before it was done.

"All right, now, we have to go in," she called. "If you want to do any more you can work after school."

So with admiring glances at their handiwork they trooped back to complete the afternoon assignments.

Before school the next morning, Bill and Gilbert, ammunition at hand, took their station behind the fort along with some of the little kids and defied all comers. However, it was too cold to form new snowballs, and though Bill and Gilbert had a few on hand, Joe and Pete lured them into expending their stores by making daring approaches to within throwing distance and dodging their missiles. When they knew the team behind the fort was without firepower, Joe and Pete, having gathered up most of the snowballs, stormed straight up to the fort. Jumping on top of the frozen wall, they pelted the helpless two until they and their entourage withdrew. So, the battle raged for a day or two, then they tired of it and turned to other sport.

Anthony Over, or Handy Over as it was usually called, was a favorite warm-weather game at the rural school. For this, two captains chose teams, each taking one side of the building. One team shouted, "Handy over," and tossed the ball onto the roof so that it rolled down the other side. If anyone on the other side caught it, he took the ball, and his team, divided into two sections, ran around the building from opposite ends. Surprised, the waiting team, not knowing who had the ball, ran to the other side of the building. The person having the ball threw it at one of the fleeing members who, if hit, became a member of the attacking team. This continued until one team had all been caught.

Another game was Pump Pump Pullaway. Bases were laid out and the person who was It stood midway between. He then called, "Pump pump pullaway. If you don't come, I'll pull you away!" The rest then ran from one base to the other, whereupon It tried to catch them. Those caught became It with him, and so on until all were caught. If anyone did not run from the base, It again called, "Pump pump pullaway, if you don't come I'll pull you away!" Whereupon, if the reluctant child did not run, It had the authority to take him by force from the base, which constituted being caught.

Another game the Harper children introduced at various schools was called Nibble. The equipment for this consisted of a hole in the ground the size of one's hand and two sticks, one about eighteen inches long and the other about six inches. The children divided into two teams. The team that was up took possession of the hole and the sticks. The other team stood a few yards in front of them. The first player laid the short stick across the hole and with the end of the long stick under it, boosted it toward the opposing team. If it was caught, the player up was out. If no one caught it, the long stick was laid over the hole and an opposing player threw the short nibble stick, as it was called, at the long stick on the hole. If he hit the long stick, the first player was out.

If he missed, the player at the hole then held up the short stick and struck it with the long one, batting the short one toward the opposing team. If one of them caught it, the player up was out. If not caught, an opposing player tossed the nibble stick at the hole and the person who was up tried to bat it away. If the nibble stick came to rest within the long-stick's length of the hole, the person up was out. If that person was able to bat the nibble stick away, he took the long stick and measured by its length from the hole to where the nibble stick came to rest. This was his side's score.

Next, the person up placed the nibble stick down in the hole, with one end sticking up above the rim of the hole. Then he struck the top end of the nibble stick so that it flew up, whereupon he batted it away from him. If he missed batting it he was out. Also, he was out if the fielding players caught his nibble, in which case the team catching it could measure to the hole with the long stick, adding that to their score. If not caught, the team up measured and added that to their score.

The final maneuver in the series of plays was to repeat the last operation but to hit the nibble stick twice while in the air, the second time batting it away. This was called the double nibble. If the opposing team caught it, they could measure with the small stick and add these points to theirs, and the nibbler was out. But if they did not catch it, then the nibbler could measure to the hole from where the nibble stick fell and add these points to his team's score. If the player up was still not out, he began at the first operation again. When all players on the team had been put out, the other team was up and the game proceeded as before.

Shinney, actually much the same as field hockey, was played in cooler weather. Sticks either bent at one end or straight were used, and the puck was usually a tin can.

A game played indoors was called Show. For this, two rooms were needed, the entryway to the building serving as one. The game required a doorkeeper and a couple, boy and girl, who would go out into the entryway. This couple gave the doorkeeper the names of a boy and girl. With the door closed, all the other children presented themselves in pairs at the door and asked, "Whole show or half show?" If neither of them had been named by those in the anteroom, the doorkeeper would reply, "No show at all." If the doorkeeper answered, "Half show," this meant that one of the two qualified. As soon as two people found that each was a half show, they appeared together as a whole show and took their turn in the outer room.

Bert, then in sixth grade, noticed that some of the older boys and girls approached the door with arms around each other. Accordingly, he tried passing his arm around his partner's waist. He was pleased when she was agreeable. When he repeated the gesture with another young lady, however, she removed his arm. Apparently she had been coached.

While arms around was the practice of older couples as they approached the door, once they were in the anteroom and the door was closed some explored other avenues leading toward closer friendship. Though Bert observed this, he did not get the meaning of what was going on behind the door that he so carefully guarded when he was doorkeeper. He mentioned this to Eddie, who was then in high school, and was interested that Tom smiled knowingly when Eddie repeated it to him.

"Le's ask if we can go after water," suggested Glenn Rutledge soon after Bert arrived at school one blustery morning in March. "We'll get our arithmetic right after readin' class, then we'll go."

Outdoors it was not as disagreeable as it looked. The sun peeked through the clouds now and then and the snow abated and returned, pelting them with sleetlike pellets, but walking with the pail between them the boys were comfortable. They cut across the pasture of the nearest farm, going through the feedlot near the barn. Here stood several small A-shaped buildings that farmers used for housing their brood sows during farrowing.

"Le's go in here," Glenn said, ducking through the low doorway.

Bert followed. Glenn produced a small cloth bag of Bull Durham tobacco and a packet of cigarette papers.

"You smoke? he inquired.

Bert shook his head. "Folks won't let me."

With feigned expertness Glenn held the paper between his thumb and the first and second fingers of his left hand while he shook out tobacco from the bag with his right. "My old man don't want me to, either, but I sneak it." He held the drawstring from one side of the bag with his teeth and pulled on the opposite one with his right hand to close the bag. He rolled the paper over, enclosing the tobacco into a neat tube. Wetting one edge of the paper with his tongue he turned it down against the side of the tube. "My big brother showed me how," he said, proudly holding it up. "He does it real good. First time I tried I spilled it all over. Takes practice." He lighted it and began to puff. "Want a drag?"

Bert declined. After several hurried puffs Glenn threw the butt through the door, stepping on it as he went out, and they proceeded toward the pump. The owner of the farm stood observing. They were near neighbors.

"Smokin' today?" he asked.

"Smokin' every day," retorted Glenn as they passed.

"Has your dad ever caught you smokin'?" Bert asked as they passed through the hog lot on their return to school.

"Yow, he caught me once."

"What did he say?"

They changed sides of the pail to rest their arms. "Well, I was feedin' some calves in a shed back of the barn. I had a pipe then, so I loaded up an' lighted 'er off. When I looked around, there the old man was."

"What'd he do?"

"By gol', you know what he done? Didn't say a word. Just grabbed the pipe. Then he stamped a deep hole in the mud, an' threw the pipe in the hole an' stamped on it. Then he looked at me again an' went away. Didn't say nuthin'."

"Boy, I bet you was scared."

"Well, I never smoked a pipe again. Cigarettes is easier to hide, an' if he throws one away I can make another one. He smokes too. What can he say?"

"What if the teacher smells it on you?" asked Bert as they approached the school. "What'll you say?"

"That's why we go for water before recess. Now we'll play outside an' by the time the bell rings she won't be able to smell it."

CALIBER OF THE RURAL SCHOOL

Requirements for rural teaching credentials in 1915 were minimal. All that was needed was to be a high school graduate and pass the teacher's examination. Even some ten years later, high school teachers often had no more than two years' preparation beyond high school for teaching certain subjects.

At that time it was the practice to employ a rural teacher for one three-month term only. If no teacher could be found, the pupils would be distributed among nearby schools. Where this plan was followed, a student might have three teachers in the same school within a year's time or he might attend as many as three different schools. These conditions, coupled with the practice of parents keeping their children out of school for weeks at a time to help with farm work, weakened the effectiveness of the rural school.

So it was not surprising that Eddie, who had stayed out of school a good deal to help at home, failed to pass the county eighth-grade examinations in the spring of 1916. Because a good foundation was needed for high school, he was enrolled to repeat the eighth grade the following fall at Deep Creek. The next fall, 1917, Bill was also in the eighth grade at Deep Creek, both boys riding horseback five and a half miles each way daily, even in coldest winter weather.

When one considers today's schools, with long class periods under supervised conditions and with supplementary materials and audiovisual aids, one wonders how children in rural schools years ago learned much. Those in lower grades could expect to have a maximum of five to six minutes for each class — no more. Likewise, older students could not expect their classes to be more than ten minutes long. In addition, there was no seat work of any kind. The bookcase that represented the library might contain a dozen or two classics and a few old textbooks. These were devoid of pictures, some containing a few pen and ink sketches.

When it was time for class the students took their places at the recitation bench. This long seat was so placed that while talking to the class the teacher faced the rest of the room. Thus her attention was never entirely on the class, for she had to keep the whole room under observation. She would ask each student a few questions about the lesson, explain hard problems or difficult answers, but engage in almost no thought-provoking discussion. It was a matter of reciting facts. When the time was up, the next day's work was assigned without discussion.

During the late 1920s many counties in the state introduced a weekly or biweekly program for rural schools. This allowed for longer class periods. It was an improvement in many respects.

But even at this later date, no money was generally provided for seat work, supplementary books, or enrichment. Parents bought the children's books, pencils, crayons, and paper. Likewise, there was no money for playground equipment. If there was a baseball or bat it was usually because the teacher bought it with his or her own money or some student brought it. If a school wanted any money for special supplies, it was expected to raise its own. A program was held once during the year, usually in the fall or early winter. The community was invited, and following a program there would be a basket social.

There was a tacit understanding that the young ladies who came would bring a box lunch for two. The boxes were beautifully decorated and contained tasty lunches. The boxes were auctioned to the men present. The purchase of a box gave the buyer the privilege of eating the lunch with the young lady who had provided it, and if it was a successful evening he might take her home afterward. Such an event might raise from twelve to twenty-five dollars, seldom more. This the teacher could use for special school needs.

In about 1920 the consolidation of rural school districts began, and with this emerged a more effective rural education.

Winter

CHRISTMAS

THE sun rose bright and clear Christmas morning. The children were excited and the household was abustle, for they had been invited to the Hammonds' for Christmas Day.

"Give the horses a feed of oats this morning, boys," said Tom at the conclusion of breakfast. "All a horse gets out of this life is what he eats and a lot of hard work. Put the harness on Hazel and Prince. We'll drive them. Turn the others out."

At nine thirty they set out. To keep Jean and the smaller children warm, two heated rocks had been wrapped in burlap and placed beneath the blankets in the carriage. The thermometer registered ten above.

The Hammonds' spacious square white house, surrounded by a large yard, stood adjacent to the road. Near it was a steel windmill with a wooden pump house beneath. Farther away was the barn and other outbuildings, all painted white and appearing well cared for. Tom let the family out near the house and drove toward the barn where Jim Hammond and Jack Fitsimmons stood talking.

"Did you get your corn picked, Tom?" questioned Jim. "Three years ago we got caught with a big blizzzard just before Thanksgiving. Had to dig the corn out of the snow with the thermometer down to zero."

"Got the last of it on Friday. It can snow, hail, rain, sleet, or whatever it wants to now. I don't care."

They put the team into the barn and walked to the house. Inside there was great activity. Tempting odors emerged from the kitchen, which was cluttered with cooking equipment. Toward the back of the range a pumpkin stood slightly drooping, its well-baked sides wrinkled and in danger of caving in. A large kettle on the front of the stove emitted gasps of steam from under its cover, suggesting a good supply of mashed potatoes. Mrs. Hammond directed operations. Going to the sink she turned the faucet. There was no water. She opened the door to the stairs and called Fred to come and pump up the pressure.

Presently Fred, followed by Eddie and Bill, emerged from the stairway and went outside and down into the basement. In one corner stood a large, round, closed steel tank containing the water supply. This was filled by operating a hand pump, which forced water into it.

Bill and Eddie stood on one side of the pump and Fred on the other. They pushed the long handle toward Fred and he pushed it back. Gradually the supply built up as indicated on the dial. When the tank was full enough they closed the valve and Fred tapped on the water pipe with a screwdriver to signal that there was pressure.

Upstairs in Fred's room, Eddie and Bill gazed in wonder. There were two beds with plenty of room to spare. By the window was a dresser with drawers on one side for Fred and on the other side for his brother. The floor was not painted but was of clean, bright wood that had been varnished, as Bill said, "just like the top of a table."

"Where does that door go to?" Eddie asked, pointing.

Fred opened it, and to the surprise of both boys, it was a closet just for this room.

"Does everybody's room have a closet?"

From the ceiling hung lamps that Fred said burned carbide gas, which when turned on could be lighted with a match. It was the nicest house the boys had ever seen.

"All right," Mrs. Hammond called at last. "Get washed, now, dinner is ready."

Everything came together at once. Boys pushed into the dining room after having washed, the men sauntered out to perform the same operation. The women and girls bustled to the dining room with steaming burdens of food and drink. Then all was quiet as each stood at his chair admiring the feast. On occasions such as this, the Hammonds knelt by their chairs to say grace. Jim Hammond led off with a quiet blessing, somewhat long, however. Then Mrs. Hammond expressed her thanksgiving for the Lord's blessings. Following her, Jean, Tom, Jack, and Opal responded. Mrs. Hammond next called on each of the children. If they hesitated, she gave them words they could repeat, until all had had their turn.

At length they took their places. Food was passed until plates were filled and refilled and the hungriest one could accept no more. The meal completed, the big boys and girls went to the pond to skate while Ernie and Bert, on the invitation of Jim, took Fred's sled and coasted down the mound over the storm cave.

"How did your corn turn out, Tom?" asked Jack as the men stood in the sun near the barn. "You said you had quite a few soft ears. Does it look better now that you're finished?"

"Well, I took your suggestion and throwed the soft ears in the back of the wagon as I picked 'em. Then when I went to unload I'd scoop 'em onto the ground an' we fed 'em right away. But it looks to me like it's too damp to sell at the elevator. I was up in the crib yesterday and it's heatin' some. Does it spoil if it's too damp?"

"Yeh," responded Jim, "it'll mold so that they won't buy it at the elevator. That's how the Henderson boys got into the cattle business. They always had some soft corn so they decided to buy cattle an' feed it."

"Come to think of it," said Jack, "Joe told me yesterday he was lookin' for corn to buy for feed. He might buy yours if you don't sell it in town."

At about four o'clock Tom gathered the family and they went home to do the chores, after which they returned to the church for the Christmas program.

When they arrived there Fred was having trouble pumping up pressure for the overhead gas lamps. The gauge on the pressure tank remained at zero when he pumped. Hearing a hissing noise when Fred pressed the pump plunger down, Tom discovered that the hose was split. With his pocketknife he cut off the end and pressed the hose into place again on the tube. Each stroke of the pump then registered more pressure. When the gauge showed that this was adequate, Fred lighted the wick on the top of a long bamboo pole and went out into the main room. With the torch held adjacent to the lamp overhead, he called to Eddie to open the valve on the tank. Promptly the lamp at the ceiling flared brightly, then glowed white and steady.

There were gasps of joy from the children as they beheld the eight-foot Christmas tree in the corner. Some of them had never seen a Christmas tree before. Parents hurried forward with packages. Jack and Mrs. Fitsimmons accepted these, hanging some on the tree and depositing the rest below.

Children in the program took their seats. The Sunday school superintendent called the meeting to order. As groups marched to the platform to perform, there were jibes from their friends in the pews waiting their turn. Teachers positioned children on the stage, gave the opening words to the first speaker, and each in turn spoke his piece. All went well until it came Ernie's turn. The child before him spoke out plainly, but Ernie did not take his cue. Members of the audience snickered; the teacher prompted, but Ernie did not respond. He stood digging at the inside of his mouth with one finger, oblivious to all about him.

At this point, Jack, who sat in the choir on the platform near Ernie, reached over and punched him. "It's your turn, Ernie, say your piece."

Whereupon, Ernie turned and said in a clear voice, "I got a piece of chicken in my teeth."

This brought the house down. At the conclusion of the program, Joe Henderson came to the front. He selected three or four big boys and girls to serve as messengers, and taking gifts from the tree, he announced the name on each package and handed it to them to deliver.

Upon receiving the gift, each person opened it. There were cries of delight as long-hoped-for trinkets or more useful gifts were unwrapped. Eddie and Bill each received a knitted cap that was worn folded up above the ears in mild weather but which could, in time of storm, be pulled down so that the face appeared in a small opening. For Jane there was a new Sunday dress with a bright red bow. For Ernie and Bert there were yellow canvas leggings with straps that went under the instep to hold them down and clasps up the outside to keep them on.

"Oh, boy," said Ernie. "I bet we can go through most any drift now, Bert."

"Yow, an' no more teasin' from the kids at school for wearin' them gum boot tops for leggin's. They never was much good, anyhow."

Tom was genuinely surprised when his package contained a beautiful black sealskin cap. He had wanted one of these fine caps but could not think of spending the money on himself when other needs were so pressing. He put it on while the family beamed with pride.

Jean was amazed when she opened her long, heavy package. It was a footwarmer. This consisted of a metal box, oval in cross section, a foot or more long, four inches high, and covered with velvet. Accompanying the footwarmer was a box of small charcoal briquets. By heating two of these in the firebox of the stove the briquets became red hot. Placed in drawers at each end of the footwarmer, they continued to burn for two or three hours, generating a surprising amount of heat when placed near one's feet under a blanket.

Too quickly the whole affair was finished. Parents gathered their families and departed tired but happy amid wishes for a Merry Christmas and a Happy New Year. As they journeyed home, it began to snow.

A BLIZZARD

The next morning they awoke to a quiet white world. During the night soft fluffy snow had covered the landscape eight inches deep. The outdoors had become a fairyland.

"I betcha there's a thousand rabbits down by the dredge ditch," said Bill. "After the last snow they had paths all over the place. Musta been a lot of rabbits to make so many paths."

After breakfast Tom called Buster, the dog, and headed toward the dredge ditch. Before they had gotten past the garden, Buster raised a cottontail from behind a bunch of grass in a bean row. The rabbit took two or three hops and then dove into the soft snow. In a trice Buster had him by the neck. Tom hit the rabbit on the head with a stick and tied him to a small rope around his waist. In half an hour he had ten. Calling off Buster, they headed for the house. There he dressed the rabbits and hung the carcasses up along the front porch to freeze. Jean would select as many as needed for a meal, and when the supply was gone Tom or the boys would take Buster and renew the larder.

When they awoke the next morning the wind had begun

to blow. By noon it had started to snow. In the early afternoon Tom called the children together. "Get on your things. We gotta get all the chickens and turkeys and ducks and geese into the hen house or barn. Roust them out from wherever you can find them. We're in for a humdinger."

They searched around every building and through the garden and the orchard, finding stranded birds in unexpected places. Often they were huddled, covered with snow, cold and in distress but not having enough sense to find shelter. When at last the fowls had been gathered in, Ernie and Jane returned to the house while Tom and the other boys milked early and gave the cattle and horses some hay.

"Well, boys," said Tom, as they sat down to supper, "it sure wasn't much fun to finish pickin' the last day or two before Christmas, ankle deep in snow, but we got it done. How would you like to go out there tomorrow wadin' in it up to your navel huntin' for nubbins?"

Outside the wind howled through the trees in the grove. The thermometer registered ten degrees above zero. On the windowpanes, spiderwebs of lacy frost spread sparkling and white.

Tom went to the porch and carried in more wood. Opening the stove door he thrust in several pieces. The heating stove stood in the corner of the living room. The ash box of the stove was eight or ten inches high, twenty-four inches square, and sat up off the floor on six-inch legs. A door in the front opened for cleaning it out. In the front of this door was an opening for regulating the amount of air admitted into the burning chamber. Above the ash box was the cast-iron bowl, or firebox, and on top of that a sheet-metal cylindrical section extended some two feet high. This, in turn, was topped by a cast-iron helmetlike section. From the top of the heater the six-inch smoke pipe extended upward and then turned into the chimney.

The stove was generously decorated with glistening, lacy steel. Its most attractive feature was the door through which fuel was introduced. This was ornamented with bright work, and in its center were four squares covered with mica. The fire within glowed red through this window, especially in the dark, giving a comforting atmosphere on a cold night.

At about seven thirty, Tom laid down his paper. "If

there's any fire left in the kitchen stove, why don't you kids pop some corn?" he inquired.

Together Bill and Eddie hurried to the kitchen as Bert and Ernie hastened after them. Eddie added kindling to the dying embers in the firebox and on top of this laid larger sticks of wood. Presently it began to crackle. Bill got down the iron skillet from the warming oven and put a large spoonful of lard into it. When Ernie and Bert had shelled two or three ears of popcorn he poured that in and put the cover on. With the stove lid removed, he placed the skillet directly over the fire and waited. From time to time Bill shook the skillet to prevent the corn from burning and sticking to the bottom.

Before long, popping noises began to come from within. Bill placed the lid back over the hole, set the skillet on the hot stove, and holding a cob down against the cover with one hand to prevent it from sliding off, shook the skillet continually with the other. Soon the popping, thumping noises were continuous as the corn popped furiously. When it stopped, Bill removed the cover and poured the popped corn into the dishpan. He continued popping until the dishpan was full. From the cupboard Eddie collected a number of serving dishes, took a salt shaker, and they carried the repast to the sitting room. Each person took a dish and scooped out a helping for himself, salted it, and settled down to enjoy the evening treat.

By half past eight the family, full of popcorn and getting drowsy, trooped off to bed. Selecting two large chunks of wood, Tom thrust them into the heater, closed the draft openings, and set the damper in the stovepipe to retard the draft up the chimney. It was a good stove. With it he and his family would be warm. Tonight he was especially glad he had it.

Heat was introduced into the boys' upstairs room by a hole in the floor above the heating stove. This opening was covered by a register, which could be opened or closed. By opening the door into Jane's room the upstairs could be heated reasonably well. On a quiet night it would be necessary to renew the fuel in the heating stove just once. But on a windy night the fire burned out sooner and required fuel more often.

When Tom was up at three o'clock the thermometer

showed five degrees above zero, and the storm was as intense as ever. In his nightshirt and overalls he stood with his back to the stove. Outside the storm raged. Upstairs his children were asleep, warm and well fed. In the barn he had five head of work horses, two of which would have colts in the spring. In the basement of the barn were six good milk cows and five calves now nearly a year old. One of the calves he would soon slaughter for meat.

The four sows he had brought with him when he moved to the place had produced thirty-one pigs, some of which he had sold. He had kept back six gilts for breeding stock and they would have pigs in another eight weeks. In the corncrib there remained six or seven hundred bushels of corn, part of which would be needed for feed, but there would be a few hundred bushels for market in the spring. He had rented the one hundred acres beyond the dredge ditch and would have this added land to farm next summer. Bert, who would be six in March, would be big enough to work in the field then. With the three boys he could handle it. He would need another boar pig and a corn plow or two. All this he could find at sales. Very likely he would have to borrow money again. Well, he had paid back nearly all he owed. It paid to keep your paper at the bank in good shape.

"You comin' back to bed, Tom?" asked Jean from the bedroom door. "You been up quite a while. Did you fix the fire?"

Chores took longer than usual next morning. With all of the livestock inside, feed had to be carried to them. Also, because of the drifts, it was not possible to follow the usual shorter routes from place to place. With a scoop, Bill removed the snow from a spot on the stock's watering tank, chopped a hole in the ice, and set the windmill to pumping. By twos and threes they released the horses and cows and drove them out into the storm to drink. With their eyes half closed against the driving snow, the stock reluctantly ventured through the drifts to the tank, took a few mouthfuls of cold water, and then hurried back to the barn. Water was carried to the pigs and chickens and corn scattered for them. When the chores were finished, Tom and the boys retired to the house.

There was really little to do there. The family did not subscribe to magazines, so aside from one or two picture-story books that had been read many times and a stack of old newspapers, there was little to interest them. Jean organized a game of I Spy, which occupied the children for half an hour. This was played by having the person who was It hide a sewing thimble in plain view while all others covered their eyes. When It called, "Ready," everyone got up and searched for the thimble. When one found it he called, "I spy," but allowed no one to see where he had observed it. When all or most all had found the thimble, the first one to have spied it was It and he hid the thimble, and so on.

After a time the game was abandoned for Button Button Who's Got the Button? To play this the children placed their chairs in a row. One person was selected to be It. This person held a button between his palms that he pressed down between the palms of the person next to him, pretending to release the button to that person, who in turn repeated the operation with the one next to him, and so on. It tried to guess who had the button, and when he was successful that person became It and the game began again.

With the coming of the first cold snap, the seed corn had been carried into the low-roofed storage space above the kitchen. Here it was spread out on the floor to dry, the husks pulled back, tied with twine, eight or ten ears in a bunch. At about ten o'clock Tom and the boys went to this room to remove the husks and clean up the room. Each took a bunch of ears and began breaking off the shucks. By noon the task was finished. The ears were neatly stacked along the wall and the husks were bagged to be taken downstairs and used for fuel. Tom had been concerned about all those dry husks in that room. If a fire had gotten started there it would have burned fast, with little chance for stopping it.

As dusk descended the wind abated, and at dawn next morning the thermometer stood at ten below zero. Bright spots showed on each side of the sun. These were called sundogs, which were said to forecast bad weather in a day or two. After chores were finished, Tom directed Eddie and Bill to take scoops and shovel paths about the barnyard.

In the meantime he walked along the lane to the road, struggling through hip-deep snow in places, to learn whether they could get to town. "Ain't no teams on the road nowhere that I could see," he reported at dinner time. "This's Saturday. We can't make it to town 'til Monday at least. We'll have to walk to church tomorrow. Me an' the kids can go — them that wants to tackle it."

At a little after noon the next day, Tom, Eddie, and Bill set out for church. As they were passing the farmhouse of Timothy Green, the Green's son, Edward, who was hitching the team to the bobsled, invited Tom and the boys to ride to church. Mrs. Green, in a heavy wool coat, stocking cap, and scarf, settled into the spring seat placed in the bottom of the wagon box, where fresh straw lay six inches deep. Over her lap they spread a robe. The men stood.

"Hey, that robe looks like it has horsehair on it," commented Eddie. "Was it made from a horse's hide?"

Edward replied that the robe was from a horse that had broken his leg, and they had had to shoot him.

"I saw a man with a coat that looked like it was made from a horse or cow," said Bill. "Do they make coats out of skins from horses or cows, sometimes?"

"Yes, they do. My mittens were made from a cow we butchered. I used to have the coat that went with them, but the rats chewed holes in it when I left it in the barn. On account of the holes, I quit wearin' it."

The chassis of the farm bobsled was somewhat like that of the wagon except that the sled had runners where the wagon had wheels. Also, it was not as wide as the wagon and it was set closer to the ground. The chassis was made of steelbound wooden parts, the runners being some four feet long and about two inches wide with thick iron soles. It pulled easily over the snow and ice, its long runners spreading the weight so that it ran over the top of the hard drifts.

"Do you think the preacher can get here from Deep Creek?" asked Tom of Timothy Green as they approached the church.

"Yes, I think so. I called him last night and he said he would be here. He sold his horse when be bought his Ford last summer, but his neighbor will lend him a horse when he needs it. I think he'll ride horseback."

Those who had arrived at the church gathered around the stove in the main room, their coats unbuttoned, their mittens and headgear laid aside.

"Poke up that fire there, Leo," said Jack Fitsimmons. "Feels about as cold in here as it was in my cow barn this mornin'. Can't you blow in the grates to get 'er goin'?"

"Sure needs somethin', all right," said Leo. "You always got a lot of wind. Why don't you get down there an' blow on it?"

"No! Don't let Jack blow on it," teased Edward. "We don't want to burn the church down, we just want to warm it up a little."

Leo had had the fire going since ten o'clock and the firebox had been red hot since before noon, but the room was large and it would take a long time to become comfortably warm on a cold day. Because the congregation was small, Mr. Green asked them to take seats near the stove, the adults on one side of the aisle and the children on the other. Thus one person could teach the adult Sunday school class and another teach all of the children.

When Sunday school was about half finished, the minister entered. Frost from his breath was white on his coat collar, and his nose and cheeks were pink from the cold. He removed his fur coat and mittens, took off his sealskin cap, and stood, back to the stove, listening.

"Well, Tom," said Jim Hammond as they visited after the service. "I was thinkin' about you yesterday, wonderin' whether you would be able to get out. How was the storm over your way?"

"By doggies, it was a stem-winder. We really needed to get to town yesterday with cream an' eggs, but we couldn't do it. We walked this morning an' scouted the prospects. I think that with some scoopin' we can make it in the carriage tomorrow."

"I was thinkin'," continued Jim. "You don't have a sled, do you?"

Tom shook his head. "Guess we'll have to make it with the carriage an' wagon this winter."

Jim had reservations. "Can't do it after this blizzard. This snow won't go off. The farmers'll all come out with bob-sleds an' you won't be able to go far with a wagon if you got a load on it. Wagons an' carriages are wider than sleds; you'd have a bad time."

Tom agreed that he had been thinking about that.

Jim continued. "We got an old sled out in the grove you could borrow for the rest of the winter if you want it. We still use it for haulin' manure an' a few things, but if you want to borrow it, why don't you bring a team over tomorrow an' have a look at it?"

Tom considered the offer. The Hammonds had done so much for them that he hesistated to accept more. He was deeply indebted to them for friendship and encouragement. He was not indebted to them for money. He was glad for this. He did need a bobsled. "All right," he said, "I'll come over tomorrow an' look at the sled."

There was a sequel to the bobsled story, which happened a year or two later. The Harpers and a neighbor family had gone to church together in separate bobsleds. On the way home the horses took off down the road at a fast clip toward the first corner, a mile away. The neighbor's sled turned the corner first. Tom gave little heed as they approached the turn, knowing that his team would follow. However, a ditch had been dug across the road just after the turn, and when it had been filled, mounds of earth were left on either side. When the horses swung around the turn the rear runners skidded in a wide arc, striking the hump of earth, and the sled overturned. Tom, with the lines around him, landed on his back in the snow. He seized the lines with both hands and the pull of the horses brought him up onto his feet, running. The wagon box flew off the sled chassis onto its side in the shallow ditch. Jean and the smaller children were hurled out, rolling in the knee-deep snow. The chassis of the sled righted, and Tom found himself running beside it with the lines still about his back. There were shouts and probably some screams as the melee came to rest. Tom turned the team back to the overturned box as the people in the first sled ran back to assist. Jean and the children picked themselves up. The men placed the box back onto the sled, and the families went happily homeward.

After the crib had been filled, several hundred bushels of corn remained. To store this, Tom set up woven wire in a circle about fifteen feet in diameter and some four feet high. Into this pen he scooped corn until it was full. On top of this he placed another smaller circle of wire and filled it also. Instead of planning to shell his corn and haul it to town, he had sold it to a cattle ranch a mile and a half away. He expected to haul a load each day. To load the corn he climbed to the top of the lower pile and snipped the wires of the upper pile from top to bottom. As he severed the last one, the whole circlet fell loose and the corn burst out, running down onto the ground by the sled.

While Eddie and Bill went about the chores, Bert and Ernie were assigned to help with the loading. Bert got up in the wagon to throw out any moldy ears that Tom scooped up. These would not be fed to cattle. When he had scooped up most of the corn that had run down, Tom boosted Ernie up onto the pile and instructed him to kick it down to him. By suppertime the sled was loaded.

It was twenty below zero the next morning as Tom prepared to start for the ranch with the load. All went well until he reached the prairie where the graded road ended and there was only a trail to follow. He had broken the track the previous day with the sled, but this had drifted shut again in several places. While the empty sled had run over the tops of the hard drifts the previous day, the load now caused it to sink in so that in places the sled frame dragged on the snow. Presently the sled stuck in a deep drift. The team stopped, their sides heaving, their breath showing white with frost. On the hairs around their flanks frost had begun to collect from perspiration, and icicles grew from the bristles at the ends of their noses.

While the team rested, Tom removed his sheepskin coat and threw it up on top of the load. Then he took the scoop and shovelled away the snow from ahead of and under the sled. Going ahead of the horses, he scooped away a few drifted spots. Returning to the rested team he took up the lines and the horses moved on. After two or three more delays he reached the ranch yard where Oscar, the foreman, stood at the open gate.

"Man," exclaimed Oscar, "never thought we'd see you today. The hands was a-sayin' at breakfast they bet you'd never make it."

"I think we agreed that I'd begin today," commented Tom.

"Yeh, we did, all right. So I told 'em, I said, 'Just wait a little an' see.' Well, pull 'er in by the first bunk an' shovel in about eight or ten bushel. We got five bunks for you to use."

As Tom turned the team toward the feed-yard gate his face was toward Oscar.

"Hey, man, ya know your face is froze?" He examined Tom's face more closely. "An' your left ear, too."

Tom looked surprised. "Never felt a thing," he mused.

"Hey, Hank! You an' Pete come shovel off this load for Tom; he's froze his face an' his ear. Gotta take him in the barn an' thaw him out."

When Tom's face was thawed, Oscar and he went to the house for a cup of coffee. Half an hour later, Hank brought the team from the feedlot and tied it to the fence. Tom rose to go. "Had a letter from my landlord. He says for me to sell as much of his crop as you want at the price you offered."

"Good," answered Oscar. "We'll need prob'ly fifteen hundred bushel by March."

"Well, that's about what me an' him's got between us."

Oscar agreed. "All right, we'll take all you've got."

SHIVAREE

One day in January a neighbor rode in on horseback to announce that another neighbor, Roscoe Anderson, had been married and that a shivaree was planned for that evening. He wanted everyone to gather by a grove near the corner after dark. Then they would drive to the house together and raise cain all at once.

"What's a shivaree?" asked Eddie when the messenger had gone. "How come they're gonna do that on account of Roscoe an' Mabel gettin' married?"

Tom smiled. "Don't know how it got started. Been a long time since I went to one myself. They generally have a shivaree the night of the weddin', but they missed out on that, so this is the next best time."

"Are we gonna go?" asked Eddie eagerly. "I'd sure like to."

Tom turned toward the house. "I think we can go," he said. "Let's go talk to Mom about it."

By seven o'clock, sleds began to assemble in the shadows of the grove. Together they drove to the barnyard, tied their teams, and gathered in front of the house.

"Hello, there," shouted Oscar, and pandemonium broke loose. Everyone screamed. They pounded on old washtubs, rattled strings of tin cans, jangled bunches of sleigh bells, and made noise by every means available. After several minutes, the din subsided when Roscoe and his bride appeared in the kitchen doorway.

"Happy married life, Roscoe!" How's married life, Roscoe?" "We just had to come an' see how ya was makin' out," various friends bantered.

The groom invited them in.

"Well, now, Roscoe," announced Oscar after things had quieted down, "we want to congratulate you an' your blushin' bride. Us married men think it was the right thing to do, and I 'spect some of the women would agree with us. So we thought we ought to come tonight an' have a party — at your expense, of course. How about it, are you prepared for company?"

Roscoe was indeed ready. From the cupboard he produced a box of cigars, which was passed among the men. He dispatched Bill and Eddie to bring in the freezer of ice cream from the side porch. Jean and Mabel, the bride, cut the cakes and put cookies on platters. They placed a bowl of hard candy on the kitchen table and took another to the living room. Everyone helped himself, pleased with Roscoe's foresight. After a bit, Oscar stood up again and beckoned for silence.

"Bring out your blushin' bride, Roscoe," he requested. "We all want to have another look at her."

Arms around each other they appeared in the doorway.

"Now, that's the way us married ones like to see it, an' it's the way the single ones hope it'll be for them someday.

An' after this nice party we want to do our part. We didn't have time to buy you a gift, so we're gonna let you do that." He held up a buckskin purse. "We passed the hat. Here's about twenty dollars your friends have chipped in. Take it an' buy yourselves a nice weddin' gift. It's from all of us."

The ice cream disappeared, the platters became bare, and the candy bowls were emptied. Children fell asleep on their mothers' laps or in corners of the room, and the conversation lagged. The guests congratulated the newlyweds again, then happily gathered up their families and went home.

Revival Time

PRAYER MEETING

PRAYER MEETING was held at the home of Ed Johnson one Wednesday night in January. As Tom was blanketing the team upon arrival there, Joe Henderson drove his sled alongside and stopped.

"Hello, Tom," called Louise Henderson as she climbed out. "Jean here?"

"Yow, she just went in."

"Is that youngster still kickin' up a storm for her? Is it gonna be a boy or a girl?"

"Boy, I hope. That's what we're figgerin' on."

"Tom, that's not fair. You already have four boys to help you in the field; you ought to allow Jean another girl for the house. You should be ashamed of yourself. Girls are nice, too."

"Yeh, I know about that," said Tom. "I'm married to one of 'em."

"Well, maybe it's a good thing that the Lord's gonna decide this one for you. You'll take what you get."

"Throw me a blanket an' I'll put it on this horse," said Tom as Joe was sorting the blankets in his sled.

Joe straightened up, his ruddy cheeks almost glowing in the moonlight. To Tom he was like a fine big brother. Tall, plump, ruddy of complexion, cheerful, and kind. It was seldom that a thoughtless word came from his mouth, and whatever he turned to seemed to make him money. Tom admired him as he emerged from the sled, a horse blanket in each hand, a round badger-fur cap on his head, and his long badger coat open down the front. He handed Tom one of the blankets. "Be sure to pin it on the crupper," he cautioned. "Don't want it to slide off an' be under his feet when we come out."

As they approached the yard gate, Timothy Green and his wife joined them. The turned-up collar of Timothy's sheepskin coat framed the oval outline of his face, punctuated by the white goatee below and topped off by his black sealskin cap. His glasses glistened in the moonlight. "Glad to see you got a sled now, Tom," said Timothy.

Tom looked at the men, one on either side of him. Joe, tall and handsome, Timothy, slender and spare, older than either he or Joe but strong and solid. Both were a head taller than Tom. His short stature sometimes made him feel insecure. He knew that he was a short man, but with these men he felt tall.

Inside the house the visiting stopped when the hostess stood up and took charge. One lady went to the organ to supply the accompaniment. Several revival-type hymns were sung. There was a scripture lesson and prayer. Following this came a period of testimonies when anyone could stand and express his thanks for God's kindness or tell some interesting event that had enriched his experience. Mrs. Henderson expressed thankfulness for their small son's recent recovery from a bad cold. Timothy Green thanked the Lord for good crops and for continued well-being in his older years. Then Jack Fitsimmons rose.

"I've got a problem an' hope you can help me with it. The pipes from the pump at my place run underground to the stock tank. During cold weather the water standing in the pipes overnight will freeze and break them. So a couple of times every day I start up the gas engine an' pump warmer water from the well through the pipes so they won't freeze. But on Sunday my wife objects to my runnin' the engine because of the noise it makes, so I have to pump by hand. Now, I can't see why it's any worse for me to start the engine an' make a little noise on Sunday than it is to pump by hand. The Bible says I'm not supposed to work on Sunday. I guess my problem is, Shall I pump by hand, which seems wrong to me, or shall I run the gas engine, which seems wrong to my wife? Or shall I let the pipes freeze?"

The matter was debated. It was pointed out that Christ approved of watering the livestock on Sunday. Operating the engine on Sunday seemed to be the problem because the neighbors, hearing the sound, might think Jack was grinding feed. If he explained the matter to them, his friends believed he would be free from question and could use the engine on Sunday.

After the testimony service, another hymn was sung, followed by a closing prayer. Coffee and cake were served. The minister did not often appear at these midweek sessions. Confident and able in their own strength, the members met and solved their problems.

REVIVAL MEETING

On arrival at home from town one day in late January, Tom announced to Jean that there was to be a revival meeting in Deep Creek. A tabernacle big enough to hold 300 or 400 people would be built right on Main Street. They had arranged for two preachers from out of town to come for a week.

"Well, I sure hope we can just plan to go every night," responded Jean. "In February, you say?"

On the first Sunday in February the minister at Fairhaven announced that the revival would commence on the twelfth. He asked men to volunteer to help build the tabernacle. Tom and several others agreed to go.

The tabernacle was really a shell of a building with a dirt floor. When the structure was complete, eight-inch drainage tiles were set on the ground inside in rows. On these, two-by-ten-inch planks were laid, serving as seats with no backs. Two large heating stoves were installed, a platform was erected for the choir and the preachers, and electrical current was brought in to supply power for light bulbs that hung from the rafters. Then sawdust was raked over the dirt floor, and all was ready.

"Well, it's wonderful to be here in Deep Creek to share with you in the work of the Lord," said the minister as he opened the first meeting on Sunday morning. "I want us to begin this first service with a favorite old song, 'I Love to Tell the Story.' Will the pianist play it through for us?" As she finished, he held up his hand for her to stop. "You know," he said, "I was here when the men were finishing the building. It's a good building. I don't think you need to worry about it coming down. So let's make these rafters ring." At the conclusion of the first stanza he again held up his hand, and the pianist halted. "Do you see these empty chairs here on the platform?" he asked. "We're going to fill these chairs with people who can show you how to sing like you never sang before. While we sing the second stanza I want forty young people to leave your places and come up and fill these chairs. Even if you've never thought you could sing, come on up here and the Lord will put a song in your heart whether you ever had one there before or not." Beckoning to the pianist he continued, "Sing it, now. And come on, fill up these seats. There's a young lady over there coming — two of them. Here comes a young man. Yes, here they come to sing for the Lord! Come on! We've got forty chairs. I know we can fill them."

The seats were not all filled, but he let it go at that. They would be filled in the afternoon. He praised them for their zeal and faith in erecting the tabernacle. He promised great experiences for them in the coming week. That first session was largely a songfest to put them into the proper mood for what was to come.

At noon they ate a basket lunch with friends in the tabernacle. At one o'clock there was a meeting for the men and boys. The minister invited them to cluster near the front, and he came down to stand in the sawdust with them. They opened the service by singing "Faith of Our Fathers." At the end of the first verse, he stopped. "The words of that chorus ought to thrill you every one," he said. "You men have such a proud opportunity. What a glorious challenge. Are you fathers setting an example of faith that your children will want to follow? You can decide here this week to make it so. Let's sing it prayerfully and think carefully of what it means to you."

When the song was finished he put the book down. He reminded them that their children were looking to them for evidence of this faith and this was the time to not be found wanting. After another song or two he pleaded with them to be better fathers to their children, better husbands to their wives, and better examples in the community. God would show them how to do this if they would trust him with their lives.

For the song of dedication to close the session they sang

"All the Way My Savior Leads Me." While they sang he spoke to them. "Won't you come? Won't you come? A better husband to my wife, a better father to my children. No more cheating on my family. Won't you come?" And they came, taking him by the hand. "Thank you for coming, brother. I'm glad you made the decision, brother! God wants you to be a better man, brother! Your family will be proud of you, brother!"

The building was crowded for the afternoon session at two o'clock. With the tabernacle full of adults and a bank of vigorous youth at his back, the minister then began. "Let's start with that grand old hymn, 'I Am Thine, O Lord.'" The pianist ran through it. At the end of the first verse he requested the youths on the platform to sing the second verse. "Aren't you proud of them?" he asked as the last tones died away. "Did you know your children could sing like that? I told you this morning that the Lord would put a song in their hearts, didn't I? Well, have you got a song in your heart, too? Now, I want you to show them how you can sing. Will you sing the third verse, and we'll have them join with you on the chorus. Let's raise the roof!"

So the week continued. The sleighing was never better. The temperature was near zero. It was the resting time of the year. Nothing of consequence had to be begun or finished on the farms nor in the town. It was the time to take stock of one's blessings and to go to meeting and give thanks.

During the sermon, stories were told of confirmed sinners who had come to Christ and had led upstanding lives from thence forward. He told of the drunks whose families had been rescued from poverty when the father, after giving his life to Christ, began to spend his money for food and clothing instead of for drink. Stories were told of people then great in the church who had been saved at such meetings and had spent the rest of their lives as ministers, missionaries, and well-known figures in their state and nation. When the sermon was finished, preparation for the altar call began.

"I want all those who have been saved to stand up," the minister announced. Several people rose. "Thank you, thank you. What a fine testimony of the work of the church." He then explained that the two of them on the platform could not do all of the work of saving souls, for the harvest truly was great. He asked those who had stood to come to the front and be ready to help. Presently ten or a dozen adults gathered at the altar.

"Now, we know that many of you in the congregation have loved ones that you want to see saved. We're going to ask these people at the front to help you. As you close your eyes so that no one else will know what's heavy on your hearts, will you raise your hand if you have a loved one for whom you want them to pray. We'll ask that these at the altar not close their eyes, for they need to know who wants help. If you will raise your hand, someone here will see it and pray for you, and a little later they will go and talk with this person for you. So raise your hands, now. Yes, sister! Yes, brother, I see your hand. We'll help you!"

After a few more minutes he asked all to open their eyes. He then explained that he knew many were ready to come to Christ and he invited them to do this as they sang the next hymn. As they came, those standing at the front were to give them the handshake of love to let them know that they were accepted.

They began to sing. He pleaded, he begged, he urged them to come. He asked parents to do this for their children. He urged husbands and wives to do this for each other and for children to do it for their parents, their sweethearts, and their friends. They sang the chorus over again. They sang the verses a second time. They stopped while he pleaded. As people came to the front, those waiting there greeted them with a handshake, and they knelt at the altar. Some of the people standing passed among those kneeling to talk with them. When they felt they were saved they could stand. If they were not saved but wanted to be, then someone would help them further.

There seemed to be more than one step or condition in the process for some people. Some came to the altar believing that they had always been reasonably decent people, but now they wanted to meet the church's requirement and have it recorded that they were indeed converted. Others came knowing that they had been sinners to some degree and now wanted to make a clean new start. Still others, after they had decided to start a new life, could not feel within themselves that they were forgiven; or if they did not doubt this, something else clogged their conscience and prevented them from clearly understanding the new role offered to them.

Such a case was a young man named Claude. When approached by a lay worker, he said he wanted to be converted. He had waited for this opportunity for some time and he felt that he was ready. But, in spite of his own prayers and the encouragement of others, he did not feel that this great alchemy had yet occurred within him. Finally, he was the last one still kneeling at the altar.

"I'm sure he's saved, but he's not sanctified yet," the lay worker reported to the minister.

"Now, Claude," the minister began, "Christ has promised that all who believe on Him shall be saved. You believe, don't you?"

Claude nodded.

The minister pulled from his pocket his gold watch. "Now, Claude, if I told you I would give you this watch if you did certain things tomorrow and you did them, do you believe that I would give you this watch?"

Again Claude agreed.

"Well, it's just that simple. You have Christ's promise that if you believe you will be saved. Now you feel within yourself that you do believe. This is all Christ requires, so all you have to do is to accept Him. Can you do that?"

"Well, I feel like I've always done that," replied Claude.

"Now that's what I think, too. And that's what your mother and father think. And that's what your friends think. And do you know something? That's what Christ thinks. Can you accept that, Claude? I don't know what it is that's holding you back unless the Devil's trying to get hold of you. But he never had a hold of you, Claude, and he's never going to get a hold of you. Christ has chosen you for His. Do you believe that?"

A smile broke over Claude's face. Slowly he rose to his feet. The minister seized his hand and they looked deeply into each other's eyes. At the back of the tabernacle several people who knew Claude sat waiting for the mesmerism to break. When he rose they moved forward to shake his hand. It had been a long ordeal. Everyone else had gone.

"I'm glad we stayed," observed Jean as she wound the clock before going to bed. "Claude has always seemed like such a nice boy. Now his folks won't have to worry about him no more. He's been saved an' sanctified."

The First Car

GOOD-BYE, BONNIE

IT was a little after eight in the evening. The June sun was almost down. From the dredge ditch came shouts of the boys who had gone there to swim. Actually they were not swimming, for at best the channel of water was not more than three or four feet wide and only a few inches deep. Together Tom and Jean sat in the shade on the porch. It had been a hot day and their clothes felt cool with the evaporation of perspiration. It was a time to relax.

Across the driveway the garden looked lush. From it they had had new lettuce, onions, and radishes for some weeks, and peas were now setting on. In another month it would supply much of the table needs. In the field beyond the yard, toward the ditch, the small corn appeared in neat rows, even and beautiful. To their right, through the trees, a field of oats stood several inches tall, green and fragrant in the evening breeze.

"I aimed to tell you," said Tom, "I met Josephine Hobson on the road the other day, an' what do you suppose she asked me?"

Jean had no idea.

"Well, I was drivin' Hazel an' Bonnie to the carriage. They was steppin' right along when she come over the ridge yonder an' stopped to talk. An' right off she asked if I would sell Bonnie. 'I been lookin',' she said, 'for a good drivin' horse so's I can get to town without havin' to take all day. We ain't got no real buggy horse, an' when the men're in the field they've got all the horses. Then I can't go at all. So,' she said, 'I just told the men I'm goin' to keep on a lookout for a good drivin' horse an' when I find one, I'm a-goin' to buy it. So what'll ya take for her? The black one?' "

"Why," exclaimed Jean, "we wouldn't think of sellin' Bonnie — what'd you tell her?"

"I told her that as soon as she could bring me a hundred an' fifty dollars in cash she could have Bonnie."

"Tom! You didn't! You can't sell Bonnie!"

Tom understood. He had thought so too, at first, but he had been looking at horses on the road when he was hauling. He had looked at Jim's horses and at Joe's. All about him he saw strong, heavy horses. And he had concluded that his horses were too light. They had been all right for the carriage and for the casual fieldwork in Indiana, but they were not up to the strenuous demands of the Iowa farm. He needed heavier horses.

"All right," agreed Jean, "but how will sellin' Bonnie help do all of this?"

Tom explained that they had to start raising bigger colts. To do this they had to buy some bigger mares. So if Josephine Hobson wanted to lay down a hundred and fifty dollars, it would do Bonnie a favor by putting her back between the buggy shafts instead of in the field, and with a little more money they could buy some larger brood mares that could produce stronger colts.

At this time Jean was like Josephine. Tom had all of the horses in the field. She had cream and eggs that should go to town, but without a horse to drive there was no way she could get there. Tom considered her problem. Cultivating corn was going well, but the grass was coming fast. They all had to keep at it. But they had to get to town, too. After further discussion it was agreed he would not go to the field Saturday afternoon and they would take his team to go to town.

"You know," he said, "if the crops are as good as it looks like they'll be, I'm goin' to buy one of them Fords in the fall. We need it bad for goin' to town."

The following Wednesday evening Tom and Jean set off to prayer meeting driving Bonnie and Hazel, but half an hour later the children were surprised to see them returning in the dusk, with the Hobsons' buggy following them. Tom unhitched the horses and led them to the barn. Soon he returned leading Bonnie. Josephine opened her purse and in the dim twilight counted out one hundred and fifty dollars. Tom counted it again and put it in his pocket. Then he tied Bonnie to the Hobsons' buggy.

"Be good to her," said Jean, her voice choking. Bonnie

reluctantly followed on the rope. As Tom walked past her, he gave her an affectionate pat on the rump.

"Good-bye, old girl," he said. "You've been a good hoss." In silence Tom and Jean walked to the house.

With the money from the sale of Bonnie, Tom bought a Percheron mare whose progeny supplied most of the horsepower for the farm for the next ten or fifteen years.

THE 1916 FORD

Threshing was finished. The stubble of the oatfield lay yellow under the hot August sun. To Tom, who had seen the field as a forest of grain shocks for the past several weeks, it now lay nude and empty. It had borne its crop, which he had cut and threshed. About the field stood a few bunches of grain missed by the binder, some scattered wads of straw, and a few bundles not collected by the bundle haulers at threshing time—small gleanings from a good crop. He would turn the cows in to clean it up and to forage on the grass that grew in the fencerows. But first he had to repair the fence. He was completing this when Mike Romier, the son of a neighbor, came by mowing the grass along the side of the road. He stopped to rest the team.

"Howdy," said Tom wiping his forehead. "You got up about as much of a sweat on the team as I got myself. Doggies, it's hot today."

Mike smiled. "Good day to cut the hay. Ought to dry fast if the weather holds out. Patchin' up the fence a little?"

"Yow. Goin' to let the cows in to clean up the field, so decided I'd better be sure the fence is in good shape. How much hay do you figure you'll get from the road?"

"Well, we generally get a small load. Don't amount to much, but we ain't got much other hay, so every bit counts. It's pretty good this year, though, with all the rain we had."

Tom thought he would pasture the cows on his side of the road after they got the oats cleaned up from the field. The little boys could watch them. In a week or so they'd have it cleaned up.

"Well, I better get this mowed, I guess," said Mike. "Gotta crank up the Kissel an' take Paw to the doctor at Antonville this afternoon. His stomach's actin' up again."

Tom looked at him interestedly. "You goin' to Antonville this afternoon, ya say? What time?"

"Oh, we generally go right after dinner. Prob'ly 'round one o'clock." Mike pulled a stalk of green standing timothy out of its joint and began to chew on the tender end. "It's twenty mile. Takes about an hour. If we go around one o'clock that gets us back about five."

"Mind if I ride with you?" asked Tom. "I been wantin' to go to Antonville."

Being the guest, Tom was invited to sit in the front seat with Mike, who drove. "Where did you get the car?" questioned Tom. "You say this is a Kissel? I never seen a Kissel before."

They had seen it at the fair in Antonville two years before. Mike's father was just starting to go to Antonville to the doctor then and it took all day to make the trip. As soon as his father saw the Kissel, he was all for buying it. It was easy to make the trip with the car.

"Where do you get gasoline?" pursued Tom.

"We always put in gasoline at Antonville. Takes maybe two gallon to go an' two more to come home. The tank holds ten gallon. The implement store in Deep Creek has a gasoline pump right on the sidewalk, now, too. You drive up in front and he'll put a hose in the tank an' pump in a gallon, then he turns the crank back an' pumps in another gallon, 'til you got as much as you want. The hardware man in St. Vincent's gettin' a pump put in, he told me. Lots of people gettin' automobiles. Pretty soon you can buy gasoline prob'ly in most any town you come to."

When he returned that evening, Jean knew by the smile on his face that he had ordered the car. He hung his pants on a nail and slipped into his overalls. Four hundred dollars was a lot of money, but the oat crop had been good and the corn was better than last year. With the hundred acres across the ditch that he hadn't farmed previously, it looked like a real good year for them. They could manage it.

It was a warm, sunny day in October. Outside of the schoolhouse the grasshoppers sang and the meadowlark warbled from the tall grass. Along the fences the goldenrod showed deep yellow in the sunshine. Bill had been restless all day. He had had more than the usual number of problems wrong in arithmetic and had not known anything about the history lesson. After the last recess he had quit work entirely, sitting most of the time looking out of the window. For a second time he asked to leave the room. At this point a sharp "Beep, Beep" sounded from the road.

"There he is," said Eddie in a loud whisper.

"Beep, Beep." This time from in front of the school.

Both Anderson boys and Eddie raised their hands for permission to leave the room.

"Well, you can't all go at once," remonstrated the teacher. At this moment a bright new black Ford turned into the driveway and stopped in front of the open door.

"That's our Pop," announced Eddie. "We got a new Ford today. It's our Pop. Can we go out an' see it?"

By this time the big boys were standing up peering out through the doorway. Perry Anderson stood by the water pail drinking slowly, admiring the scene outside.

Emerging from the car, Tom approached the entrance and knocked. "Is it about time for school to be out?" he inquired. "If you could let my kids out now, they could ride home with me 'stead of walkin'."

TEACHING JEAN TO DRIVE

The next morning Tom took Jean out to the barnyard to teach her how to drive, for he would depend on her to go to town when he was busy in the field. He had her turn the ignition on. Then she pushed the spark lever up, and it was ready to go. "Do I have to crank it?" she asked. Opal Fitsimmons says crankin's awful hard."

Tom insisted she would have to learn to crank. If she had trouble she might get a man to crank it for her if she was in town, but if she killed the engine while out on a country road she would have to start it herself. He showed her how to engage the crank, then lift it with the right hand while she pulled the choke wire with the left. It was an ordeal, but the new car was easy to start.

"Now, get under the wheel," he instructed, "an' we'll drive around the barn lot a few times."

Almost petrified, she complied.

"Pull the spark lever down so's to give it more power. Now, that pedal on the left side is the low pedal. You step on that for goin' slow or when it's hard pullin'."

Uncertainly she began. She pressed too hard on the low pedal and the strain killed the engine. She got out and cranked. After killing the engine a few times she learned to give it more gas and to press more cautiously on the low pedal until the car was in motion. Around the barnyard they went in low, stopping to back up from time to time. Then it was time to go down in the lane and try it in high gear. Jean objected, but Tom insisted that she could not drive all the way to town in low gear, even if it was easier.

Changing into high gear was difficult. After gathering momentum in low, she thrust the high lever forward, then removed her foot from the low pedal so as to give an easy transition. If it was traveling too slowly, the shift would cause the car to jerk or stall. A half dozen times she threatened to give up, but each time Tom persuaded her to try again. He had had the same problems when Jack Fitsimmons had taken his Ford out into the pasture one Sunday afternoon and taught Tom to drive.

WHEN IT BALKS

"What's the matter, Pop, won't it go?" Eddie peered over the front fender at Tom, who for several minutes had been cranking. "Can't ya get it started?"

Tom shook his head. He reached under the dash and turned the carburetor adjustment rod. Returning to the front he cranked some more, but to no avail. In desperation he instructed Eddie to get on a horse and go see if Harry Jorgeson could come and give him a pull.

In half an hour Harry appeared, driving his new Reo. "What's the matter, Tom? Can't get her started?"

"By doggies, no, I sure can't. Cranked an' cranked on her. She coughed a couple of times at first, but then she never snorted again."

They tied the cars together with a rope and Harry drove around the barnyard, pulling the Ford in high gear in an attempt to start it. But there was no response from the Ford. Thinking that it needed choking, Tom asked Eddie to lie on the front fender and choke it a few times. Around they went again, Eddie lying half over the fender pulling the choke wire—but it did not start.

"Tell you what le's do," offered Harry. "Maybe if we go out on the road where we can get up a little speed it'll get goin'. An' if that don't work, we'll haul it over to Green's place. If Ed is there, he'll likely know what to do. He's pretty good with a Ford."

In a few minutes they arrived at the Greens' place and fortunately Edward was at home. After raising the hood for a look beneath, he took the crank in one hand and the choke wire in the other. Then planting his feet wide, he whirled the crank a dozen times, pulling the choke wire now and then. It did not go. In amazement Eddie witnessed the speed with which Edward had spun the crank. It was unbelievable.

"Boy, can he spin it!" he exclaimed.

Edward looked under the hood again. "Not gettin' gas," he said. "Got any in the tank?"

"Four inches of gas in the tank," said Tom.

After so much choking, there should have been gas dripping from the carburetor, but there was none. Edward took hold of the carburetor adjustment rod to turn it. The carburetor was shut off. He opened the valve, then again spun the motor. It fired a couple of times but did not go. With a wrench he loosened a bolt behind the fan, slipped the spring clip to one side, and removed the timer. Taking a glove from his hip pocket he wiped around the inside of the timer.

"Look at that. Dirty. Oil gets into the timer, water splashes on it and some seeps inside, and pretty soon you got this goop in it. Current can't get through."

He replaced the timer, tightened the bolt, and signaled for Tom to crank it. After a few turns it began to go. Everybody smiled. Edward advanced the spark and the engine settled to a steady hum. He raced the throttle up and down several times and then shut it off. "It's O.K. now," he said.

"Was it just that dirty timer?" asked Tom.

Edward explained that this probably was why it wouldn't go in the first place. Then Tom didn't know what was wrong, so he tried this and that, and one thing he did was to shut off the carburetor with that rod under the dash. He probably thought he was opening it, which was the right thing to do. But he had turned it the wrong way and shut it off completely. Then it would never go. Edward had done the same thing himself. There was a lot to learn about these cars. Saying "get up" and "whoa" wasn't enough any more.

"Pop, can I drive?" asked Eddie expectantly when they were on the way home again. he had rehearsed this moment for weeks. He was then fourteen. Other boys' dads allowed them to drive now and then. He had screwed up his courage for this opportunity. "Ain't nobody comin'. Can I drive?"

Eddie often cranked the car for Jean. Tom knew that other boys his age had begun to drive; in fact he could see that within the near future he might need Eddie to take the car on errands by himself. "All right, Eddie," he said, as he brought the car to a stop and climbed out from behind the wheel. "We're gonna teach you to drive."

A Larger Family

THE BIRTHING OF MATTHEW

BERT awakened slowly one April Sunday morning in 1915. Something was not as it should be on that morning. It was daylight. They generally arose about six thirty or seven on Sunday morning, and it seemed like it was time to get up, but Tom had not called them. Eddie and Bill lay whispering in bed. This was unusual.

"What day is it?" asked Bert, raising up on his elbow and looking at them. "Is it Sunday?"

"Yow, it's Sunday," replied Bill. "Why?"

Bert thought it over. Downstairs people were moving about — several people. There were quiet voices. He listened.

As the spring nights became warm, Tom allowed the fire in the stoves to go out. This required that he light them again each morning. Upon arising he would select a dry piece of wood; with one end of it resting on the floor he would take a butcher knife and cut long shavings from it for starting the fire. This made a reverberating noise throughout the house as the floor amplified the sound.

Following this there would be other noises as he lighted fire in the heating stove and kitchen range. Presently he would call, "Eddie, Bill. Time to get up."

"Awwwnnngg!" They would turn over, yawn, and relax again into a semistupor.

After a bit the call would be repeated with more urgency. "Eddie! Bill! Come on now, time to get up!" ·

But all of that was missing this morning. Suddenly Bert was wide awake. That sounded like Mrs. Hammond's voice downstairs. How could she be there before time for them to be out of bed? Then vaguely it occurred to him that he had heard sounds downstairs for some time before he had been fully awake. "Hey, you guys," he said, addressing Eddie and

Bill, "What's goin' on downstairs, anyhow? What's Mrs. Hammond doin' here before breakfast, I'd like to know."

At this point the door at the bottom of the stairs creaked. "Don't you kids get up yet for a while," said Tom. "Don't come downstairs."

Bill and Eddie looked knowingly at each other. From the next room, Jane emerged in her nightgown.

"What's goin' on?" she asked. "I been hearin' people downstairs an' it ain't even time for breakfast. There's people in Mom an' Pop's bedroom right under my room. I been hearin' 'em."

Bill grinned and pulled the covers over his head. Eddie looked sheepish. "Sure sounds like somebody's down there. Must be somebody's sick."

Presently there was the sharp, short cry of a baby. From her position by the door, Jane dropped to the floor and searched the limited area in the living room below the register. Bert and Ernie sat bolt upright.

"I heard a baby cry!" said Ernie.

"Mrs. Hammond just went by with a pan of water an' there's a man down there with a bald head," announced Jane, standing up and whispering at the top of her voice. "There's a baby all right." She looked at the boys in amazement. "Are we gonna have a baby?"

"All right, you can get up now," called Tom after a time. "You can come downstairs."

They raced down the stairs, their bare feet making soft whispering sounds on the wooden steps. The children had seen new little calves, colts, chickens, and other animals, but this was the first brand-new baby they had seen. They stood in silence, each with his own thoughts.

Mrs. Hammond bustled back into the bedroom. "The doctor says I can ride with him, so I'll go now. I'll come again if you need me. Just telephone from the neighbors an' Jim'll bring me in the car, day or night."

The bald-headed man waited at the kitchen door, valise in hand, pulling on his gloves as Mrs. Hammond approached with her coat over her arm. The doctor put on his hat as they went out. Tom followed onto the porch.

"Thank you for comin', Edith," he called. "G'bye, Doc, hope we never need you again."

The doctor turned, walking backwards for a step or two. "Well, this's only six, I think you said. I'll probably be back again a time or two." He chuckled as he opened the car door for Mrs. Hammond.

The new baby proved to have a lusty voice and a strong pair of lungs, for he kept them awake at night occasionally. He was, however, a good baby, needing little special attention. Life agreed with him. They named him Matthew. For presiding at the birthing the doctor charged Tom fifteen dollars.

GRACE

Tom and Jean's seventh child, Grace, was born during the night in 1916. Her arrival did not disturb the rest of the children. When they awoke in the morning, there she was.

JOHN

When the eighth child was born, it was a different story. Tom met Bert and Ernie at the foot of the stairs when they got up that morning. "You boys an' Jane are goin' to the Harmonson's—right now. Just hike right across the field. Mrs. Harmonson'll have breakfast for you. I'll call you when it's time to come home."

The boys looked at him blankly. It was quite unheard of to just walk off without a pretense of helping with the chores.

"How come?" asked Bert.

"Well, Mom don't feel well this mornin'. I'm gonna stay in the house an' get breakfast. You kidlets run on now."

The Harmonsons expected them. After they had eaten, the boys busied themselves about the barnyard. They seemed to be in a sort of suspension until they returned to the house at about eight thirty. Here they found Jane and Gloria Harmonson hovering near the telephone, listening every time anyone on the party line had a call.

Presently there was one long ring for the operator. Jane took down the receiver to listen, her hand clasped over the hard-rubber cup on the mouthpiece of the phone. A sly smile spread over her face. "He's callin' the doctor. He's supposed to come right away."

Meanwhile, at home, Eddie and Bill had gone to the barn to milk, a sizable job for the two of them by themselves. When they came from milking, Tom met them at the kitchen door and directed them to separate the milk and then get the horses ready for the field. He would bring their breakfast to them at the barn. Their mother didn't feel well. He would have to call the doctor for her.

At about ten in the morning a phone call to Harmonsons notified the children that they were to come home. Expectantly they hurried across the fields. The new arrival was a boy. They named him John.

This birth, however, had not gone well, and in a day or so a nurse arrived.

"Which one of the children was it that went to the hospital?" inquired Jean of Tom when he returned from church on Wednesday night.

"What are you talkin' about?" asked Tom. "Ain't none of the kids in the hospital."

"Well, I'm thankful for that. It just seemed from the way the horses was runnin' across the creek that somethin' was wrong."

"What have you been givin' her?" asked Tom sternly of the nurse. "Did you give her a hypodermic?"

"Well, who's going to be the doctor here, you or me?" asked the nurse. "If you want me to take care of the patient, then I'll have to do it according to doctor's instructions and as I find best."

"Well, you're not to give her no more dope unless the doctor tells me she should have it. Not if you're gonna stay here," responded Tom firmly.

A bed had been made for the nurse on a cot in the front room. In the meantime, Tom slept in the room with Eddie and Bill upstairs above the living room. The following night he was awakened by talking from downstairs. Jean seemed to be protesting, her voice coming quite plainly to him through the heat register in the floor.

"No, I don't want any of that tonight."

"Yes," countered the nurse, "I have to give it to you. You have to have some sleep and so do I, so give me your arm."

Almost before the conversation had ended, Tom was down the stairs. "I told you she wasn't to have no more hypos unless the doctor told me so himself. Do you hear me?"

In a pet the nurse put down the needle and went to her cot. She advised him that if he wanted to be the nurse for the rest of the night he could have the job, but she would not be responsible for what happened. He replied that if she couldn't do what the doctor had sent her to do she could just go to bed and he would take the job. And in the morning he would take her back to town. This closed their conversation for the night. The nurse, who had been on twenty-four-hour duty for two or three days and was probably tired out, took him at his word and went to bed. He took a rocking chair into the bedroom and remained there for the rest of the night.

"I'm gonna bring your nurse back to town," announced Tom to the doctor over the phone the next morning. There was conversation from the doctor's end of the line.

"Well, I took care of her from midnight on. There ain't nuthin' she needs that I can't give her just as well as the nurse, I guess. Maybe I can do it better." Whereupon the doctor asked to talk to the nurse.

"Well, doctor, there doesn't seem to be much that I can really do for the patient. I think I'd better come back to town."

"Well, you're goin' back because I'm gonna take you," interrupted Tom.

"No, doctor, there's just too many fingers in the pie here for a nurse to take proper care of the patient."

"Get your bag packed. I'll be ready to go in fifteen minutes."

In about three weeks Jean was on her feet again, and the family resumed its usual operation. For the next several weeks Tom, when not in the field, spent most of his time in the house helping with meals and encouraging Jean to rest as much as possible. He was neither a good cook nor a good housekeeper, but when she was not well Jean always said she would rather have Tom look after her than anyone else.

Interesting Events

Tom had sent Bill to the pasture to bring in the horses. When he finally arrived with them, Bill was not in a happy mood. "That Jake and Rolly would gallop along with the other horses up to the pasture lane an' then they'd duck out and kick up their heels an' away they'd go to the back of the pasture again," he complained.

"Yeh, I know," agreed Tom. "They're gettin' real foxy, them two."

The colts, Rolly and Jake, were two years old. He would break them to work in the spring, but before doing this he would have to castrate them. The young stallions were full of fire, burning up with energy, playing and chasing each other continuously. At times they would rear up on their hind legs, striking at each other like boxers, snorting, biting, and kicking until Jean had questioned whether the small children were safe with them free in the barnyard.

"Let 'em have their fun," Tom told her. "We'll need all that vim an' vitality when I harness them up for work next spring. Before I do that, I'll get the vet'inary out here an' he'll cool 'em down so's they won't feel so frisky."

On Saturday morning a few weeks later, the veterinarian drove into the barnyard. Tom brought Rolly out first. He was a sturdy bay, medium of build, with a strong, arching neck. He shied nervously away from the vet, prancing lightly about.

The veterinarian placed on the horse's back a long, wide leather band having a four-inch iron ring on one end. He buckled the ends together under Rolly's belly. Next he placed his hand on Rolly's upper foreleg and slowly moved it downward to below the knee, where he placed a leather band around the leg, with a rope attached. He slid this down to the fetlock, just above the hoof, buckled it, and repeated this operation on the other front leg. Going toward Rolly's flank he patted him gently. The horse shied away. Tom held the bridle with both hands, but so excited was the horse that he lifted Tom bodily off the ground as he backed and tried to rear. After a time the vet was able to buckle a similar encircling band about each rear fetlock.

They passed the four ropes, each from a different foot, through the iron ring on the band under the horse's belly. The vet then took two ropes and gave two to Tom. They pulled them taut, then instructed Eddie to back the horse. As Rolly lifted his rear leg to move backward, they pulled in the slack to hold that leg off the ground. Off balance, the horse soon went down on his belly, his four feet pulled together beneath him. Straining and threshing he rolled over on his side.

Tying the ropes to the steel ring, the vet moved to the horse's rear, where he crouched down against his haunch. Seizing a testicle in one hand and a knife in the other, he made a quick slicing cut some three inches long in the outer skin of the goose-egg-sized mass. The wound opened, showing whitish tissue below, which was soon overrun with a crimson sheet of blood that oozed from the cut and dripped from the vet's fingers. He made another quick slash, cutting completely through the tough membrane that enclosed the testicle. This he followed with a third cut, slicing into the soft mass of the organ which gaped open, looking pink and beady like a cluster of fish eggs. Pressing back the cut flesh, the vet squeezed the testicle out through the opening, then pulling it slightly away from the horse's body he severed the connecting cords and threw the excised organ to one side. In a few minutes he had removed the other testicle also. Buster, the dog, sniffed at one of the testicles, then took it gingerly in his mouth and trotted away.

"Well," said Eddie, who with Bill and Bert had stood watching, "Buster won't need any supper tonight."

The men removed the ropes and Rolly got slowly to his feet, shook himself carefully, and with drooping head tested his legs. He moved a few paces, then turned and looked at the men.

"You can go on, now," bantered Tom. "Kick up your heels an' have your fun. Next spring I'm gonna put the harness on you an' learn you a couple more tricks."

In much this same manner, dozens of hogs and calves were castrated every year, though these smaller animals could usually be held without ropes. In a week or so they would generally be healed and ready to perform as before, except for breeding purposes. The farmer usually performed the castration on the calves and pigs himself before they were a year old.

SKUNK BUTTER

Being late for milking was a serious breach of responsibility. Each person had his own cows to milk, and no one was apt to milk them for him unless there was a good reason. So when Bert and Ernie returned late from an errand one evening they burst hurriedly into the cow barn.

"Wheeeeou!" exclaimed Tom as they walked past him. "You fellows have been mixed up with a skunk. Go out an' take them jackets off; the smell'll settle into the milk. Go on, get 'em off outside."

"Where'd you run into that skunk, anyhow?" pursued Tom when they had returned.

Ernie explained. "We was about halfway down the pasture lane when right in front of us this skunk ran out of the grass an' started down the path."

"He wasn't goin' very fast," added Bert. "We could easy catch him."

"Well, just for your information," interjected Bill, "a skunk is one of the last things you want to chase."

"Yow, we found that out," continued Bert. "Just when we was about to catch up with him, he stopped right in front of us an' let us have it. There was a broken-off fence post along there, so I grabbed that an' we went after him. Just as I was ready to lay him out with the post, he stopped an' sprayed us again."

"Sounds like you kids learned about skunks the hard way," chortled Eddie.

During breakfast a few days later, while Jane was eating a piece of toast, she commented that the butter tasted strange.

"Tastes like skunk," observed Eddie. "How'd it ever get to taste like a skunk, anyhow?"

"Did you churn yesterday?" inquired Tom.

"Yeh," replied Jean. "It sure does taste like skunk, all right."

Tom smiled. The smell was from the skunk Bert and Ernie had met. When the boys had milked with their skunk-smelling clothes on, the milk had absorbed the odor, which finally showed up in the butter. Tom wondered whether some of that cream was mixed with what they had taken to the creamery. Jean assumed that it probably was. He laughed.

"Well, somebody's sure gonna be surprised when they get a pound of skunky butter all done up in a nice clean package from the creamery."

A RUNAWAY HORSE

During the summer of 1917 Mrs. Hammond was involved in a serious accident. Driving her favorite horse to the buggy she had gone on an errand; on the return she had approached a section of road that was being graded.

At that time, road-grading equipment consisted of a gasoline tractor, about the size of a steam threshing engine, which pulled a grader behind on a steel cable. The plowlike blade of the grader cut the soil loose from the roadside and moved it up onto the roadbed. After a few days of grading, a ditch had been cut along each side of the road and the soil from this was piled up on top of the grade. It stretched in long tongues of sod and loose dirt like the squirming arms of some monster that might lie beneath. The snorting tractor rolled over it, packing it down and hauling the grader some thirty feet behind on the cable. The men were making good time. In another day or two the job would be finished, smooth and beautiful. But just then it was impassable.

As Mrs. Hammond approached this mile of road she had two choices — go all the way around the section, three extra miles, or pass the grading equipment on the sod between the ditch and the fence. This she chose to do. The horse was gentle and dependable. He was used to the Buick and gave little heed when he encountered cars on the road. But he was not acquainted with large tractors. As the horse approached the tractor, which was snorting irregularly and ejecting black exhaust, it all became too much for this trusted animal. He bolted as he came abreast of the equipment. Away he went, his mistress shouting, pulling with all her strength on the lines, her feet braced against the front of the buggy. But it was of no use. The terrified horse lost all reason. He shied away from the machinery and ran along the fence. The hub of the front wheel struck a post, twisting the front axle and breaking the shafts between which the horse was hitched. The buggy turned over, throwing Mrs. Hammond out. Freed from the buggy, the horse raced toward home a half mile away.

When the men from the equipment reached her, she was semiconscious, with a cut on her forehead. A neighbor and her son came running to the scene, and she dispatched the boy to hitch a team to their spring wagon and return. They made Mrs. Hammond as comfortable as they could. By this time Jim Hammond had returned home, and when the horse came galloping into the barnyard he climbed into the Buick and started out to investigate. Leaving the car at the corner, he ran to his wife. He instructed the neighbor lady to return to her house and call the doctor. Placing Mrs. Hammond in the spring wagon, they took her home.

Several stitches were taken on her forehead, a collar bone was broken, and she had many bruises. She had lost some blood, but the doctor thought that after a week or so in bed, she would be all right. During the days following there was hardly an hour when there was not a car or buggy from the neighborhood standing in the barnyard. Friends brought food; they came to offer their help and understanding. Tom and Jean went to see her on Sunday after church. Mrs. Hammond was cheerful and able to sit up in bed. The worst was over.

"Sure glad my woman learned to drive the car," Tom confided in Jim as they stood in the barnyard by Tom's Ford.

"Yeh, I got a good drivin' horse somebody can buy real cheap right now."

THE CURSE OF THE PRAIRIE

In 1914, when Tom began to build up his stock of work horses, Maude was the first colt. She was a beautiful, gentle, black Percheron, and a few years later she had become a fine young mare. One Sunday afternoon they heard the fence squeaking repeatedly where the horses were grazing; when Tom arrived at the scene he found Maude caught in the barbed wire.

Crawling through the fence, Bert and Ernie hurried toward the mare as she stood with a loop of the wire around her hind leg. Tom held her by the nose with one hand and by the foretop with the other. She had apparently kicked at another horse and her leg had come down across the wire. Running away from the fence pulling the wire caused the barbs on the wire to saw into her leg at the joint. As Tom backed her, Bert and Ernie seized the wire on each side of the leg to remove it. The cut oozed blood, which ran down over her hoof. The wire made a sickening, sucking sound as they thrust it out of the wound. Hair from her tail and bits of flesh clung to it.

"Go tell Mom to call the vet'inary," instructed Tom as he took Maude by the foretop and led her toward the barn.

By the time the veterinarian arrived, the bleeding had stopped and clots of blood hung in the mouth of the cut. Maude stood quietly switching flies as if she understood that something serious had happened and that the men would do what was best. Several tendons from the lower leg had been cut through. Had it happened to a person, a surgeon could have spliced the tendons together, but with a horse that could not be done. The vet consoled Tom by pointing out that she would still make a fine broodmare even if she was unable to work in the field. The wound was not bandaged. Daily they sprinkled it with disinfectant powder. To keep the flies away they coated it with pine tar, a pleasant-smelling black preparation. The leg healed, but it remained swollen from the hock down to the ankle during the rest of her life, and it was stiff so that she always dragged that foot slightly. In a couple of months she was back in the harness again, as steady and dependable as ever.

When a Farmer Moved

LOCATING ANOTHER PLACE

It was toward the end of August in 1917. Tom was working about the barnyard when he noticed a man slowly walking over the farm. As he was crossing the field below the house, Tom realized that this was Pete Smathers, who owned land in that part of the state. There was but one reason for his being on the place.

"You goin' to buy this place, Smathers?" Tom asked as the other man approached.

Pete looked at him briefly, then turned his eyes away. "Nope," he said. "Kind of thought I might, but don't guess I will." They exchanged a few more words and then Smathers left.

"Well, you got a new landlord," greeted Strane as Tom entered the bank the next afternoon.

Tom stared at him in amazement. "Did Smathers buy my place?" he asked.

"Yes, he signed the papers this morning."

Tom's face became tense. "I asked him point-blank yesterday if he was gonna buy that farm an' he denied it. Funny, Oberly never told me he was gonna sell." Tom was not pleased. "Well, I gotta move. Know of a place that's for rent?"

Astounded, Strane looked at him for a moment. Slowly he shook his head. "It's the end of August—pretty late. Pretty late to find a place that's for rent now. Look, why don't you stay where you are for another year? Things are going all right for you. Next winter or spring something good's bound to turn up that you can rent.

Tom considered this. "Nope," he said decisively, "I don't

81

aim to do business with no man that lies to me like that."

George Harmonson, a renter of one of Smathers's farms, had entered the bank in time to overhear these remarks. He followed Tom outside. "You gonna move?"

Tom nodded. George was agitated.

"You know, things are not goin' very good for me. I'm lookin' for another place to rent, too."

Together they considered their plight. Both agreed to tell no one but to start looking. They examined the many-sided aspects of their dilemma. George, who had lived several miles to the southwest a number of years before, then remembered that a man named Sam Magnussen owned a number of farms there. If they could find him, he might have land to rent. In considering how to go about this, they decided to ask Strane to call a bank in Westover, some twelve miles away, where Magnussen would be known. The president of the bank in Westover assured them that he believed Magnussen did have a farm or two for rent. They agreed to go to Westover in Tom's car the next morning.

For Tom, the problem was further complicated because school had begun and Jean was at that time visiting in Indiana. At suppertime he instructed Eddie that when he went to school the next morning he was to send a telegram to his mother. Eddie read the words written in Tom's uneven hand. "Come home immediately by train We have to move Reply"

"We gonna move, Pop?" he asked incredulously. "Are we gonna move away from here?"

"We're gonna move, but I don't want you to say nuthin' to nobody about it yet. Just keep still an' don't say nuthin' at all."

He looked around the table at each of them. They were wide-eyed at these instructions, but they did not question him. He would leave in the morning right after breakfast. Jane, then ten, would stay home from school with two-year-old Matthew. The boys would do the chores and go to school as usual. Tom expected to be home again the next night, Friday, or if not, he would return on Saturday. He had to find another place for them to live.

When Frank Berg, president of the First County Bank in Westover, unlocked the bank at eight thirty Friday morning, the men climbed out of Tom's car and followed him into the bank.

"We called you yesterday from Deep Creek. I'm Tom Harper an' this's George Harmonson."

"I remember. You're lookin' for Magnussen?"

"If he's got land to rent we're lookin' for him," said George. "I used to live out south of there several years ago. Never talked to Magnussen, but I know he's got land."

Berg agreed. He had done some inquiring after they called. So far as anyone knew, a farm of about five hundred acres called the home place and a nearby quarter section were for rent, but Magnussen was not in town. Berg told them where the farms were, and they decided to go look at them.

They briefly surveyed the farms and learned that Magnussen was probably at Empire, twenty miles away. It was then eleven in the morning. They set out for Empire. Walking down the street in that city they noted a man with a beard sitting in the sun on the bank steps. As they walked past him, George punched Tom in the ribs and gestured toward the man. "That's him. That's our man. Sam's got a beard an' he's about seventy years old. I know that's him."

As they turned back and approached the older man, he looked up at them. "Are you Mr. Magnussen?" asked George.

The man got up. "Yes," he said in a firm voice, "I'm Sam Magnussen."

"You got land for rent?" asked Tom.

"I've got two farms for rent near Westover. You men interested?"

"We're interested, an' we've seen the farms," replied Tom. "We want to rent them." Tom invited Magnussen to ride with them to Westover, where they signed the leases.

It was nearly dark when Tom reached home. He had been gone thirteen hours, and during that time the world for him had changed beyond anything he could have dreamed a week earlier. The boys had done the chores, supper was finished, and Jane and Bert were doing the dishes while the others played in the yard. Going to the bedroom he deposited the lease in a box in the dresser drawer and sat down to a cold supper, tired, but pleased.

As they had driven home, Tom and George reasoned that they would have to take horses and plows as well as feed and stay at one of the places to do the plowing. On the farm Tom had rented was a large cattle barn where the horses could be kept. The men could sleep on the hay there and do their cooking on a kerosene stove, placed in a wagon box for safety.

As Tom considered the day's events, Pierre Romier appeared in the doorway with a telegram from Jean that had been phoned to his house from the depot in Deep Creek. She would be on the train that reached Deep Creek at four in the morning on Wednesday.

On Monday morning at daylight Tom, mounted on a load of oats for feed, and George, on a load of hay, departed for Westover to plow. The horses they were not driving, along with the plows, were tied behind their wagons, while on top were piled bedding, groceries, and harness. They would be gone for over a month.

The children had their instructions. Jane would stay at home with Matthew until Jean returned. The small boys would walk to the rural school, and Eddie with Bill would ride horseback to school in Deep Creek.

At two thirty on Wednesday morning Eddie, aged fifteen, and Bill, twelve, took the car and set out to meet Jean's train. The road was passable, but there was one bad mudhole. As they approached this, Eddie put the car into low so as to race through it. The ruts were deep, and when the axle began to drag, the Ford stuck. Bill got out and pushed from the front and then from the back, but they could not budge it. They had tire chains in the car but could not put them on in the deep ruts.

"Maybe if we pulled grass and laid it under the back wheels, it would help," suggested Bill.

"We can sure try it," responded Eddie as they began to pull the long dead grass from the roadside. After packing this under the back sides of the rear wheels and laying it in the tracks for two or three feet, they were able to back the car. They then laid grass in the ruts ahead of the car, and with Bill pushing they made a short run that carried them through the rest of the mudhole. In town, while waiting for the train, they put the chains on and had no trouble going home.

During the winter months Tom made frequent trips to move equipment to the new place, eighteen miles away. Before daylight he would be off, the load jolting on the frozen, rutted roads. Since a team could make about three miles per hour, he reached his destination at noon. On the first trip he took his dinner in a syrup pail, but the tenant at the place insisted that he come into the house and eat a hot dinner with him and his wife. This he gladly did from that time on. By the time he was ready to start home, it was one thirty or two o'clock. Returning, he trotted the team slowly for most of the way, reaching home sometime after dark.

To move the seed corn, Tom decided to shell it and put it into sacks. They worked at this during Christmas vacation. As soon as morning chores were finished each day, he and the boys gathered in the room over the kitchen amid a clutter of milk pails and cooking pots into which they shelled the corn.

"Boy, this hurts my hand," complained Ernie, aged seven, when he began to shell an ear the first morning. "I'm gonna put on a pair of mittens. This corn'll wear my hands out." He shelled off a few more kernels and paused to look at his hand.

"You can't shell corn with your bare hands," said Tom. "It sure enough will wear your hand out. You have to use a cob."

"Yeh, the corn'll make your hands look like mincemeat," agreed Bill.

"Let me show you how," suggested Tom. He broke two or three cobs in two, giving a half to each boy. "Ya hold your cob in your right hand between your thumb an' first finger, with it hangin' down in your palm." He held up his hand to show them. "Then you hold the ear in your left hand. You start at the top of the ear and press the cob against the kernels and push away from you, toward the right."

When Ernie tried this, his cob turned and popped out from his palm. They showed him how to hold it at the top with his thumb as he let the bottom hang free.

"Hey, I get it!" exulted Ernie as he began to shell his ear. "Boy," he said looking at the cob, "You're sure gonna take a beatin' today." When they had finished the pile at their feet,

Eddie reached for an ear from the row by the wall.

"No, you can't take them 'til I shell off the butts and tips," objected Tom.

"How come you do that?" asked Eddie.

Tom explained. At the large end of an ear the kernels are extra large, while at the opposite end they are quite small. The planter would drop three or four normal-sized kernels to each hill of corn, but it might drop only one of the large kernels or too many of the small ones. So it was better to shell them off and not use them.

There were on the market hand corn shellers consisting of a boxlike unit eight or ten inches thick and three and a half to four feet high. These were operated by a hand crank geared to a flywheel and this to a large flat steel disc inside. On this disc were pyramidlike teeth. As corn was fed, one ear at a time, into an opening in the top, the teeth on the disc pulled the ears downward into the machine, tearing off the kernels. The cob was ejected on the opposite side and the shelled corn fell out at the bottom. The shellers split some of the kernels, and because these would not grow, Tom preferred to shell his seed corn by hand. After several days of shelling, the seed corn was neatly bagged, ready for moving.

FAREWELL

One Sunday in January, Bill Green and his wife approached Tom after church. "We'd like you folks to come to our house some evening before you move," explained Bill. "I think Jean said you like oysters, Tom. How about your family an' ours havin' a nice oyster stew?"

He had hit on Tom's weak spot. He did, indeed, love oyster stew. So they agreed on the night. The family set out in the sled soon after dark for the Greens' place, the boys riding on the runners or jogging behind in the smooth, hard track. The temperature was five degrees below zero, and Tom cautioned the children to be alert for frostbite. The full moon reflecting from the snow made the night brilliant.

"Bet I could read a newspaper if I had one here," suggested Eddie. "Man, I never seen it quite so bright at night." The landscape was visible for miles, almost as clearly as in daylight.

Upon reaching their destination, Jean and the small children got out and hurried toward the house. Tom and the boys tied and blanketed the horses. Mr. Green came out from the house to greet them as other sleds began to arrive.

"Well," said Tom, as women from the church emerged from their respective sleds carrying covered pans and dishes. "This looks like a party."

Mr. Green smiled, and others gathered about, gleeful that the event had come off as a complete surprise. When all had arrived the repast was served. First came generous bowls of oyster stew followed by cake and ice cream, fruit gelatin, and other delicacies. When everyone had finished, Joe Henderson, beckoning for silence, turned to Tom and Jean. "We're sorry to have you folks move away, but sometimes that's the best way to get ahead. We want you to know that we'll miss you, an' as a token of our remembrance, we have a gift for you." He beckoned to Fred Hammond, who with some other boys brought in six beautiful oak dining room chairs.

Jean burst into tears. They needed chairs so badly, but she saw no way they could ever get a good set. Often she had looked at them in the catalog but had always put the book away, knowing that dining room chairs would have to wait. Tom rose to accept the gift but was unable to speak. His eyes brimming, he smiled, looked around at these their friends, hesitated in one more effort to respond, then sat down. Understandingly, people gathered around, happy that they had thought of the one best gift, and happy, too, that they had thought of the party at all.

While the ladies cleared the tables and washed the dishes, the children went outside to play Hide-and-Seek in the moonlight and the men visited.

"With 120 acres of corn to plow next spring, you'll prob'ly be teaching Ernie to use a cultivator," suggested Jack. "He'll be eight, I believe. How soon do you start the boys workin' in the field?" He smiled questioningly at Tom.

"Just as soon as their legs is long enough, so's their feet'll touch the ground," rejoined Tom. "No use waitin' any longer."

After an hour of visiting, the parents made their parting remarks, gathered their children, and went out into the beautiful night, homeward.

March first was by tradition the day when farmers moved. In addition to transferring his machinery, most of the seed oats, and some feed grain to the new farm, Tom had also been busy all winter hauling shelled corn to the grain elevators in town for various neighbors. They, in return, would haul a load for him on moving day.

At three in the morning the family was astir. Breakfast and chores were soon finished. Bedding was folded into dresser drawers, the fire was removed from the stove, and the stovepipe was taken down. Each person had been assigned a few tasks, which, when completed, left the house ready for the movers. Anderson's wagon appeared at four thirty and backed up to the porch. Into this was loaded the kitchen range, dishes, food for noon, the dining room table, and cooking utensils.

Soon after breakfast Eddie and Bill assembled the cattle and each on a horse set out driving them down the lane, assisted by Perry and Jim Anderson. Other neighbors arrived and with Tom's direction began loading their wagons with furniture, crates of poultry, tools, and small pieces of machinery. At about seven thirty the loading was finished. Tom, driving one wagon, and nine-year-old Bert, driving another, brought up the rear as the procession took to the road. When the house was empty, Jean and Jane swept it. Then, loading the dishes and cooking essentials into the car and taking Ernie, Matthew, and Grace, they set out at eight o'clock for their new home. At ten o'clock, after the long ride over rough, frozen, rutted roads, they arrived. Two men who had loaded their wagons the night before had arrived and were waiting there. Jean set them to laying the rag carpet on the front room floor while she and Jane unpacked food and peeled potatoes. Roscoe Anderson arrived with the kitchen equipment at eleven o'clock. They installed the stove and lighted the fire in it.

As other wagons arrived, Jean instructed the men where to place the furniture. Half an hour later the last wagons arrived and Tom took charge of unloading. After a time the boys appeared with the cattle.

By twelve thirty, dinner was ready and by one o'clock

the men began to disperse. By two, the last friend had wished them success in their new home and had gone.

When Tom counted the livestock in the afternoon he could find but thirty-three cattle. They had counted thirty-four when they set out that morning. They searched the barns and the corners of the premises for the missing animal. They named over the milk cows, each looking for the ones he usually milked.

"It's old Holstein," said Bill. "She's mine to milk, an' she's not here. She was givin' us trouble all the way, always tryin' to go the wrong way at a corner or to turn around an' go back."

"Get on a horse an' go look for her," Tom instructed Eddie. "Stop at every farm an' ask if they saw a Holstein cow. She prob'ly got away amongst the wagons without us seein' her an' she's started for the other place. Hurry up, now!"

Much dismayed, Eddie bridled up a horse and set out. A mile up the road he made his first stop.

"Hello, there, young fella," the farmer greeted him. "You lookin' for a Holstein cow?"

In amazement Eddie gaped. He had had visions of riding miles in the search and perhaps not finding her by nightfall. "Yow, I sure am," he replied. "She got away from us somehow."

"Well, cows'll do that. They'll break out an' head for home if they get a chance sometimes. C'mon, we'll get her, she's in the barn."

Seeing him returning, Tom came out into the lane to meet him, much relieved to have recovered his cow so readily. It was apparent that they would have to count livestock every day for a week or so until the animals got used to the place. They did not let them into the fields for a few days for fear some of them would find a weak spot in the fence and escape.

The children stayed home from school the rest of the week to help establish themselves in the new home. Machinery was put away in the large shed, pigs and cattle were apportioned space in the barns, furniture was positioned in the house, and canned goods were placed in the storm cave.

After supper a few nights later, Jane collected the table scraps into a dish, which she carried out the back door. She called the dog but he did not come. "Have you kids seen Buster?" she asked, returning to the living room. "I took his supper to him an' called, but he didn't come."

Tom and the boys looked at each other. No one had seen the dog since noon. Tom went to the door and called, "Huow, Buster! Huow, Buster! Huow! Huow!" He returned to the room. "You know, I bet that dog's run off an' gone back to the other place."

The next evening he telephoned to Romier's in Deep Creek and was relieved to learn that Buster was there. Tom returned to their former place in a few days, at which time he brought Buster back with him.

"I'll bet his feet was tired," mused Jean.

Chores of Early Spring

A WEEK after Tom was settled at the new place, farrowing time began. Two or three times each night he went to the barn with a lantern to look at the sows. On the third night he found that one sow had had two pigs. One of these had located the sow's belly and was busy getting its first meal. He found the other up behind the sow's ears, lost, far from the feeding station, weak, and getting cold. He placed it in position to nurse, and when the pig had its fill he put the young porker into his jacket pocket and took it to the house. There in a covered box behind the warm stove the piglet grunted and squeaked contentedly until morning, when Tom returned it to its mother.

By this time there were four more little pigs in the pen, all doing well, nestled down against the warm pink belly of their mother and making contented little-pig sounds. In all, eight sows produced fifty little pigs. Tom examined the mouth of each newborn pig, rubbing his finger along its gums in search of needle-sharp teeth. Because these small teeth would cut the pig's tongue until it would not nurse, he broke them off with pliers. By the time the teeth had again grown out, this danger was past.

If a sow was slow to deliver her pigs, he might stay with her all night. Dressed warmly, he continued the vigils during the nippy nights of late winter. Often the kitchen was a miniature pigpen of boxes containing half a dozen little pigs. If a runt was crowded away from its mother at feeding time it might starve. He took these to the house and fed them cow's milk, first with a spoon and later with a baby bottle, until they were strong enough to fend for themselves. Thus with the hope of springtime a renewed and enlarged life on the new place began.

BREAKING ROLLY TO WORK

"Eddie, you put the harness on Mabel an' I'll throw it on Rolly," said Tom one Saturday morning soon after moving. "We hafta break these colts if we expect to have them ready to work in the field." Taking the harness on his right arm, he walked slowly up along Rolly's left side toward the manger. The colt shied away over against his stall mate. Crouching slightly just behind Rolly's shoulder, Tom swung the harness upward to slide it across the gelding's back. At this point, Rolly, his eyes rolling wildly, hauled back on the halter. He braced his feet toward the manger as he pulled with all his might, twisting his head from side to side with short pivoting yanks. He snorted and jerked. Tom lowered the harness. Rolly relaxed.

"Shut the barn door, Bill. If this rascal gets loose an' out of the barn, we'd have a time just to get him back in here."

With the door closed Tom approached Rolly again. As he raised the harness the colt panicked again, this time ripping the halter to pieces. He popped out of the stall, but having no place to which he could flee he returned to his stall and stood nervously eying the situation. Carefully Tom approached him again and tied him to the manger with a rope around his neck. "There, now," he said quietly, "I don't reckon you're goin' anyplace for a little while."

After considerable jerking and yanking they got the harness on him. Tom led him to the water tank, where amid much champing on the bit he took a few swallows. Then he became obstinate and would not lead. Tom passed the lead strap under the colt's jaw through the ring on the other end of the bit. When he pulled on the strap the two rings came together beneath the horse's chin, pinching his mouth. When Tom tried to lead him again, Rolly balked, standing stone still. When Tom pulled harder, Rolly stretched out his neck and shook his head, but he did not move. Suddenly the horse plunged forward, only to be stopped short by a stern yank on the strap. Angry now, the gelding threw back his ears, braced his feet, and snorted.

"Oh, you ready to talk a little bit, are you?" jibed Tom. "Well, c'mon, then, tell me some more. If we can get to talkin' it over, maybe we can agree on somethin'." He yanked the lead strap with short, stern jerks. "You been your own boss for quite a while," he bantered. "Now le's see who's in charge!"

Suddenly Rolly snorted again, then reared up on his hind legs and struck Tom just below the eye, cutting an inch-long gash on his cheekbone. Thoroughly angry now, Tom seized the bridle by both rings and shook the horse's nose from side to side as through his teeth he muttered, "You bow-necked devil, I'll show you a couple of things yet!"

At this point the horse began to plunge and tried to rear up. Tom held to the bridle with both hands. Though short, he was no lightweight. Rolly tossed him up and down several times but soon found that this man was not going to let go and that he was not going to give up. The colt pranced and danced, but gradually he quieted, so after careful maneuvering they were able to hitch him to the older mare. Using a heavy strap, they fastened Rolly's bit to Mable's hame so that if he tried to rear or plunge he would be securely anchored.

They hitched the team to a flat sled loaded with rocks, and Tom led Rolly by the bridle while the boys rode on the stone boat. When it appeared that the colt would not bolt, Eddie took Rolly by the bridle while Tom rode on the stone boat and drove. Up and down the lane they went, smoothing the ruts left from the winter's mud.

After half an hour of this, they hitched the team to a wagon. By this time the horses were perspiring freely and Rolly was puffing hard. He twisted and squirmed in the harness, trying to run, but the strap to Mabel's hame stopped him cold. At last, getting tired, he settled into a pattern of trotting, halting, and bolting and finally quieted into reasonably good behavior.

"He'll be a good horse," commented Tom, as they unhitched the team. "The rascal's strong, an' that's just what we need. I'll put him on the seeder along with Prince when I start sowin' oats. That'll give him all the fancy walkin' he wants."

Rolly proved to be a good work horse. He was always a little nervous, but he was strong and reasonably dependable. Most of Tom's colts were quiet and easy to break, but being fractious by nature, Rolly was an especially difficult case.

THE INCUBATOR

There was plenty of space on the new farm for chickens and there was a good hen house to shelter them in the winter. Since the sale of eggs supplied considerable cash income, the Harpers decided to substantially increase the flock by hatching more chicks.

About the middle of March Tom brought an incubator into the house and placed it on the floor of the downstairs bedroom where he and Jean slept. Incubators came in several designs, but all served the same purpose, namely, to provide the proper temperature for incubating the eggs and to shelter the new chicks for a short time.

This incubator consisted of a round, lightweight, insulated sheet-metal shell some thirty inches in diameter and twelve to fifteen inches high. Inside, about halfway between the top and bottom, was a wire-mesh floor with a three-inch hole in its center, which was closed by a removable disc of wire mesh. The removable top had a glass for viewing the interior. Beneath this glass, inside, stood a thermometer with a heavy mark at 103 degrees, the proper temperature for incubating chicken eggs.

A low kerosene lamp placed beneath a small water tank outside the incubator heated water, which circulated inside to keep the egg chamber warm. About a day was required for the lamp to bring the water to the desired temperature and to stabilize the adjustments. Jean placed a hundred fertile eggs on the wire-mesh floor and closed the lid. Several hours were required for the eggs to become warm, but after that the incubator operated with little need for adjustment. Each day Jean removed the cover, and with her palm resting on the eggs she rolled them to one side to turn them. The eggs had to be cooled daily, and to do this the cover was left off for the prescribed time.

After about three weeks, cheeping noises could be heard

from inside the incubator as chicks started to pip (peck) open their shells. For this the embryo chick came equipped with a special point on the end of its beak with which it struck the inside of the shell until the shell cracked; then by stretching and kicking it ruptured the shell, which popped open. Wet and gangly at first, the chick dried and gained strength as it began to move about. The wire disc was then removed from the center of the floor on the egg level, and as the chicks wandered about they fell through into the bottom compartment. From there they were removed.

By this time a number of hens would be ready to set. Jean placed about fifteen chicks with each of several setting hens in coops and observed them until certain that each hen had accepted her brood.

Instead of using hens to care for the chicks, large numbers of them could be sheltered under a brooder. This was a metal hood having warmth supplied by a kerosene lamp or a very small stove.

After about 1920, live chicks could be bought from commercial hatcheries, which sold them by the hundred and shipped them by parcel post or railway express.

FANNING OATS

It was necessary to have clean oats for sowing. For this reason seed oats were run through a fanning mill to remove trash and weed seeds. This machine consisted of a wooden frame some thirty inches wide, five feet long, and four feet high. A gasoline engine supplied power by use of a belt. Oats were scooped into a hopper on top of the mill, from which they flowed through a slot onto the vibrating sieve below. The oat kernels passed through this top sieve, but weed stems and other large debris slid along the top of it to be ejected onto the ground at one side. The oat kernels then rested on a finer, lower sieve through which only the small undesirable kernels and weed seeds would pass. The full-bodied seed grain moved along on top of the screen to where a blast of air from a fan removed the dust and chaff. Then the clean oats fell into a box below from which Tom scooped them into a wagon.

Spring Fieldwork

Tom used different teams for casual work during late winter in order to keep all of them in touch with the harness. Toward spring he brought them into the barn daily to feed and curry them and to remove burrs from their tails and manes.

Before taking a horse from the stable for work, it had to be harnessed. The first item of harness to be mounted on the horse was the collar. This was a hollow leather U-shaped tube, of varying contour to fit the horse's neck, filled with hard-packed straw. With the open end up, it was pushed upward onto the horse's neck and buckled together at the top. Between the collar and the horse's shoulder, a thick felt pad was often placed to ease the pressure when pulling.

Next came the two hames. These were of hollow steel or iron-shod wood, shaped to fit the collar. They were fastened together with a strap at the top, and after they had been set into grooves on the collar were buckled together at the bottom.

Backward from the lower part of the hames ran the tugs, or traces, reaching beyond the horse's heels. At the ends of the tugs were metal pieces called cockeyes for connecting the tugs to the singletree of an implement. Some tugs ended in several links of chain instead of the cockeye.

Just behind the horse's withers, which are on its back directly above the front legs, was placed a wide piece of leather called the back band. From its right side a heavy strap that hung down was pulled under the horse's belly and buckled loosely. This was the bellyband. It held the back band in place and assisted in backing a load. Backward from the top of the back band the crupper strap ran toward the horse's tail, where it split into a Y. Each end of the Y was buckled to

96

a round-formed strap called the crupper, which passed under the horse's tail.

From the top of the horse's rump a strap passed downward over each hip, the straps having loops on their lower ends through which the tugs passed. At the top of these straps, on the horse's rump, there were usually two steel hooks. To these the cockeyes at the tug ends were attached after unhitching. This prevented the tugs from dragging on the ground where the horse could step on them.

Some harnesses also had what was called the breeching, commonly referred to as brichen. This thick band also hung from the crupper strap and passed around the hind legs of the horse a foot or so above the hock, parallel with the ground. From the front end of the breeching on either side, a strap ran forward along the horse's belly to snap onto a ring at the back end of the pole strap at the bellyband. Thus, when the horse sat back into the breeching, his weight was carried directly through the pole strap to the neck yoke, which backed the implement.

The bridle was put on last. The most essential part of this was a steel bar called the bit, which was placed in the horse's mouth. From large rings on each end of the bit a band passed up over the top of the horse's head behind the ears. The bridle was prevented from slipping off over the ears by a strap called the throatlatch, which passed under the throat and buckled to the headband on each side. The checkrein, its ends attached to the rings of the bit, passed back between the tops of the hames to a hook on the back band. Thus the horse was harnessed, ready for work.

When driving just one horse, long reins, called lines, passed forward along the horse's back through rings on the back band and the hames and were snapped to the rings on either end of the bit. Thus one drove the horse.

In assembling a two-horse team, there was one line on each horse. Each line formed a Y behind the back band. The short leg of the Y, called the outside check, passed down the right side of the right horse to his bit. The long side, called the inside check, passed through the inside rings to the inside of the bit of the opposite horse. The left-hand horse was rigged in the opposite manner. When the right line was pulled both horses were directed to the right and conversely.

When hitching up three horses, the lines were made up in

the same way as for two, the inside checks being fastened to the center horse. But to control the three as a unit, a strap or rope was tied continuously to the bit of each horse so that all were turned together.

A four-horse team was sometimes made up as two two-horse teams, using four lines. But usually they were assembled in the same way as three, all four being tied with one continuous rope or strap.

Five horses were assembled as one three-horse team and one two-horse team, with the two in the lead. This required two pairs of lines. It was the most difficult of these arrangements to handle and was generally used for plowing.

SOWING OATS

Examination of the fields during late March confirmed Tom's hope that the time to sow oats was at hand. The oats had been fanned and the discs made ready.

Tom and the boys carried the oat seeder to the double-box wagon used for sowing oats. They set the board on which the seeder was mounted into the slots that held the rear bottom endgate. Then they screwed in the endgate rod to hold it securely and scooped some twenty bushels of seed oats into the front of the wagon. At the field, Tom turned onto the fifth row of standing cornstalks and stopped to make preparations. Attached to the endgate was a bushel-sized metal hopper. Below the hopper a mechanism fed grain from the hopper downward onto two horizontal whirling fans, which threw the kernels of oats over four or five rows on each side, sowing nine rows at a time. The seeder was powered by a chain running over a large sprocket mounted on the wagon wheel. With the hopper scooped full of grain and the seeder in gear, Tom started the team at a brisk pace.

Behind him, Eddie entered the field riding the disc. This machine consisted of two cutting sections, each four feet long. Each was composed of eight concave steel discs, twelve to fourteen inches in diameter, mounted with six-inch steel spacers between them. The concave faces of the discs of each section faced outward from the center. The driver's seat was directly above the center. The eveners were attached to the trucks, a pair of small wheels, ahead of the seat. From the trucks a tongue passed forward between the middle horses. When not in operation the two cutting sections of the disc lay in a straight line, but when in use the two halves were adjusted by levers to form a shallow V, the outside ends pointing forward. When the team moved, the discs dug into the soil, chopping up the clods, cutting the vegetation, and burying the seed. The disc cut three rows of cornstalks each time it crossed the field. Following the first discing the field would be disced again, usually crosswise to the first cutting, then it would be dragged with the harrow to level the cornstalks and leave a smooth surface.

"Boy, I sure had a rough ride this mornin'," announced Eddie as he rubbed his bottom after the first morning of riding the disc.

"It's a good thing you got your seat toughened up a little from ridin' horseback with no saddle," replied Tom. "Ridin' a disc is kinda rough the first time over. After that it'll be smoother. You'll get used to it in a little while."

"An' my legs won't reach the footrests, so I have to brace myself by puttin' one foot up in front of me against the lever. That way I can stay on the seat pretty good. Once I tried slidin' down with my feet on the footrests an' my back against the iron that holds up the seat, but the horses kicked so much dirt in my face I got back up on the seat."

"Yow, I saw you tryin' to figure it out. I hadn't thought about how short your legs was. But I decided you'd manage it after a while."

Harrowing was the last operation. The harrow consisted of three or four sections, each about four feet square, having a total length of twelve or sixteen feet. Running longitudinally across each section were wooden or steel bars to which were secured square steel teeth four to five inches long. When using the harrow the teeth were set to tear the soil and level it. The sections were attached to a long timber, and to this the eveners were fastened. Three or four horses pulled the harrow. Walking behind the harrow was a dirty job because the harrow created a lot of dust. However, by walking at the windward end considerable dust could be avoided. Some farmers rode on a high-wheeled cart that traveled behind the harrow. This kept the driver up out of some of the dust, but in an hour or two his face would be well-covered with it and in the corners of his eyes small lumps of hardened dirt would form. He would find himself blowing small clots of wet dirt from his nose for several hours after harrowing, whether he walked or rode.

PLANTING CORN

After the first of May the weather was warm in the daytime and the soil pregnant with small grass and weeds. This was corn-planting time; the beginning of a long, busy season. Both Bill and Bert stayed home from school to disc and harrow. They arose at four thirty in the morning and Tom expected to be in the field with the planter by six. He drove one team in the forenoon and a fresh pair after dinner, and he worked until dark. The weather was right. There was no time to waste.

The frame of the corn planter was about four feet square. It was pulled by two horses, traveled on two wheels, and planted two rows at a time. The driver's seat was located in the center at the back. Directly ahead of the wheels, just behind the eveners, were two gallon-sized metal boxes that held the seed corn. Beneath each box and extending forward was a runnerlike steel device called the shoe, which was connected to the corn box by a tube. When in operation, the shoes ran submerged through the soil to provide a trench into which the corn dropped.

At that time in Iowa, corn was planted in hills of three or four stalks, and to insure uniform distance between hills a check wire was used. This was a soft iron wire composed of hundreds of lengths, each about three feet. Each length was connected to the next by a flexible knot known as the button. Before starting to plant, the check wire was laid along the edge of the field and secured to a round steel stake, called the anchor, set in the soil at each end of the field. When planting, the wire ran through a carriage of roller guides just ahead of the planter wheel. This passed the wire through a movable steel fork. When the button struck the fork, as the planter passed along, the fork was pulled back, releasing kernels of corn through the bottom of the box down the tubes through the shoes and into the soil.

To plant the first two rows, Tom placed the wire in the fork and carriage and drove across the field alongside the fence. Attached to the frame of the planter was a device called the marker, having on its end a disc or blade that dragged in the soil to make a small furrow called the mark. As he planted the first two rows, the marker was turned away from the fence to guide his return.

As he reached the end he stopped the team and pulled the rope, releasing the carriage, which dropped the check wire. He then turned the team and placed them astraddle the mark he had just made. Dismounting, he pulled up the anchor, brought it behind the center of the planter frame, pulled the wire tight, and set the anchor in the sod. Going to the carriage he placed the wire in the fork and the roller guides, locked the carriage, and proceeded back across the field.

A RUNAWAY TEAM

The last forty acres to be planted was two miles from home. The boys walked behind their four-horse teams to and from the field—morning, noon, and night. Because he had to take seed corn to the field, Tom hitched the planter team to the buggy to haul the bags of corn. At about four o'clock the first afternoon, he realized that he would not have enough seed to finish the day. Not wanting to quit early, he directed Bert, who was harrowing, to hitch his four horses to the buggy and go to the house for more corn.

When driving four horses to the buggy, only the two middle ones could be hitched to the singletrees, leaving the two on the outside with nothing to pull. With the early quitting and lightness of the buggy, the horses started off for home at a smart trot. As Bert turned the first corner and started toward the next turn a mile away, the two horses on the outside began to gallop. He pulled on the lines to slow them. Then the two at the tongue also began to gallop. This did not concern him much at first because the horses had always been dependable. He continued to pull and then to yank and finally to seesaw on the lines to no avail. Then he realized that he had a runaway team on his hands.

Along one side of the road was a four-foot woven-wire

fence with a strand of barbed wire at the top. He decided to stop them by running them into the fence. Accordingly, he turned them across the shallow ditch toward the fence, but the team shied away toward the direction they had been going and ran parallel with the fence. He then understood what a mess there would have been if they had run into the fence. Some of them might have tried to jump over it and become entangled in the wire, and the buggy would probably have turned over, throwing him out. It would have been a glorious melee. He was glad that the horses had had better judgment than he. He guided them back to the roadway shouting, "Whoa," at the top of his lungs and pulling on the lines, feet braced against the steel footrail on the floor of the buggy.

Presently he observed that not one horse remained hitched to the buggy. The steel cockeyes on the tugs of a work harness fit loosely on the steel prongs of the buggy's singletrees. His pulling on the lines with his feet braced had pushed the buggy up onto the horses. He was pulling the buggy with his arms and the slackened tugs had dropped from the singletrees and were dragging on the ground. If he relaxed his pull on the lines the horses would run away from the buggy, the tongue would fall out of the neck yoke and probably run into the ground and break off, and the team would be free from the buggy, going pell-mell down the road. His only hope was to hold on to the lines and keep his feet braced. The horses maneuvered the next turn with only a little skidding of the rear wheels; then they took off up the road toward home, half a mile away.

A neighbor along the road alerted Jean by telephone about the runaway. She came out into the lane, waving a broom in front of the team, but they shied around her and continued toward the barn. Not wanting to run the four horses through the opening into the barn, Bert turned them toward a gateway that led into the grove. He would drive them in among the trees; that would stop them. But as he approached that gateway he realized that to do this would tear the harness to pieces and probably wreck the buggy. There was no point in ruining the equipment if there was any other way. If he did not go through the gateway into the grove, he would have to drive them around the granary, which stood nearby. He had driven a wagon around that small building many times to load oats. To maneuver a wagon around it between two or three good-sized rocks was a little tricky when he had but two horses and plenty of time. How the four horses at a dead run, with the buggy careening behind them, managed to do it with no smashed wheels, he could not answer later. But presently they were around the granary headed again toward the barn. As they approached it the team suddenly stopped as if to say, "This is as far as we intended to go." By this time Eddie had arrived home. He helped Bert unhitch the team and they took the seed corn to Tom in the car.

Bert was then in the sixth grade and weighed no more than eighty pounds. He could not have been any kind of match for an unruly four-horse team. That the incident did happen and occurred so casually was witness to the fact that farm life was sometimes precarious. It was made further so because immature youths were often a main supporting factor in the farm economy, sometimes at risk to their own welfare.

REPLANTING

Walking over the fields several days after planting, Tom found that seventy acres had germinated poorly and would have to be replanted. He always tested his seed corn early in the spring by planting it in a box of soil that he put in the house in a window where it would get sunshine. If he found poor seed he discarded it. Unknowingly, he had not taken samples from a few bags when testing and thus had planted some poor seed.

Upon discovering that the corn was not sprouting, he bought a fresh supply of seed, and when the boys returned from school they found him preparing to replant. Bert would stay home for two or three days. Tom had borrowed a planter for him to use and they would work together, both planting on the same wire.

"Gee, I never planted corn," remonstrated Bert. "I don't know whether I can set the anchor or not, an' I don't know how tight to pull the wire."

"Ain't no trick to settin' the anchor. An' anyhow, I'll be settin' it half the time."

"I never heard of two planters goin' on one wire," objected Bill. "Bet you'll get the world's crookedest check by doin' that. How'll we ever plow it crosswise?"

"I ain't worried about the check nor the plowin' right now. What we have to do now is plant it, an' the sooner the better."

At six o'clock the next morning they were in the field. The operation they then performed, while quite simple, few farmers had witnessed before. Starting his planter along the fence, Tom planted for a few rods into the field. Then he went back and showed Bert how to place his team on the mark, reset the anchor behind Bert's planter, and place the wire into the carriage. Bert then followed him. At the other end the procedure was repeated. It was surprising how little time was lost at the ends with this double maneuver. In two days they were finished.

CULTIVATING CORN

As soon as the corn was an inch or two high it would be time to plow, or cultivate, as this operation was called. The small grass and weeds grew fast in the warm, damp ground, and no time could be lost if the field was to be kept clean.

The cultivator was built on two steel wheels some four feet high and pulled by two horses. Attached to the frame of the plow by pivots, about a foot above the ground near the front, were two steel beams, one on each side and each extending backward. Beneath the axle, each bent outward toward the rear of each wheel. Along this outward-flaring section, three small steel shovels were mounted on steel shanks below each beam.

The driver sat on a seat two or three feet behind the axle where he had a clear view of the row beneath the cultivator. With the lines tied together and passed over his shoulders, he directed the team. He controlled the shovels with his feet set in steel stirrups on the beams and his hands on vertical bars above. Fenders of sheet iron hung between the front shovels and the corn row so that the operator could roll the dirt carefully up around the young corn plants, covering the grass in the row without covering the corn.

When beginning to plow in a new field, one person plowed the row next to the fence. Each person following left nine rows and turned onto the tenth, and so on. Thus each plowed his own parcel, called a land. In that way they did not interfere with each other when turning at the end. If one stopped, the others could continue independently. Each person carried a stick three or four feet long. If he covered a hill of corn, he stopped the team and turned around on the seat to flick the soil off. At about nine thirty, when they stopped to rest the teams, the men drank from the water jug and walked about to relax. At noon they left the field and drove in a trot to the barnyard, lining the cultivators up in a row and unhitching the horses.

When the corn was being plowed the second time, the teams went at right angles to the first cultivating, plowing it crosswise. If the check was straight, plowing crosswise was easy. But if the man on the planter had been careless in setting the anchor, two hills would be in line but the next two would be set to one side by as much as two or three inches, in which case the person cultivating had to be alert to avoid plowing out the next hill.

At the third plowing, which was lengthwise, the corn was high enough so that the fenders were removed. For the fourth and last plowing the shovels were purposely kept away from the rows to prevent cutting off the lengthening corn roots. By this time some of the corn would be two or more feet high, brushing against the seat as the plow passed over it. During this plowing the man on the cultivator often got his pant legs soaking wet during the early morning when heavy dew hung onto the long corn leaves. This last plowing was sometimes left to the smaller boys to finish while Tom and the older ones began haying.

One year, ten-year-old Bert was assigned to plow the last fifteen acres. It was a lonesome job. The surface cultivator he was using needed little control, so to add variety to his tasks he sometimes walked up the tongue of the plow, after the team started down the row, and climbed onto a horse, where he rode until reaching the end. For some unexplained reason he left a row unplowed here and there, and at one point he skipped twenty rows. Before Bert was finished, haying was completed, so Tom sent Eddie and Bill to help complete the plowing. It looked as if they would be through by three thirty and all were jubilant at the promise of part of the afternoon off.

In turning the cultivator at the end of the field the driver seldom got the plow immediately aligned on the row, hence the first rows at the end would need additional cultivating. For this reason they always plowed across the ends before leaving the field. As Eddie was leading the others in doing this, he was surprised to find the unplowed rows. "You little baby," he stormed at Bert. "Why didn't you plow these rows? Now we gotta stay here an' plow about thirty more rows when we thought we was all ready to go to the house."

Bert had not a word to say. He knew it was wrong to leave the rows, and he did not know why he had done it, but there it was.

"You know what I've got a notion to do?" stormed Eddie. "Well, I gotta good notion for me an' Bill to go on to the house an' let you stay here an' plow 'em by yourself! You know Pop'd not let you do a thing like this!"

Still Bert had no answer. He took his medicine. But they stayed and helped him finish. When Tom heard of it he was not sympathetic with Bert.

"You know the landlord's gonna be here most any time, an' he always walks around over the fields when he comes. What would he think if he found a lot of rows not plowed?"

Again Bert had no answer. The matter was dropped, and never again was there need for Tom to be disappointed in him for such an obvious breach of responsibility.

A runaway that might have turned out seriously occurred a few years later while they were plowing corn. At noon when they drove to the house, Ernie was the last one through the gateway leading from the cornfield into the pasture they crossed to approach the barn. When he had passed through the gate and stopped to close it, his unattended team began to follow those ahead. Ernie hollered, "Whoa!" to them, but instead of stopping they began to trot and then to run. They soon passed Bert and overhauled Tom, who was driving a pair of colts; as the running horses came alongside, Tom's young horses also began to run. Tom held them in check and Ernie's team passed by, going through the gateway into the cattle yard. There they stopped at the closed gateway leading to the barn.

By this time Tom, bracing himself to control his team, had run his feet through the steel stirrups on his plow. He then could not brace himself to control his team, nor could he remove his feet, for his shoes had become caught on the back side of the stirrups. He turned his horses away from the standing team and drove the colts around a pond in the cattle yard. Then he realized that the team was going to run among a clump of trees. At about this time he managed to withdraw his feet from the stirrups and slide off the seat backwards, where he rolled on the ground unhurt. The team passed between two trees, but the corn plow stuck there. The hooks on the singletrees bent out straight, releasing the horses, and they raced on through the trees without the plow.

Tom and the boys repaired the harness, pried the cultivator out from between the trees, bent the singletree hooks so that they would hold again, and appraised the damage to the sprung plow frame. Tom took the same colts back to the field at one o'clock, hitched to the same plow, which seemed none the worse for the episode. Ernie's team appeared docile and safe to drive again in the afternoon, but the experience made a Jekyll and Hyde out of one old mare, for from that day on she would run at any pretext.

"By doggies, boys, we gotta get out there an' strip that corn. The wind's comin' up an' the sand's startin' to blow." Tom had come in from surveying the fields lying out beyond the pasture. They were plowing the corn for the first time, and because of a hard rain they had not gone to cultivate that day.

"Do you think it's dry enough?" asked Eddie. "That was a pretty big rain."

"It'll not be wet on the high ground. The rain beat the fine soil down, so the sand's come to the top an' the wind's whippin' it along up on the ridges just like snow."

They got out their teams and drove to the first field where billows of sand blew across the ridge as the wind slid the sand grains along the ground, cutting loose more sand.

Each person plowed two rows and left eight unplowed. Then the sand could move only until it struck the freshly plowed strip, where it lodged. Hence it gathered little momentum and would not be hazardous to the crop.

"Well, we got that stopped," said Tom when they had plowed the sandy strip along the ridge. "Le's leave this field an' go over yonder to the north eighty. We'll spend the rest of the afternoon there, an' by quittin' time we'll have it stopped."

Thus they waged the contest with wind and sand. This continued until the corn was several inches high, by which time the corn itself shielded the ground from the wind. If the above precautions were not taken after a heavy rain when the corn plants were small, the sand damaged the tender leaves until they dried and dropped off.

"Sure looks like we're gonna catch it this time," said Bert to Bill as they were plowing corn one day a mile and a half from home. "That's a bad-lookin' cloud comin' up."

They scrutinized the approaching storm clouds. Sometimes such storms contained wind but no rain, or sometimes they went in another direction. As they turned at the far end, however, it was apparent that this time they would get wet. When they were less than halfway back across the field, it began to sprinkle in large, heavy drops and they heard the roar of the coming storm. Before they had gone far the ground became so wet that all they could do was to raise the shovels and head for home.

Both boys were drenched within the first minute. Huge drops struck them in the face, so that in order to see they squinted through nearly closed eyes at the road ahead. The teams trotted toward home a mile and a half away. The lightning flashed, and at times its fierce zip could be heard as it struck in the fields. The odor of ozone permeated the air. Thunder was deafening as it crashed and rumbled near and far. At one point, lightning struck the ground and rolled out across the field in a bright orange ball.

The teams slipped and splashed on the muddy road. The water stood in the shallow ruts and ran down into the ditches. As the teams hurried on, chunks of mud slithered off from the wheels to spatter the drivers and to plop into the puddles beneath the cultivators. The boys clung to their seats, the lines around their shoulders and tied behind their backs. With their hands on the frame of the cultivator to brace themselves, they could control their teams.

Having experienced thunderstorms, the horses did not panic. It was true that now and then an animal and even a person was struck by lightning, but many of these events were so bizarre that it seemed futile to take precautions. It was unthinkable to leave the field every time a dark cloud appeared, and besides this, the warm summer rains were not uncomfortable. Unless one was working near the house, he would be soaked before he reached shelter anyhow, so he waited it out and headed for home when this was the only thing left to do.

At the barnyard the teams were unhitched and taken to the stable and the boys went to the house for dry clothing. It was all a part of the summer's work.

In the Heat of Summer

HAYING

Toward the end of June or early in July, when the corn had been plowed for the last time, it would be time for haying. For cutting hay the mowing machine, or mower, was used. This implement consisted of a cast-iron frame mounted on two wheels with a seat at the back and a tongue bolted solidly into the frame. It was pulled by two horses. A cutting bar was activated by a power train driven by the wheels. It extended six feet to the right of the right wheel at ground level. As this bar moved forward, fingerlike guards along the front penetrated the grass. Through these guards the sickle, or knife, oscillated, its triangular knifelike sections shearing off the vegetation, which fell onto the ground behind.

In good weather, cut hay would dry in the field in a day or two, after which it would be gathered into windrows with a hay rake. The rake consisted of a heavy angle iron ten or twelve feet long having a high steel wheel at each end. At intervals of about four or five inches along this angle iron, teeth were attached. These were spring-steel rods shaped into a semicircle of perhaps thirty inches. The teeth curved backward and downward from the frame, turning forward at ground level. Two horses pulled the rake.

The driver's seat was mounted on the tongue midway between the wheels. To operate the rake, one drove across the mowed field with the teeth down to gather the hay. When enough was collected, the driver stepped on a lever beside his foot, rotating the teeth upward and dumping the hay. When a field had been raked, long windrows of dry hay lay across it, ready to be stacked or hauled to the barn.

If the hay was to be stacked, it was left in the windrow. If it was to be loaded onto a hayrack, it was bunched for easy pitching. To bunch the hay the driver turned the rake astraddle the windrow, let the teeth down, and drove, periodically dumping the hay in piles. Thus the men pitching it onto the wagon did not need to gather it into bunches with their pitchforks, a time-consuming operation.

To gather the hay from the windrow for stacking, the hay buck was used. This implement consisted of a row of long wooden teeth lying flat on the ground much like a huge comb. It was pulled by two horses and moved on two small wheels. The horses were hitched to the ends of the buck, ten or twelve feet apart. To turn the hay buck the driver pulled on the appropriate line, checking one horse. As the other horse continued, the buck swung in a semicircular manner. The horses soon learned the signals.

To collect a buck load of hay the driver drove the buck with the teeth sliding under the windrow, piling the hay up between the horses. When he had enough he drove to the stacker. The base frame of the stacker was a rectangle of heavy timbers some eight feet wide by fourteen long. This was staked to the ground. Outside the frame lay the timbers of the lifting arms, which were anchored to the frame at the rear by a two-inch pipe. On this pipe the lifting arms could pivot upward into a standing position some twelve or fourteen feet high. Hay was deposited on long wooden bars at the front of the lifting arms by the hay buck. Then a team attached to a rope pulled the lifting arms with its load into a vertical position, and the hay slid onto the stack. The team on the rope was then backed and the lifting arms returned to the ground.

A man working on the stack leveled and built it up to ten or more feet, then drawing in the corners he piled the center full and rounded out the top. The sides of the stack were dressed by raking downward with a pitchfork until they were smooth all around. Thus finished, the stack would shed rain and the hay in it would remain dry.

If the hay was to be hauled to the barn, it was bunched in the windrow ready for loading into a hayrack. The hayrack was a slatted basket of boards about thirty inches deep, eight or nine feet wide, and twelve to fourteen feet long. It was mounted on a regular wagon chassis, which often had small steel wheels that set it near to the ground for easy loading.

With the hayrack alongside the windrow, one or two

men pitched the hay into the rack while another drove the team, tramped the hay, and built the load. The man pitching up the load from the ground would approach a bunch and thrust his pitchfork deep into it. Then laying the midpoint of the fork handle across his leg above the knee, with one hand toward the top of the handle and the other toward its base, he would throw his weight backward, heaving the load upward over his head into the wagon.

Prairie grass held together poorly because it was short, and pitching it was slow work. Red clover was likewise slow to load because the short stems did not hold together. Timothy and alfalfa, however, having rough, coarse heads and long stems, held together quite well and could be loaded faster.

During the early 1920s Tom's hay consisted mostly of alfalfa. When hauling it to the barn, Ernie usually loaded the hay while Bert and Tom pitched it up. Together Bert and Tom approached the bunch of hay with their backs to the wagon, one at either corner of the pile. They stuck their forks into it at separate points, then with one coordinated heave they rolled it up into the rack or up on top of a high load. They could pitch up a load of alfalfa weighing a ton or more in twenty minutes. By taking two racks to the hayfield, loading them both, then bringing them to the barn for unloading, they could deliver four loads to the barn in the forenoon and four in the afternoon.

At about this time the mechanical hay loader came into use. Towed behind the hayrack, it gathered the hay from the ground and delivered it into the hayrack. Different makes of loaders were basically alike. The wheels were geared to a shaft to which were fastened a series of small rakes or to a drum that gathered the hay from the stubble and transferred it to a conveying system that moved it up an incline onto the back of the wagon. One or two men tossed it forward and spread it over the load.

To facilitate use of the hay loader, the side-delivery rake was developed. This rake was so built that it made a windrow each time it crossed the field. With the wagon straddling this row of hay, the loader, attached behind, gathered it up. By using the side-delivery rake, the farmer with the hay loader could begin to load the wagon immediately after the first pass of the rake across the field.

Inside the barn was a large central room called the haymow. High up under the roof at one end was the hay door. This was ten or twelve feet wide and some ten feet from the bottom to the highest point. It usually was hinged at the bottom and opened by swinging downward. A heavy timber ran the full length under the peak of the roof and extended about five feet outward beyond the wall of the barn over the hay door. Attached to the timber under the roof was a steel track, and hanging from this on small wheels was a steel carriage. The hayfork hung from this carriage, and from it a rope passed through pulleys to the ground beside the barn, where a team could be hitched to it. The loaded hayrack was placed beneath the open hay door and the man on the load pulled a rope that moved the carriage and fork to the outer end of the track above the load. At that point the carriage locked to the track and the fork dropped down to the load.

A U-shaped steel fork called the harpoon was often used for unloading hay. It was about thirty inches long and fifteen inches wide. When the fork had been thrust deep into the hay, three-inch steel barbs near its points were turned crosswise and locked so that the fork could not pull out. The team on the rope then pulled the fork laden with hay up to the carriage, which carried it into the barn. The man on the load allowed the trip rope, attached to the fork, to slide through his hands until the fork reached the right spot within the mow, whereupon he pulled the rope, which unlocked the barbs and dropped the hay. To properly place the hay in the mow, one man worked inside and directed this operation.

Another type of fork used for lifting hay from the hayrack into the haymow, or loft, was the grab fork. It resembled one's hands placed with the wrists together, the palms facing each other and spread apart, cuplike. The two halves were hinged, and when spread wide apart the steel fingers were set deep into the hay, which was lifted into the barn by rope and pulley.

Another method for quickly unloading hay was to use slings. These consisted of four ropes running the length of the hayrack, spaced evenly apart by wooden bars. The ends of the ropes were attached to steel castings hung over the front and back of the rack with enough slack so that the castings could be drawn together over the top of the load. One sling was laid on the floor of the rack and about half the load was built up. Then a second sling was laid on that and the load was completed. If the hay was heavy or if a large wagonload was expected, three slings could be used.

Upon arriving at the barn the ends of the sling were pulled to the center over the top of the hay, coupled together, and connected to the pulley. The team on the rope was started and half a load of hay rose from the wagon up to the carriage and went into the mow.

Loading hay in the field was hard work, but because there was usually a breeze it was not uncomfortable. However, unloading at the barn, which was inside the grove where there was little or no breeze, could be a very hot job.

One day when haying, Bert and Tom found themselves in this kind of situation. Bert was sticking the fork on the load at the south end of the barn where there was no shade. It was ninety degrees or hotter and there was no wind. The sun was hot, the hay was hot, and handling the fork generated a good deal of heat within his body. He perspired profusely. After sticking the fork he slid from the wagon and went to the stock watering tank, where he doused his head with water, while Ernie, who was driving the team on the rope, pulled the load up. When Bert had tripped the load and pulled the fork out, he went again to the tank, doused himself a couple of times, and went back to stick the fork.

Tom was working in the mow, which was getting full. The warm hay and the absence of air circulation in the mow, added to the heat that came through the roof, made it hot as an oven.

"By doggies, this is a hot one," said Tom, appearing in a small door near the load. "I feel like I'm burnin' up." He mopped his head, neck, and face as his shirt dripped with perspiration and his chest heaved. "Toss me the jug, will ya?" He drank steadily from it until out of breath, rested a moment, and drank again. "Boy, that's good. Never knowed I could sweat so much."

"I been dousin' my head in the tank after stickin' the fork," said Bert. "I sure am hot, too."

At about this time Jean came to the well for a pail of water. "You fellows look awfully hot," she called. "Don't you want a drink of cool water?"

Leaping from the door onto the half-unloaded wagon, Tom slid to the ground and taking the pail he drank without waiting for a cup. He then poured half of what was left over his head. "That sure feels good. I feel about the most tuckered out I can remember. This heat must be gettin' me. When you go back to the house, will you fix us some bacon an' eggs? I need somethin' to eat."

When the load was off they removed their shirts, dipped them into the water tank, wrung them out, and put them back on. They rested until Jean came with the food. They ate leisurely and then went back for the final loads of the day. It was quite probable that they both were near heat exhaustion that afternoon.

HARVEST TIME

Soon after the Fourth of July the weather was hot and humid. The long bright days and warm nights forecast a strenuous two weeks ahead. It was time to begin cutting oats.

For this operation a large machine called the grain binder was used. It had a cutting platform eight or ten feet long that ran through the standing grain six to twelve inches above the ground. The weight of the platform was carried on a small wheel at its left end. The remaining weight of the machine was carried mostly on the thirty-inch bull wheel under its center. This wheel was about ten inches wide and studded with iron cleats to give traction. It powered the machine by use of a heavy chain that ran on sprockets. The binder was pulled by four horses.

Along the front of the platform an oscillating knife similar to that on the mowing machine cut the grain. Above and in front of the platform was a reel of long horizontal wooden slats, which as it turned pressed the grain stalks backward and deposited them onto the platform when cut. There a moving canvas, with thin wood strips attached, carried the grain toward the machine proper. Here two similar canvasses caught the grain between them and carried it upward, throwing it onto a downward-slanting deck at the right side of the binder. At that point it was formed into a bundle, tied with twine, and ejected onto the bundle carrier.

The first operation when beginning to cut grain was to open the field. Since the grain was sowed close to the fence, the first trip around the field was with the platform wheel near to the fence, while the rest of the machine and the horses traveled over the standing grain. This placed the bundle carrier some fifteen feet out in the field, where it dropped the bundles. These had to be picked up and carried to the fence so that on the next round, going in the opposite direction, the horses and binder would not run over them.

When Tom had cut two rounds, the boys began to shock. The driver of the binder usually dropped the bundles four to six in a bunch in a straight windrow so that the shockers could gather them easily. The grain shock was composed of six to ten bundles that were placed standing with the heads upward. Any one of several methods for building a shock was acceptable so long as the finished product allowed the grain to dry and remained standing until time to thresh. The last bundle in building a shock was the cap. This was laid on top, its spread-out heads and butts pulled down at the sides to prevent the wind from blowing it off. It held the shock together and protected it from the weather.

After a few rounds, Tom climbed down from the binder and asked Eddie, then sixteen, to cut for a few rounds. "He does it just as well as me. Gonna need him to cut when we get into the late oats. We'll let him get used to it for a day or two now." Tom assisted Bill and Bert at shocking until noon.

In the afternoon, while the other boys hitched up the horses, Tom gave Eddie the oilcan and went about the machine with him, pointing out the oil holes. Seeing there was but one ball of twine in the twine box, he had Eddie remove it and showed him how to tie it to a new ball, using a square knot, then place the fresh ball in the bottom of the box with the used one on top. Eddie cut again for about half the afternoon. Soon after they finished the early oats they expected to start cutting ninety acres of late oats.

"That's gonna keep us hoppin' for a week or more," predicted Tom. "The forty acres on the far eighty is about as ripe as the fifty acres here at home, so once we begin, we'll step it off like we mean business. It's a good thing we didn't get hail with that big rain we had on the Fourth. We've been lucky this far. It's ripe now, so we'll go out there an' cut it. Once it's in the shock we got nuthin' to worry about."

"Does hail knock the oats off the stalk?" asked Eddie. "We never had hail, did we?"

"I guess you never saw a field that had been hailed out, did you?" asked Tom.

"I remember it hailed when you was plantin' corn an' I went out in the yard and picked up a hailstone as big as a goose egg."

"Well, hail will ruin any crop. It'll even take all the leaves off the trees. Hail went through a strip about a half a mile wide, north of Deep Creek, the second year we lived there. Hank an' me went to see it. The oats was just about ripe, an' you wouldn't believe the way the fields looked when it was past. Oats was beat into the ground 'til it looked like it had been plowed. On the other side of the road there was a cornfield that had been cultivated for the last time, an' I don't think it would have paid to have turned the cows in to clean it up. There was just nuthin' left."

They opened up the late oats in the afternoon and cut a couple of rounds. Tom walked through the grain to examine it. It was a good stand and it was ready to cut. "Now in the mornin' we'll get up at four thirty an' be out here about six thirty. I'll cut 'til noon. At eleven thirty you boys'll go to the house for dinner while I keep cuttin'. When you come back after dinner, you bring the other four horses an' Eddie'll take the binder. I'll go for dinner an' leave my team at the barn. We'll cut 'til dark."

So they went to it with a will. By working the split shift they could cut forty acres in two days. The boys worked relentlessly at shocking, and usually there was no more than an hour of this left to do when the last bundle had been cut.

Several years later, when Bert and Ernie were in high school, they had almost finished cutting the last field when a casting on the binder broke. The next morning they were having trouble adjusting the repaired part when a neighbor came along the road with his team to cut in his own field. His crop was ripe, but he came to their aid and spent an hour helping them make repairs.

When they had finished in their field, Bert and Ernie

117

agreed that since this man had helped them repair the binder and since he had no one to shock, they would show their appreciation by shocking for him until noon. He had dropped the bundles in straight windrows, and they decided to line up the shocks in nice straight rows that would look good from the road.

"Well, I didn't expect help," said the neighbor, as he came cutting past where they were working. "Say, you're makin' it look pretty nice. I seen fields shocked up in straight rows like that but never took time to do it myself. Looks good."

"Well, we was finished," said Bert. "An' you took time to help us with the binder so we decided we'd shock for you 'til noon, if that's all right."

"Sure," he answered. "That's fine, especially since you make it look so good."

At noon he offered to hire them to complete the shocking, which took until about four o'clock the next afternoon. There were smiles on their faces when he offered them five dollars apiece for about a day and a half's work.

"It sure looks nice from the road," he said.

IN TIME OF SORROW

After Roscoe Anderson married Mable, her parents continued to live with them and her children. During the summer of 1918 her father died suddenly one Saturday. When Tom and Jean received the news, they took the family on Sunday to be with their bereaved friends.

The procedures were as one would expect. The family, shocked and grieved, did the routine things to keep the farm going. A neighbor lady set about to make a black dress for Mabel.

"Did they get all the early oats cut?" Tom asked of a neighbor who was present during the afternoon.

"Early oats is cut an' shocked. They was puttin' up a few loads of hay from the road, waitin' for the late oats to be ready. They aimed to begin cuttin' them on Monday—tomorrow."

"I see they're ripe," answered Tom. "Funeral's not 'til Wednesday; that's gonna throw 'em three days behind."

The neighbor agreed. "Yeh, a bad storm or a little hail could ruin it for them, but I don't guess they'll do any cuttin' 'til after the funeral. At least I never knowed anybody to go ahead with fieldwork with a corpse in the house."

Following the funeral, as people were leaving the cemetery, Tom and the neighbor approached Roscoe. "I suppose you'll be startin' to cut in the mornin'?" inquired the neighbor.

"Yow, that eighty is dead ripe. We should have been in there on Monday, but of course we couldn't. But we'll be at it first thing tomorrow."

"Well, we're finished an' so are some other neighbors. I'll see if we can get you some help."

"Well, that'd be great. Another binder in there would look pretty good to me an' the boys tomorrow."

At six o'clock Thursday morning Roscoe and his stepsons were in the field. As they turned to come down the last side to complete the first round, they saw a second binder waiting at the entrance and with it was another man to shock. Neighbors smiled as they greeted each other.

They started around the field, one binder behind the other, and the shockers set out after them. As Roscoe turned at the far corner he saw two more binders beginning to move along the first side of the field. The machine on which he rode blurred before his eyes. By the sound of the equipment he knew that it was working properly, but he could not see it. With one hand he seized the binder seat to stabilize himself, then taking his bandana he blew his nose vigorously. When he had wiped his eyes, the world again came into focus. The four binders would cut every stalk of the eighty acres in one day. Suddenly Roscoe had no problems. It was a bright day and the world was a good place in which to live.

SETTING THE GRAIN ELEVATOR

As threshing time approached, Tom considered the two places available for storing the grain. One was a building called the granary, into which oats would be scooped by hand. The elevator would be set to deliver the rest into a bin in the barn through the haymow door.

The portable grain elevator had a long chassis of heavy

wood mounted on steel wheels. Attached to this chassis was a troughlike conveyor of wood or metal having vertical sides eight or ten inches deep and a flat floor some fourteen inches wide. It was assembled in sections that were bolted together to make the desired length. When ready for use, the bottom end of the conveyor rested on the ground while the top was positioned in a door along the wall of a building or over an opening in the roof. By turning a hand winch, cables raised the top end of the elevator into the air. With a team of horses it could then be backed into position at the building. When in operation, two chains having steel cleats between them moved up the incline. Each cleat, called a cup, pushed a portion of grain ahead of it to the top where it slid down a spout into a bin.

When unloading grain at the elevator the front of the wagon was lifted by a jack and the grain slid out the back end. There were two syles of jacks for doing this. One consisted of a platform that lifted the wagon up under the front wheels. The other was an overhead framework having cables that attached to the hubs of the front wheels. When the cables were wound up they lifted the front of the wagon. The jack was driven by a short, one-inch tumbling rod connected to the bottom of the elevator. When ready for unloading, the elevator hopper was set under the rear of the wagon and the rear bottom endgate was opened to allow the grain to flow out. The hopper carried the grain to the inclined section of the conveyor.

The elevator was activated by horsepower. The power unit consisted of a wood and steel frame having a large cast-iron cogwheel lying horizontally on its top. Bolted to the top of the cogwheel were two timbers called the sweep. These were parallel with the ground and were bolted together at their outer ends. A team of horses hitched to the end of the sweep walked in a circle, turning the large steel wheel. This, through a series of cogs, turned a one-inch tumbling rod that was connected by a knuckle to the shaft on the bottom of the inclined section of the elevator.

A few farmers used a large gasoline engine and a speed jack instead of horses to power the elevator, and a very few had inside vertical elevators like those used in elevator buildings in town.

Threshing would begin early in August. It was the first gauge of the year's success, a change in the routine of going to one's own fields daily, and an interlude in the long, steady, hard summer routine.

Each farmer calculated how much help he would need for threshing, and the ladies contacted friends to exchange kitchen help. When it began, the men would be on the way by six in the morning and they would not be home again until dark. For the women this was a less strenuous season, for there were no noon or evening meals to prepare for the men. They worked in the garden, maintained the house, and did some canning as they laid plans for the day or two they would have threshers.

"Looks like the machine'll pull in here about Thursday night," announced Tom on Tuesday when he reached home.

"I'll have to go to town on Thursday, then, to get groceries," observed Jean. "What kind of meat have they been havin'?"

"Roast beef, mostly, so far as I can remember," replied Tom.

"They had fried ham an' gravy at Cummings'," interposed Eddie. "That was pretty good."

"It'll take a good deal of meat to feed twenty men two dinners an' two suppers." Jean considered the problem. "But we won't have to buy too much else, with potatoes an' other things from the garden an' plenty of canned vegetables in the cellar. I better bake bread tomorrow. It'll prob'ly take fifteen loaves."

"Well, get what you need an' write a check for it. Le's not skimp on the food. The men get hungry."

"No, I don't aim to skimp. I remember when you come home from some place threshin' last year complainin' because the food was scarce. I'll need a pile of wood split for the stove—an' it would help if you could spare one of the boys to stay near the house to get water for us an' bring in wood."

"All right, Ernie, you're chief cook an' bottle washer for your mom when we thresh. Eddie an' Bill'll haul grain, an' Bert, I want you to run the blower. George Harmonson'll divide the grain an' I'll stack straw. So everybody's got their job. How're you fixed for kitchen help?"

"Well, there's Jane an' me. Mrs. Peterson's gonna come an' bring Alice, so that's four, countin' the girls. Mrs. Hanson said she would come about ten an' could stay 'til supper. I think that'll be enough."

Thursday evening about dusk the steam engine pulling the canvas-shrouded grain separator chugged up the lane. Behind them came the water boy driving a team hitched to the water wagon. This was a half-round barrellike tank mounted on a wagon chassis with a hand pump on top. It would be filled from the stock tank to supply the steam engine with water. The men parked the equipment in the barnyard and went home.

When they had gone, Ernie and Bert stood admiring the steam engine. It was the most powerful thing about which they knew. Above the heavy steel front wheels was the boiler, some three feet in diameter, the top standing eight or more feet above the ground and extending eight or ten feet back to the firebox. The rectangular steel firebox hung to within about thirty inches of the ground and reached to the top of the boiler. The huge rear axle was just behind the firebox, and mounted on its ends were wide drive wheels five or six feet in diameter. Between the rear wheels was the cab, a steel deck about four by five feet, where the engineer stood. Behind that was the covered water tank, holding about a hundred gallons, the top of which served as a coal bin, holding a few bushels. Over the machine a metal canopy provided protection from rain and gave shade.

The boys climbed up into the cab. In the twilight they could dimly see the details of the machine. The rear wheels on each side were chest high. On the end of the firebox toward them they could make out the waterglass, showing the amount of water in the boiler, the steam gauge, and various hand wheels and hoses. Above the firebox was the throttle, a handle about fifteen inches long; the clutch lever; and a lever to reverse the engine. They could almost feel the quiet power of this monster.

Ahead of the left drive wheel above the top of the boiler was the cylinder. Steam was introduced into it from the boiler, first at one end and then at the other, driving the piston back and forth to supply power. The steam was then exhausted through the smokestack, producing the chug that is the hallmark of the reciprocating steam engine.

The piston moved in the cylinder and was connected by a pitman rod to the flywheel behind it. This wheel was mounted on one end of the drive shaft, which crossed the top of the boiler and carried the drive pulley on its other end. The drive pulley was some three feet in diameter, having a flat face perhaps eight inches wide, and from this the belt ran to drive the grain separator when threshing.

Daybreak showed dimly in the east when the family arose the next day. Soon Odie, the engineer, arrived and began preparing for the long day ahead. Opening a door on the front of the engine beneath the smokestack, he revealed a honeycomb of holes in the boiler. These were flues. Through each hole he ran a long steel rod having on it a round steel brush to clean it. If the flues were not cleaned, the heat passing through them could not properly heat the water in the boiler.

Presently Sam, who tended the grain separator, arrived. He removed the canvas covering from the machine, pulled a multitude of belts from an opening near its rear end, and placed these on the pulleys. He adjusted idlers, repaired belts, filled grease cups, and squirted oil into bearings until Tom called, "Breakfast!"

After breakfast the men drove the equipment into the feedlot. Here they uncoupled the engine, backed it some forty or fifty feet away, and set it in line with the grain separator. Unrolling the drive belt, they lifted it into place on the drive pulley of the engine and backed the engine to tighten the belt. Then, placing a block in front of the rear wheel of the engine as a chock, they operated the equipment slowly until satisfied that all was in order.

Ernie and Bert stood fascinated as they watched. The separator stood on four heavy steel wheels, its bottom some thirty inches above the ground. The top was still far above Sam's upraised hand as he made adjustments. The main body of the machine was probably thirty feet long and up to eight feet wide, and when the feeder at the front was swung out to full length and the blower at the rear turned pointing backward, it indeed seemed huge.

At about six the first bundle rack appeared, towing a buggy in which the man would ride home at night. In the field of shocked grain the driver tied the lines to the top of the front ladder of the bundle rack, climbed out, and began to load. Taking two or three bundles at one stab of the pitchfork, he filled the basket of the hayrack. Then pushing each shock over as he approached it, he thrust his fork into the bottom of each bundle and placed it flat on those in the rack so that its butt extended a few inches out over the top board of the rack. He laid up two or three rows of bundles on one side, then pressing his fork against the line he directed the team through the windrow and built up the other side. Tossing the middle full, he continued. When it was as high as he could reach, he threw his fork onto the load, climbed up, and drove to the machine.

Bundles were carried into the maw of the separator by a ten-foot-long conveyor called the feeder. One wagon drove up on each side, and the men tied up their lines and waited.

Standing on top of the separator, Sam surveyed the scene to be sure that all was ready. "Aaalll riiiight!!" he called.

Odie, his hand already on the throttle, jerked it with short, easy yanks of his wrist. Slowly the wheels began to turn. When he was certain that all was in order, Sam moved his arm in short quick circles. Odie opened the throttle and the engine snorted as it picked up momentum. The throat of the separator emitted a low soft hum, which increased in tempo and volume. At full speed the whir of the cylinder plus the throbbing of the machine and the whine of the blower blended into a humming, thumping crescendo. A few straws swished up the blower and floated away and puffs of dust lifted and scattered around cracks in the wood frame of the separator as the equipment voiced itself in a tumultuous concert. Sam signaled to the men on the racks. They could begin.

With his fork, each seized a bundle and flicked it head first into his side of the feeder, to be followed by another and another. At the maw of the machine, knives chopped at the bundles, cutting the twine and shoving the straw down the monster's throat. The cylinder whined and groaned.

The cylinder was the vital organ of the grain separator. Mounted on the drive shaft, it was some two feet in diameter and thirty-six to forty-two inches long. Set in rows around its periphery, a few inches apart, were heavy steel teeth. Below the cylinder was a stationary steel plate having similar teeth mounted on it. This was called the concave, being slightly concave in shape to match the cylinder. The cylinder teeth caught the straw and yanked it through the concave teeth, threshing the kernels off. The grain and straw were then tossed toward the back of the machine where the oats passed through oscillating sieves to a deck below. The straw remained above the sieves and was carried toward the rear.

The blower fan was housed in a circular sheet-metal form at the rear of the separator. Above it a circular metal tube some fifteen inches in diameter carried the straw, propelled by the fan, upward to the strawstack. The fan not only delivered the straw to the blower, it also created a draft through the body of the separator so that after the cylinder released the straw and grain, the suction from the blower drew them toward the rear of the machine. It was tossed along by the action of the sieves, which were operated by long shaker arms driven by a crankshaft below.

The grain, having passed through the sieves, moved toward the center of the separator, where a blast of air blew the chaff and dirt from it. Then it was carried to the top of the separator, automatically measured, and emptied down a spout into a waiting wagon.

When one man had finished unloading his bundles he drove back to the field to reload, and the next man took his place at the machine. When one grain wagon was full, it was driven to the elevator where a man recorded whether that load went to the tenant or to the landlord and unloaded it.

At about midmorning, ladies appeared with the lunch, which was usually placed in the shade near the engine. Thereupon Odie gave the whistle a short toot, and the pitchers on the bundle wagons stopped. When the bundles had passed the cylinder, Odie shut down the engine. Refreshments consisted of sandwiches of cheese or cold cuts, cookies or cake, and coffee or tea. About ten minutes was given to this rest period; then with another toot they began again. Those not at the machine during the lunch rest had their refreshment when they arrived.

At a little before noon, Odie signaled to those bundle

haulers who were waiting to unhitch and go to dinner. When those unloading were finished, he shut the equipment down. Wash pans, pails of clean water, soap, and towels were placed near the house in a shady spot, and here the men washed up.

The dining table seated ten to fourteen men. In about twenty minutes they began to come out, toothpicks in their mouths, joking about how full they were. Others took their places, and those who had finished rested in the shade until one o'clock, when Odie tooted the whistle for operations to begin again.

When they had begun that morning, Bert had taken his place at the rear of the machine on top near the blower.

"You gonna run the blower?" Sam inquired.

"Yeh, I guess. Pop told me to do it, but he didn't show me how."

"Not much to it. Here, I'll show you."

The blower tube emerged from the top of the fan housing to point horizontally away from the rear of the machine. When in operation it swung slowly from side to side, depositing the straw evenly in a wide arc. As the strawstack grew, the blower could be raised by turning a crank and lengthening it to some eighteen feet by a telescoping section. It could deliver straw to the top of a stack some twenty or more feet in height.

"All you have to do, Bert, is to hold this rope so that the straw hits the stack toward the front or the back as your dad motions to you. See, like this." As Sam pulled and relaxed the rope, the hood at the top of the blower opened and closed much as one might open and close his hand with the palm turned down. This turned the straw downward onto the front of the pile; or when raised up, it allowed the straw to soar back toward the far side. "Or," continued Sam, "you can fasten the rope to this doodad an' it'll hold it wherever you set it."

The rhythm of the machine was interrupted at this instant by a sudden whack, whack, whack. Sam, standing on top of the separator, yelled, "Whoa, whoa," to the engineer.

Tom, from the straw pile, also joined in calling, "Shut 'er down."

Odie, who had been filling a grease cup on the engine at

126

the time, stopped and scanned the area as his hand went to the throttle. He knew the sound to be that of a loose or broken belt. This they could repair. The only thing that mattered was whether anyone was in danger. He could not shut down the engine with grain going into the cylinder unless safety required it, for to do so would clog the cylinder and require another fifteen minutes to clean out. At this point the feeder belt broke; the long end slapped hard on the corner of the separator and the feeder halted. The two or three bundles that were beyond the knives slid into the cylinder and went ripping through; then the drive belt fell slack and Odie shut it down.

Sam secured tools for repairing the belt as Odie came to help. They cut the belt off where the lacing had torn the holes out, made new holes, and laced the ends together. With repairs complete, they began again.

Toward midmorning the next day Tom began to bring the corners of the strawstack in, keeping the center full, and before the last wagons began to unload he had topped it out, round and high. Sam then turned the blower to one side and the rest of the straw was blown onto a small pile by itself. At noon the job was completed, and after dinner the equipment was moved to the next farm.

There were two kinds of threshing rings, or organizations. In one type the machine was owned by one man or a family who solicited about a dozen neighbors to join the ring. This would comprise enough farms to supply ten bundle racks, two grain wagons, and a man to operate the elevator. Each farmer in the ring paid the owner so much per bushel for threshing.

The other type of ring was a cooperative, in which case a group of farmers formed a company, each buying a share of stock. The company was often known by the last name of one of its prominent families. In the cooperative ring there was no charge for the use of the equipment, since each was part owner; however, each member was required to pay his share of operation and maintenance expense.

In the operation of either ring each farmer supplied enough suitable coal to thresh his own grain. Often they would pool their funds and buy a carload of coal at reduced rates. Each supplied a source of clean water for the engine, and each provided dinner and supper for all hands as well as lunch in the morning and afternoon.

A week or two before threshing began, the group had a meeting. The farm where they would start and the one to thresh last would be determined as well as the succession for moving from farm to farm. The number of hands available from each farm would be agreed upon and the overtime rate established. Overtime was paid by those whose total threshing time was more than that of the others. The hours for starting and quitting were set and other details determined. The separator man kept a record of the number of bushels threshed and the hours worked at each farm. The engineer was usually the director of operations.

Within about two weeks after completion of the last job, a closing meeting was called. The separator man gave each the record of time worked at his place and each paid to or collected from each other any overtime. This meeting was a social event. The women visited and the children played while the men transacted business, after which ice cream and cake were served. If the ring was a cooperative, the cost of the ice cream was prorated among the members. If the machine was privately owned, the owner stood this cost.

THRESHING ACCIDENTS

When unloading at the machine a bundle would sometimes slide from the load and lodge on the drive belt. As soon as the wagon was unloaded far enough to get at the bundle, the man on the load would lift it off from the belt with his fork. In an attempt to do this one time, Bert stabbed so deeply that one tine of the pitchfork stuck into the belt. The fork was carried toward the rear of the load and jerked out of his hand. Luckily, it fell behind the wagon. There were cases in which the fork was carried all the way to the engine, and as the belt whirled around the drive pulley the fork was flung backward and landed on the ground. For this reason the area behind the drive pulley was kept clear. Spearing bundles from the drive belt was a precarious business unless done properly. It is said that the engineers usually sat on the side behind the cylinder, rather than behind the drive pulley, so as to avoid pitchforks on the belt.

Another near accident involved Tom. Repairs had to be made while he was unloading bundles. To give the men room to work he pulled his team a few feet forward, after which he stood talking and watching at the back of his wagon with one foot on the top board of the rack. Unexpectedly, one of his horses jerked forward and yanked the wagon ahead. Leaning over the back of the wagon, Tom was catapulted head over heels, turning a somersault in the air, his head barely missing the heavy front wheel of the separator. He landed on his seat where he sat stunned for a moment; then he remounted the wagon without a word. Had his position been but a few inches to one side, his head would have struck the edge of the steel wheel with perhaps sad results.

When threshing at a neighbor's a few years later, Ernie was involved in an accident. While a man was unloading at the separator, several bundles from the front corner of a load slid off and became entangled in the belts, which made a terrific noise and threw straw into the air. The team attached to the load turned away from the machine and started to run in a circle back toward the barnyard.

Several people who saw this develop began to shout. The engineer looked up from delivering a scoopful of coal into the firebox, and saw the team turning away from the machine, but he could not see the driver. He saw the straw whirling in the wheels, but the load was in the way so he couldn't understand what was happening. He thought the driver might be entangled in the belts. With several men shouting for him to stop the machine, he closed the throttle with one hand and with the other pulled the clutch lever to reverse the drive wheels. Thus he stopped the whole operation dead. But as the wagon turned away from the machine he saw that the driver was still up on the load and that no one was involved at the separator.

In the meantime, the team ran toward the barnyard. Ernie came out from the barn just as the team burst through the gateway. The stampeding horses ran astraddle of him, knocking him down, and the wagon passed over him. The tenant on the farm picked him up, put him into the car, and raced to the doctor in town three miles away. It proved that there was nothing wrong with Ernie except shock and a good scare.

At the separator a casting supporting the cylinder shaft

at the pulley had been broken and the shaft sprung. Since it would take hours to remove the cylinder shaft, it was decided to try to repair it in place. The cylinder was rotated to allow the bent shaft to make a mark on a timber pressed against its end. This showed a small deviation from center. With the sprung section of the shaft turned upward, a timber was chained beneath it, extending outward from it. Three men pulled down on the timber while one man struck the top of the sprung shaft with a sledge. This bent it downward, and the men's weight on the timber prevented it from vibrating back upward. After one stroke of the sledge the timber was unchained and the shaft tested. This was continued until the shaft was straight. The repaired casting was replaced and threshing was resumed after a stop of only a few hours.

Another incident that could have been serious involved a man temporarily acting as engineer. He was ready for the separator man to hand the drive belt up to him so he could mount it on the drive pulley. He closed the throttle and climbed up out of the cab over the front of the drive wheel in the usual manner to take the belt. The drive pulley was bright and smooth on the surface where the belt ran and its edges were true, so even when in motion it appeared to stand still. Had he made note of other moving parts near him he would have realized that the machine was still in motion, but being intent on getting the belt he moved forward down the front of the drive wheel toward the drive pulley until he was at a point where his next move would have brought him to rest against it. If he had let his weight down onto the moving pulley, it would have thrown him over the pulley and he would have fallen onto the front wheel of the engine.

The instant before he came to rest against the drive pulley, he realized his danger but could not retreat. Quickly he withdrew his hands from touching the wheel and thrust himself sideways from it. His stomach and chest came down against the wheel lightly and the wheel took hold against his overalls, pulling him somewhat toward the top of the wheel, but his evasive action also thrust him to the side so that he was able to leap away from the engine, landing on his feet to one side, shaken but unharmed.

Strenuous Tasks of Autumn

THE STRAWSTACK

AFTER threshing, the strawstack stood proud and tall, well rounded, bright and golden in the sunshine. With the coming of cold weather the farmer began to haul or carry straw from the stack to the barn to be used for bedding animals. As he cleaned the stables he threw the old bedding out upon the manure pile. Many farmers did not bring all of their livestock into the barn at night except in severe winter weather, leaving them instead to seek shelter around the strawstack.

With a winter's topping of snow and ice to depress the pile, and with the farmer carrying portions of it away as well as the livestock eating from it and eroding its base by rubbing against it, the stack gradually shrank during the winter. Often by March it resembled a very large toadstool, decimated at its base, with the heavy top lurching toward one side and sometimes sliding off.

One day in February Tom received a phone call from Norman Chrysler, who stated that the top had slid off from his straw pile. He needed help to find whether some of his animals might be buried under the straw. Tom and Bert hurried to their neighbor's, where at the straw pile Norman, pitchfork in hand, stood appraising the situation.

"I knew the top was gettin' too heavy, an' I should have pushed some of it off a day or two ago. But I let it go, an' at noon today I saw that it had slid off."

"Are there any cattle or pigs under it?" questioned Tom. "Have you counted your cows?"

"We counted the cows an' sows. Near as I can figure, two sows are missin' an' I'm short one cow."

"No way to tell where they would be under there, I guess," commented Tom. "Just have to start diggin' an' hope we find 'em." He walked along the mass of frozen straw that had cascaded down and covered the undercut section of the stack. With his fork he tentatively attacked the debris. "Been an hour or more since it tipped over, did you say? A cow could still be alive if she was layin' up against the stack an' it didn't fall on her. She'd be all right if she could get air."

"Yow, we hope that's what happened," rejoined Norman. "But if she started to run out an' it fell on top of her, then she might be good an' dead by now. Pretty late in the spring to butcher if she's dead; neighbors might take some of the meat, though."

Tom agreed. "Pretty warm weather for keepin' beef 'less you could fry it an' can it. Well, le's get after it an' see what we can find." He heaved aside an ice-laden hunk of the top cap.

After working for a few minutes, Norman paused and listened. "I hear her gruntin'." Forks poised, they waited. From under the pile they heard a firm, faint grunt.

"She's still alive," shouted Bert. "I can hear her up this way. She's right about in here." Approaching the end of the slide where the base of the stack was exposed, he found a small tunnel into which he crawled. "I've found her. She's still breathin'! Can you hear me?"

"We can hear ya," replied Norman. "Careful, now. I'm gonna dig right about where you are. Don't wanta stick ya."

"You're right about on her. I'm gonna get out of here now."

Outside, Bert took a fork and assisted. As they dug away chunks of the frozen top they came to soft straw beneath. Presently Norman uncovered the cow's foot. In an instant she sprang forth none the worse for the experience. They continued to work along the side of the pile until presently a pig squealed as one of them pricked it with his fork. In a flash it leaped out, followed by a second.

"Well," commented Norman, "we've made pretty good money here in half an hour." He leaned on his fork to rest. "We've saved a cow and two sows."

"Yeh, that's not bad for thirty minutes' work," returned Tom. "Good thing you noticed it when you did. If you'd been away, they could have been under there all afternoon, or even all night. That might have been another story."

Norman agreed. "We was lucky this time. A man that goes to our church had the top of his pile slide off last year an' he lost three cows. Well, le's go to the house an' have a cup of coffee."

By the time spring planting was finished, last year's straw pile would often be so decimated that only a wide circular pad of waste straw might remain. This became a wet, spongy, compacted mass, accumulating offal and urine as the animals browsed over it and slept on it. When there were a few days between field operations, the farmer hauled away the manure from about the stables. Through decades this was hauled to the field in a wagon and thrown upon the ground with a pitchfork. This slow, laborious process was made easier by use of the manure spreader.

This machine was built low to the ground for easy loading. It had a box somewhat like that of a wagon, eight to ten feet long, three feet wide, and two feet deep. The wheels were of steel, the rear ones having cleats to give traction. The front wheels were usually smaller to make sharp turning possible when working about farm buildings. Two to four horses pulled the spreader. Mounted on the axle at the rear of the box was the beater, a cylindrical framework of steel bars on which teeth were set. The movable bottom of the machine pushed the load backward and the beater, powered by the rear wheels, tore the manure from the oncoming mass, throwing it out onto the ground. Some spreaders had a second rotating shaft on which were mounted sheet-metal fins to scatter the manure further.

A day or two of hauling pretty well cleaned up the piles that had accumulated around the barns. But when it came time to work on the strawstack bottoms it took several days of continuous work.

Out behind the barn in the corner of the grove, Tom surveyed what was left of last year's strawstack. It represented a mass of straw about 100 feet in diameter, up to a foot and a half thick in the center, and thinning out to nothing at the edges. In the center a cow stood switching flies and chewing her cud. Nearby two sows rooted leisurely in the dry top straw as two or three pigs tugged halfheartedly at her teats. Along the thin edge of the straw where the dust began to show through, a rooster and two hens scratched and pecked for what sustenance they could find. In two weeks school would begin, and as soon as the boys were off to school Tom would begin to plow. It was time to get after the straw pile bottom.

"That's four loads so far this mornin'," said Ernie as he wrapped up the lines and climbed down after taking a load to the field. "What time is it?"

"Ha' past nine when I stopped in the house just now," responded Tom. "Here, do ya want a drink of water? I filled the jug."

Ernie drank thirstily, then held the jug aside to catch his breath. "How many loads do ya think we'll get out this mornin'?"

"Oughta get at least ten," responded Tom. "Should get twenty or twenty-five by quittin' time if we're gonna get this stack bottom out before school starts."

"It'd go faster if we didn't have to haul it so far," commented Bert. "It's quite a way out to where we're spreadin' it."

"Yow, it is fu'ther, but we covered this end of the field last spring, so I thought we oughta put this fu'ther down the field where we ain't spread none lately."

Standing between the spreader and the stack bottom, their backs partly toward the spreader, they began to load. On top the straw was dry and light, but the weight of the stack upon the base, the tramping of cattle, and the moisture the straw had absorbed made succeeding layers wet and heavy.

"Hey, that smells like kraut," suggested Ernie as they exposed the lower portions.

"Well, if you're hungry for some I'll lay a forkful on the seat where you can help yourself when you go to take out your next load," chortled Tom.

"Don't think I'm quite that hungry yet." Ernie paused to wipe his dripping brow. "Boy, but it's a hot time for this job."

"Yow, August is a hot time for haulin' manure, but it's about the only time for stack bottoms. It'll be time to start plowin' in a couple of weeks. We gotta get the stack bottom out on the stubble in order to plow it under. It'll be real good for next year's corn crop."

The thickness of the pile varied from twelve to eighteen inches. Thrusting their forks into it horizontally a little below the top, they pried with a twisting motion, tearing out the straw and pitching it sidewise into the spreader.

"How many loads do ya think there'll be in this bottom?" asked Bert as they put away their forks when they had finished at six that evening.

"Well, don't look like we made a very big dent in it today." Tom surveyed the expanse of straw. "I'd say there was 150 to 200 loads."

Ernie inspected his blistered hands. "At that rate it'll take a week at least. Man, my hands is sure blistered. That blister busted this afternoon, an' this one hurts like it was about ready to break. It'll prob'ly bust tomorrow. Ain't your hands blistered, Pop?"

Tom held out his hand, yellow and hard with calluses. "They used to blister like yours, an' I suppose they still would if I didn't keep doin' some fork or shovel work about every day. You'll get some blisters for a few days an' then your hands'll get tough."

"Sure wish I had some gloves or mittens to wear," suggested Ernie. "I saw the men at threshin' here last week and lots of them had leather gloves. Bet you wouldn't hardly ever get blisters with leather gloves."

Tom considered this. "Well, there's some old huskin' mitts in the drawer in the kitchen. They're kind of worn out at the fingers, but they would sure help. You boys has all got good hands like mine. They'll be tender for a day or two, but they'll soon get used to it. But use the mitts if you want to; they'll make it easier 'til your hands get toughened up."

Bert examined his hands. A blister had formed at the base of one finger. It hurt when he pressed it. Along the base of his other fingers calluses showed where there had been blisters during haying. Along the inside of his thumb was a spot half as large as a dime where that digit had adjusted to the use of the fork handle by developing a tough shield. "I noticed Jim Hanson's hands when we was threshin'. He wears leather gloves all the time. Man, his hands looked as soft as a baby's. Bet he'd have blisters in a hurry if he didn't wear leather gloves."

Tom agreed. "Some people's just naturally got soft

hands, but wearin' gloves keeps your hands damp an' they stay soft so's you can't work without 'em. Now, my hands is hard, an' the skin's so thick I never have no blisters."

"I looked at gloves in the store the other day," said Bert. "Pete Simpson was buyin' a pair that cost three dollars. Man! Who's got money to pay that for gloves, anyhow? I'll take a few blisters for a day or two 'til my hands get toughened up to it."

So they went at it day after day. They could pitch a load onto the spreader in eight to ten minutes; then, taking turns, Ernie and Bert hauled it to the field. In twelve minutes they were back. After a drink from the water jug they began again. Twenty minutes to the load, three loads per hour, twenty-five loads in a day. Loading up was hot, hard work. Then, during unloading they relaxed. It was a relentless pace, but it was the way to get it done.

FILLING THE SILO

It has long been known that when green plants such as corn are compacted to exclude oxygen and stored for a time the vegetation passes through a fermentation process similar to curing kraut. This produces a palatable, nourishing food for livestock. The Egyptians, it is said, understood this and buried such green plants in covered trenches to produce this type of feed. The original term for it was ensilage, the common term for it now is silage. It is usually cured in wood, clay tile, or sheet-metal cylindrical towers called silos, though it is reported that pit silos lined with sheet plastic are again coming into use.

"I never hauled green corn for filling a silo," Bert said when Tom informed him that he was to take a team and help a neighbor do this. "How do you go about it anyhow?"

It was much different from hauling oat bundles when threshing. One could not throw heavy bundles of green corn into the rack with a pitchfork. Instead, they were lifted by hand and slid onto the wagon. For this reason the sides of the hayrack were removed. Tom went with Bert to help him with the first load.

At the turn of the century, farmers cut corn by hand

with a knife similar to today's machete, and they still did so when cutting small amounts. But when cutting for the silo, the corn binder was used. This machine was pulled by three horses. Most of its weight was carried on a bull wheel that supplied power. Two long snouts at the front gathered the stalks between them. Inside each snout an endless chain, with lugs attached, moved toward the rear, stabilizing the stalks until the knife, similar to the knife on the mower, cut them off. As soon as the stalks were severed they were passed backward in a standing position and were tied, kicked onto the bundle carrier, and dumped into windrows. Driving alongside a windrow Bert tied the lines up on the front ladder and he and Tom climbed down.

"Now don't forget it's heavy. You'll get tired enough by night, so don't hurry."

"It sure ain't no picnic," breathed Bert as he seized the first bundle by the twine and hoisted it up onto the rack.

Tom advised against lifting bundles by the twine. This would cut his fingers, and it might break the twine. He recommended taking hold of two or three stalks on each side of the bundle near the twine with each hand. Then by lifting the lighter top end up over the edge of the rack, he could slide it onto the wagon.

As soon as they had laid a couple of layers on one side they turned the team through the windrow and laid up a like amount on the other side. Failure to do this would overload one side, causing the rack to tip off from the running gears. When both sides had been loaded to the top of the front and back ends they drove to the barnyard.

The silo was commonly fourteen to eighteen feet in diameter and up to fifty or sixty feet tall. The top might be covered or left open. Down the side from top to bottom was an opening about eighteen inches wide. Across this opening, on the outside, steel rods were mounted to be used as steps for climbing to the top. The steps and the opening were enclosed by a half-round sheet-metal cover. When a person climbed up the silo he was inside this protective shield, and when silage was thrown out it cascaded down this chute to fall in a pile at the bottom.

At the base of the silo on this day stood the silage cutter, considerably smaller than a corn sheller, mounted on a chassis somewhat like a wagon and standing on four small steel wheels. At the end of the chassis toward the silo was a round sheet-metal housing perhaps three feet in diameter and a foot or more thick. It enclosed the knives that were fastened to paddlelike fan blades mounted on the drive shaft. This shaft passed through the housing, and on its end outside the housing was a pulley driven by the belt from the tractor. The knives sheared off the stalks as they entered the housing. Then the fan propelled the chopped stalks up a vertical pipe, eight or ten inches in diameter, to the top where a semicircular hood turned them downward into the silo.

As Bert stationed his wagon alongside the cutter, the operator of the tractor let out the clutch. The heavy fan and its attached knives emitted a soft whirr that gained in intensity as the cutter gathered speed until at full throttle it became a steady, growling whoosh. The long pipe reaching up the side of the silo rattled and vibrated as the air pressure inside shook it gently. A few bits of dry silage still in the fan housing went rattling up the tube, and a pair of pigeons perched atop the silo eyed the goings on and then flew away. As the conveyor moved the bundle into the fan housing the knives emitted a quiet staccato sound as they clipped off the small tops. This grew in intensity as the bundle moved forward and became a thumping crescendo as the ears and thick ends of the stalks passed through the knives. The tractor growled and snorted. As the last of the stalks disappeared the tumult subsided, the thunder of the tractor diminished, and only the soft whirr of the fan and the hum of the tube were heard. It was time for another bundle.

One by one Bert dropped them in, lapping each a little on the one ahead to keep the machine working near maximum. He removed bundles from all over the load to avoid lightening one side too much and tipping the load over. When he had finished, the man following him took his place at the cutter.

Inside the silo a sort of green snowstorm floated down. Equipped with pitchforks, Tom and a companion began their endless round of walking. They distributed the silage evenly with their forks and tramped it down. Keeping the bed level, they moved in a circle, then crisscrossed over the center, spreading and testing it to insure uniform firmness.

"By doggies," commented Tom, "guess I should have worn my old felt hat. The stuff's goin' down my neck."

"Better be careful when you go home or the cows'll try to eat the shirt off your back, what with all the corn juice an' silage dust you'll accumulate on it," joked his helper.

"What in the world're they puttin' through that cutter, anyhow?" chortled Tom presently. "Felt like a rock hit me on the head that time."

His partner held up a whole circular cross section of an ear of corn some two and a half inches in diameter and half an inch thick. "Just a slice from an ear of corn. Lots of ears go to pieces when the knives hit them, so they come down light an' easy. But when the knives get a square chop at the ear they slice it off like this piece. I'll get you an old straw hat to protect your head an' keep it out of your neck."

As the silo filled, the men placed precut boards into the slots along the opening in the side to close it as they worked their way toward the top.

When the silo was opened for feeding, the top few inches of silage was discarded because it was moldy and tasteless from having been exposed to the air, but below this it was of good quality. Once the feeding began, the process was generally continued daily, or the top section would again spoil in a few days.

The early part of the fermentation cycle of silage generates a type of alcohol. If the silo leaked there might be puddles of this alcohol in the livestock tracks about the base, and more than one farmer found his pigs staggering about intoxicated from drinking out of these puddles. During the period just after World War I, when it was illegal to sell alcoholic beverages, an occasional farmer was hailed into court for tapping his silo during the fermenting period and selling the liquid harvest.

HUSKING CORN

In 1915, Tom's second year in Iowa, he looked forward to husking corn. This would be his first real money crop, and to him it looked bountiful. By early October the plowing was finished. The corn leaves that were not already brown showed white and limp from frost. The silk on the ears was dark and the dry husks hung loosely on the ears. It would soon be time to pick.

To protect his hands the farmer wore husking mittens, or mitts, and a good man would go through two pairs in a day. They were made of heavy cotton flannel with the nap turned outward.

For husking, the triple-box was used. To prevent the husker from throwing ears over the wagon, the bangboard, about three feet high, was mounted on the right side of the wagon box. This consisted of boards three-fourths inch thick and as long as the wagon box, which were nailed or bolted to two-by-four-inch cleats that extended down astraddle the right side of the wagon box about to the floor. On top of this there was often an additional board, usually six or eight inches wide. If the husker filled the wagon box he could take this down and place it on top of the side nearest him to prevent ears from falling off. A man who could husk 100 bushels per day would need this extra board, and he would have similar short ones on top of the front and rear endgates.

Attire commonly used for husking was blue jeans or overalls, a blue denim jacket, and a cap. When the husker reached the field he put on his mitts and strapped on the hook. The husking hook, made in several designs, consisted of a metal plate attached to a leather band that strapped to the palm or wrist. The chief feature of the metal plate was a sheet-iron hook attached to it for tearing the husk from the ear. To use the hook the man grasped the ear with his left hand without bringing the fingers completely around it. Thus his left fingers were not in the way of the hook. He drew the right hand with the attached hook across the ear, gathering a section of the husk in the curve of the hook to pull it aside. He then closed his left hand, which gathered the rest of the husk and pulled it back to expose the ear. Next he grasped the ear with his right hand, gave it a twist or a straight jerk that severed it from the stalk, and flipped it into the wagon, almost in one motion. As he did this his left hand reached for the next ear. Once this routine was established, a man might work for several minutes without looking toward the wagon. The team moved slowly along munching cornstalks, and a regular staccato was heard as the ears hit the bangboard.

On a Saturday morning soon after the middle of October, Tom announced that they would begin husking. Tom, Eddie, and Bill—each equipped with a new pair of husking mitts and a hook, and taking a jug of water—climbed into the wagon and set out.

Opening the field consisted of husking the rows along the side next to the fence as well as husking down through the field some forty or fifty rows away. This laid out a land around which to work. The team straddled the row next to the fence, which was called the down row. The name described it suitably, for as the wagon passed over the brittle cornstalks they broke down or bent toward the ground, the ears remaining on them. These ears had to be husked from behind the wagon. Tom assigned this task to the boys, then ten and thirteen, who soon found it to be a difficult one. After breaking the ear from the stalk they stood up, removed the husks, then threw it into the wagon over the rear endgate. Tom, husking two rows alongside the wagon, had the length of the wagon at which to aim his ears. The boys, being behind, had but a width of three feet at which to aim, and they often missed the wagon completely. Tom could work at the front of the wagon or near the back of it. But the boys were continually faced with being too far behind for easy throwing; or if the horses had not moved forward, they found themselves working under the back endgates so that they had to straighten up, step back, and then throw their ears. There were stops to straighten the mitts, to take the kinks out of their backs, and to just sit down in the shade of the wagon and rest. Husking the down row was not an easy assignment.

At length they completed the first round. The boys hoped that they would go to the house then, but Tom had other ideas. "It ain't much of a load yet," he said. "Get up there and look at it—see how much we've got." They complied and were surprised at the small amount of corn their combined sweat and effort had produced. "I think we might as well at least go back to the other end," he said. "Bill, you go get another jug of water an' Eddie an' me'll begin."

In spite of frost and ice on the water tank at night, it was quite warm in the cornfield by ten thirty in the morning. They perspired and went to the jug for water. They took off the mitts to inspect for blisters. They kept at it. It was eleven fifteen when they completed the second round and headed for the house. The wagon was full almost to the top. Proudly they posed on the load as Jean and the little children came out to inspect.

Corncribs were intended to hold ear corn, and because the ears needed to dry after being cribbed, the boards on the sides of the building were spaced about an inch apart for ventilation. High up along the sides, near the eaves, hinged doors opened by swinging downward. Placing the wagon beneath these, Tom prepared to unload the corn.

To begin scooping off the load, he removed the rear bottom endgate and dug out the ears with a scoop. He swung the scoopful upward, tossing the contents into the opening in the wall some eight feet above the ground. When there was room in the wagon he continued to work from there.

Husking was hard on clothing, for corn leaves and husks have burrlike edges that although seldom cut the skin soon wore the finish from clothing. Before the season was finished, a man could wear out a couple of pairs of overalls and a jacket or two, and the sleeves of his shirts would have holes in them. First the garments took on a smooth, whitish look, then a threadbare appearance, and finally holes appeared where the wear was most pronounced. Against these drawbacks they tasted the satisfaction of harvesting a bountiful crop.

"You said you was goin' to open up a new land this mornin'. How does the corn look over there?" asked Jean as Tom sat down to dinner a week later. "Is it as good as where you've been pickin'?"

"Oh, yes! Fact, it looks better. That strip down the center of the field is sure good." Tom filled his plate with potatoes, spread over them a generous helping of gravy, and took a slice of meat from the platter. "I been pickin' eight rows in the mornin' an' eight in the afternoon. Ten would be an acre. I been havin' about thirty bushel or a little more to the load, so that's better'n thirty bushel to the acre. This mornin' I figured it was more like thirty-five. Hank never had an acre that was as good as that last year, an' that forty acres we had only made about twenty."

"How long do you think it will take you to finish that field? Can you make it by the end of next week?"

Taking a biscuit, he broke it in two and eased the halves one at a time down into his cup of coffee edgewise. He wiped his forehead, still perspiring from scooping off the load. Slowly he shook his head. "This the nineteenth of October?" He pressed the biscuits down and poured coffee from the saucer back into the cup until it was full. "'Nother week'll be October twenty-sixth. If I get out of there by November I'll be doin' good. I'll not make it in a week an' maybe not by the first if the corn holds up like I think it will."

"Well, I hope the corn is good. That would be seven or eight hundred bushel from that field. That's more than you had altogether last fall, an' you still got forty acres yet to pick. Looks like it would be December by the time you're done."

Tom turned the coffee-soaked biscuits out into his saucer and spread butter over them. "An' you know what that means?" He looked at Jean. "That means I may be wadin' in snow half up to my knees to get it finished. So, only thing I can see is that Eddie'll have to stay out of school, startin' Monday, an' me an' him'll go down them rows. With him helpin' we can pick twenty rows a day instead of sixteen. In a month that saves us a week's time. I had a taste of 'rasselin' nubbins out of knee-deep snow last fall when I was pickin' for the Schultz boys. It ain't no fun, 'specially if the thermometer is ten above."

With large mouthfuls he consumed a second helping of canned peaches and then pushed back his plate. He paused for a moment, picking his teeth. "Ha' pas' twelve. Gotta be goin' or I won't get the afternoon load scooped off before dark."

Occasionally one heard about a man who, if the yield was good, could husk 100 bushels in one day. With Tom's corn making less than 35 bushels to the acre, he had not been able to husk more than about 70 at the most. Later, during the early 1920s, with the corn yielding 50 or more bushels per acre, both he and a hired man set records for themselves by husking 100 bushels per day for several days.

It was commonly accepted that 100 ears would produce a bushel of shelled corn. Thus to husk 100 bushels, one would have to husk and throw into the wagon 10,000 ears. This meant that he husked an ear every two and a half to three seconds for eight hours. Because of limited daylight during husking, a man would be in the field for about eight hours. He would arrive there at about daylight, seven o'clock, and would have to be on the way to the house to unload by eleven. He would be in the field again soon after noon. This allowed him to leave the field no later than four so as to be unloaded before dark.

THE HUSKING MACHINE

Cornhusking was one of the longest continuous activities of the farm year and for the men it was the most strenuous. During the rest of the year the farmer rode the machines and the horses did the hard work, but during cornhusking the horses pulled the wagon across the field only a few times each day, munching cornstalks, while the man sweated at the task. Because husking was slow and strenuous work and because he wanted to keep the boys in school, Tom decided in the early 1920s to buy a mechanical cornhusker.

The horse-drawn husker took one row at a time. It had a pair of small wheels in front attached to a tongue for steering, and two bull wheels supplied the power.

On the left side, two long snouts sloped downward near the ground on each side of the row to collect the stalks. Mounted in each snout was a moving chain with lugs attached that held the stalks so that the gathering rolls on the machine could seize them. These rolls discharged the stalks onto the ground, pulled the ears from the stalks, and carried them upward along the inclined rolls.

At the top of the rolls an endless chain discharged the ears down an inclined chute onto the husking rolls. These rolls were studded with steel blades that protruded about a quarter inch. As the ears passed over the rolls the blades cut the husks loose and the rolls expelled them onto the ground. The ears dropped into a bin from which a chain carried them up an inclined spout to a wagon.

The driver sat in the center of operations. To his left were the snouts that gathered the corn. To his right within easy reach were the husking rolls. Ears often piled up on these rolls, and when this happened, some operators prodded at the ears with their hands. This was an unsafe procedure; many a man had his mitten pulled off by the rolls and some had their hands caught and mangled. This problem arose because the ears sometimes came from the gathering rolls faster than the husking rolls could handle them. Some farmers solved this by mounting a Model-T motor onto the rear of the husker. The horses then pulled the machine and the motor operated it. When the rolls became overloaded the operator stopped the team and allowed the machine to run until it had cleared itself. A few years later, tractors with power takeoff equipment came into use. With this the tractor pulled the machine and the power shaft operated it. Sad reports of accidents involving the cornhusker continued with the use of this equipment. If a man's hand was pulled into the husking rolls it could be mutilated before the machine could be stopped. Tom used the husker for a few years, then discarded it, preferring the safe procedure of husking by hand.

A SHORT RUNAWAY

When unloading at the elevator it was Tom's practice to leave the team that was hitched to the wagon attached to the singletrees. However, one night the team walked away with the wagon while it was hoisted in the overhead jack. The wagon came down with a bang and the frightened team then went tearing toward the barn.

When the horses had pulled ahead, the overhead jack tipped forward and fell with its top across the front of the wagon. As the team ran with the wagon, it dragged the jack along on each side. The wagon was about empty, and because Ernie, who was unloading it, could not get hold of the lines he elected to abandon the team and wagon. The bangboard was high up on one side—there was no escaping there. The top board had been set down on the other side, so he could not readily climb over it, and anyhow, the jack was dragging alongside. There was no hope there. The rear bottom endgate had been removed, leaving an opening fourteen inches high at the floor level. He dashed to the rear of the wagon box and slid out through the opening, rolling unhurt on the frozen ground.

The team stopped at the barn door, where Tom and the others took control of them. The jack was lifted from the wagon and found to be little damaged. From that time on it became standard practice when unloading to unhook the tugs of the team that was hitched to the wagon.

No School until Christmas

FALL PLOWING

WHEN school opened in September 1919, ten-year-old Bert stayed home to haul several hundred bushels of oats to town. While this assignment lasted he scooped 100 bushels of oats into the wagon each morning, made a trip to town and back by noon, then repeated the operation in the afternoon.

In the meantime Tom had begun to plow. When Bert had completed the hauling, Tom set him to work with the sulky plow in a small field by himself. The sulky plow was basically the same equipment that farmers had used for 100 years except that a frame having three wheels had been attached to the beam and moldboard. Also, there were levers for adjusting the depth of plowing and a seat for the driver. The front wheel ran against the bank of the last furrow plowed and was attached to the tongue for steering. A second wheel was directly below the driver's seat. The third wheel ran on the stubble to the left of the moldboard. The tongue ran up between the two right-hand horses and eveners were attached to the front of the beam.

Attached to the bottom of the beam, as the back end of it curved down and forward, was the moldboard. The plowshare was bolted to the bottom of this. The share was really a huge knife, with the front point hooked slightly downward. Mounted in a vertical plane below the beam was a flat steel disc about fourteen inches in diameter called the rolling cutter. It penetrated the soil ahead of the plowshare, cutting a smooth furrow bank. The plowshare cut the soil loose and passed it backward onto the moldboard, which as it curved upward and outward turned the soil upside down, depositing the vegetation beneath it in the last furrow plowed.

"Now, you need a furrow across the end to help make a

147

nice even start every time," instructed Tom. He took the lines and drove across the end of the field, plowing a furrow some fifteen feet from the fence. Then he went to the side of the field and stepped off thirty-five strides, walking parallel with the road. "Now put your plow here an' wait 'til I go to the other end." When midway in the field, he went to the fence and again stepped off thirty-five strides, and there he placed his hat. At the far end he again stepped off the same distance and stood there.

When traveling with the plow or turning at the end of the field, the beam was raised so that the moldboard was carried above the ground. To start plowing, a foot was pressed against a pedal to force the share into the soil as the team moved forward. At Tom's signal, Bert kicked the top pedal forward and started the team. He pressed the pedal with all his might, but the share skidded along the top of the ground. Realizing that he did not have enough weight to force the share into the soil he stopped the team, hopped from the seat, and standing by the left side of the plow took hold of the lower pedal. Lifting this up he forced the upper pedal forward until it was locked. This lifted the rear wheel of the plow off the ground, the weight of the plow resting on the plowshare. When the team started, the plowshare penetrated the soil properly. He used this method for sinking the plow into the ground all fall. From the seat of the plow he sighted along the tongue past the hat to Tom, while with the lines tight he drove as straight as he could to the other end.

"Well, that's pretty good," concluded Tom as they looked back along the furrow. "Maybe I better have you do the sightin' when we get to plowin' together."

Turning the team they placed the plow so that on the return trip it cut a second furrow parallel with the first. The soil from this was thrown in a ridge against that plowed out during the first crossing. This was called the back ridge.

The sulky plow cut one furrow, usually fourteen inches wide, and required three horses to pull it, while the gangplow such as Tom used had two beams and two moldboards, each of which cut a furrow ten or twelve inches wide. The gangplow required five horses. When Bert had finished the small field he joined Tom, and with his team behind the gangplow they worked together.

"Whoa," shouted Tom as the eveners dropped to the ground with a clash and his plow stopped. "I hit a rock an' broke my wire. Come help me fix it."

"Boy, there's a lot of rocks in these fields," commented Bert as they set about to repair the break.

"Yeh, I keep watchin' for 'em. Usually you can see 'em. If not, there's usually a bunch of grass where they are so you know to stop. But some of 'em's buried an' you never know where they are 'til you hit one."

The five-horse team used on the gangplow had two horses in the lead and three behind. The eveners of the lead team were attached to a chain that ran back under the tongue to the evener assembly. Here a wire was run through the chain and a clevis to connect the eveners. This was not intended to be a breakpoint, but it served that purpose, for when the plow struck the rock the wire broke. Had there been no breaking point in the evener assembly, striking a large rock might spring one of the beams, causing that moldboard to turn the soil improperly.

Sitting on the ground side by side they pulled the evener assembly into position and attached another wire. Then, seated on the plow, Tom depressed the pedal to lift the plowshare free of the rock. It would not come up.

"She's run right in under it," he concluded. "Must be a big rock."

"We could take the lead team off and bring 'em around back of the plow an' pull it back," suggested Bert.

"Yow, I had to do that one time," agreed Tom. "But le's see if we can lift it with a lever."

The large wheel that ran on the stubble was mounted on an offset axle that could be adjusted by a lever to raise and lower the left side of the plow. With the added lifting power of the lever, Tom forced the point of the plowshare backward a little and they were finally able to free it.

"We oughtta mark these rocks an' come out here sometime an' pull 'em out with a team," observed Tom when they were ready to go again. "We'll hit 'em with the disc an' with the cultivators every time we work in the field."

Plowing was often done in hot weather, and when the men stopped for repairs or to rest the horses, the teams frequently became uncomfortable because of flies. To defend themselves the horses stamped their feet, shook their heads, and flinched their skin, causing it to vibrate. They switched their tails to the side, whipped them down between their rear legs, and occasionally one horse would rub against his teammate to dislodge the flies. The most common method for repelling flies was to place fly nets on the horses.

Binding twine that farmers bought for harvesting came in burlap bags, which when cut open and stitched together made a sort of lightweight blanket through which the flies could not bite. More sophisticated nets consisted of a network of cords or leather thongs an inch or so apart. They were mounted on the harness, the ends hanging down beneath the horse's belly and in front of his chest. The thongs slithered over his skin as he moved, dislodging the flies. In spite of nets, flies could annoy a horse unmercifully.

Botflies, or nose flies as they were also called, were another irritation to the horses during summer and early fall. From time to time the nose fly would dart up past the horse's chin and sting him on the nose. Then the horse would start violently and rub his nose on anything near. Often he would stop for a moment and hold his nose in a protected position lest the fly should attack again. Nose flies could drive a team crazy.

This insect laid its eggs where the horse ingested them. The eggs then hatched within the digestive tract. There the grubs attached themselves to the intestine walls where they remained until the end of the incubation period. The adult nose fly looked like a wild honeybee and some people called them nose bees. They often remained stationary in the air about the horse's nose or legs or they darted here and there. They would fly along with a team and pester it for hours if there was little wind to blow them away. It was possible to go to the team's head and after watching carefully catch a botfly by grabbing it as it was motionless in the air. Often there would be but two or three of them, and a few minutes spent in killing them would release the team from its torment.

There were two or three common methods for protecting the horse's nose from nose flies. One was to fasten a band of leather having closely set leather thongs to the bridle, with the thongs hanging down over the horse's nose to discourage nose flies from attacking. Also available were nose baskets.

These were six-inch cups of screen wire that could be attached to the bridle so that the horse's nose was inside of it. A third device, less used, was a sort of muzzle having a solid piece of leather that protected the end of the horse's nose where the nose fly struck.

About 1920 the Farm Bureau contracted with local veterinarians to administer a capsule down the throat of each horse to kill the grubs—if the farmer wished. This reduced but did not eliminate the nose fly.

Battling the flies, they proceeded to plow. If the soil was too wet the moldboards did not scour, that is, the soil stuck to them instead of turning off cleanly. This prevented the soil from completely turning over, which made a messy looking field. To correct this the operator would stop now and then to dig the gumbo from the moldboard with a paddle.

One field had a good deal of long straw on the ground; this clogged up under the plow, causing the men to stop repeatedly to dig it out. Because there was quite a bit of this long straw, Tom decided to burn it. Going behind the teams, he lighted it and then drove away. When they reached that end of the field again, the fire had spread into a wide path and was moving with the wind toward a meadow beyond the fence where there was a haystack.

"The stubble's short in the hayfield an' I doubt it'll burn," said Tom. "But if the fire gets a good start it might run through the stubble anyhow and set the haystack on fire. We'd better plow a few furrows ahead of it."

Plowing along the end of the field they drove beyond the fire and started up through the field, laying out a strip for a firebreak. As they came back down the field, the newly plowed strip had checked most of the fire, but the wind had carried sparks and in several places had started fires beyond the firebreak.

"We'll have to put it out," decided Tom. "If it gets into the hayfield we'll have a stack of hay to pay for." Going to one of the horses, he removed the burlap fly net and cut it in two with his pocketknife, giving half to Bert. "You go toward that end an' I'll go this way an' we'll beat it out."

They almost had to run along the fire line from one burning spot to another, beating the flames back toward the burned area. When Bert reached the far end it was burning again in a few places, but he hurried back, beating it out with the folded burlap. "By doggies, that could have been a close one," commented Tom, mopping his brow when they met. "Le's plow back to the other end an' we'll walk over to the flow an' get a drink."

The basin within which some two or three sections of land lay was so geologically constructed that there were several artesian wells thereabouts. These were spoken of as flowing wells, or simply as flows. One of these was a quarter mile across the pasture. A neighboring family that had a contaminated well in their barnyard carried all of their drinking water from this artesian well, and the school at the corner used it for many years as a water supply. Leaving their teams at the end of the field, they walked across the pasture, drank their fill, and returned to the afternoon's work.

COLD DINNER

Tom did not hire a man when he had lived at Deep Creek; however, at Westover, with 140 acres of corn to husk, he had to have more help. Accordingly, he directed Eddie to go to both restaurants and the hotel every day before he came from school and ask whether anyone had come to town wanting work. Eddie would probably have to stay out of school for a few weeks to help, but it would not be for long if they could find a man.

A man was found, but he stayed only two weeks. When he left, Eddie stayed home for two weeks, after which he went back to school. Bert had been out of school all fall to haul, plow, and husk, but he had hoped he would not need to stay out after Thanksgiving. When another man could not be found, Bert's prospects for school that fall vanished. He would stay home until husking was finished.

The last forty acres was land one and a half miles away that Tom had rented from another owner. To give this owner his share of the corn, they scooped the morning load into the owner's crib near the field. The afternoon load they took home. Because they did not go home at noon they carried their dinner in a syrup pail.

"Well, what's for dinner today?" asked Tom as he sat in

the sun beside the crib. "Come on, open it up. I'm hungry."

Bert pried open the bucket. "Looks like fried ham sandwiches." He handed one to Tom.

"I expect it will taste good as soon as I get it thawed out," said Tom as he chewed slowly. "The meat's actually froze."

"Well, what did you expect? It's been in the wagon since we left home at six thirty this mornin' an' it was ten degrees above, then."

"A cup of hot coffee would taste good now," mused Tom. "Wisht we had a way to heat some here. I'd have had her put some in a bucket for us."

"There's plenty of time while you're scoopin' it off for me to make a little fire of corncobs an' heat up a bucket of coffee. Sure would taste good to have somethin' hot."

"Well, what do you know! Here's a piece of raisin pie for each of us down in the bottom. That'll taste good, even if it is froze."

Tom lifted out the pieces of pie. They were flat from the weight of the other food on top of them. "Well, they don't seem to be froze much after all. I'll bet they're just as cold as if they was froze, though." He handed one to Bert.

"Too bad she didn't put in two apiece; that's the best part of the lunch."

They had endured a week of cold weather. It had been down to ten or fifteen degrees above zero when they left home each morning, slowly getting warmer until about noon. Then the temperature would recede, and by four it was quite cold again. In addition, the wind had blown a gale almost continuously for the whole week.

On Saturday Eddie and Bert took one wagon while Tom and Ernie husked in another.

"I just hate to see you all go off with a dinner that I know will be froze by the time you eat it," said Jean one Friday night. "If there's any way one of you could come home an' get it, I'd fix you a nice dinner tomorrow."

"Hey, that sounds good," encouraged Bert. "Why not tie Toots behind the wagon an' I'll ride her home while you guys scoop off the loads."

Accordingly, at noon Bert mounted Toots and set off the two miles home for the lunch. They had the wagons unloaded before he had returned and Tom was growing impatient. "I'm warmed up good now from scoopin', but if I have to sit here very long waitin' I'm gonna get chilly. If he don't show up pretty soon we might as well go back to the field an' get to work. When he comes we can eat there." However, the sunny side of the corncrib appeared more comfortable than the cornfield, so they tarried a little longer.

"Whatever took you so long?" asked Eddie when Bert finally arrived. "We was about ready to go back to the field and get to work just to keep warm. How come you brought it in a milk bucket?"

"I don't care what it's in," interrupted Tom. "Le's see what she's got for us." He removed the dish towel and peered within.

"For gosh sakes," said Ernie scowling. "What sort of a lunch do you call this? Looks like some kind of sandwiches all mixed up with grass an'—what the heck! Looks like peach cobbler."

"Well, Mom had a swell lunch for us like she said. It was all fixed up in the basket real nice. Made me want to sample it as soon as I looked at it. So I got onto Toots an' started back."

"Well, where'd the milk pail come from?"

"I was tryin' to tell you. I got about halfway to the mailbox when the bottom fell right out of the basket an' the whole thing went down on the grass."

"Why didn't you have your arms under it?" asked Tom.

"Well, I didn't think about the bottom fallin' out, so I was holdin' it by the handles. Anyhow, there it was in a mess on the ground. So I went back to the house an' told Mom what'd happened."

"Maybe you guys want to talk about this, but I'm gonna start on it an' get what I can," said Tom as he began to sort out the food. "Le's eat."

They began as Bert continued between mouthfuls. "Mom said there wasn't time to fix more an' she asked if I could pick it up from the ground. I took the milk pail and went back an' scooped it up best I could an' come ahead. It fell on the grass, so it's really not dirty."

"Well, it ain't so bad as it looks," agreed Tom. "In fact, if you don't look at it you might think it was pretty good."

"Never had peach cobbler smeared over ham sandwiches an' grass before," smiled Ernie. "But like you say, it ain't so bad."

"Let me tell you boys, I've seen the time when a feed like this would have seemed like a banquet to me, an' I wouldn't have looked the other way while I was eatin' it either."

To celebrate the end of the husking the family always had oyster stew. A dishpan full of whole milk was placed on the range and oysters added. Meantime, in lieu of soup bowls, empty serving dishes of every kind and size were placed about the table. A meat platter was piled high with crackers, and all made ready for the feast. Bowls were filled and refilled upon request. The cracker supply was replenished until each had had as much as he wanted. There was no dessert. They had had oyster soup, and that was enough.

One week before Christmas, husking was at last finished and Bert went to school. Since the pupils had already drawn names for gift giving he missed out on those festivities, but he was so glad to finally be in school that missing this event seemed of little importance to him.

Except for the two weeks when there had been a hired man and the two weeks Eddie had stayed home, Tom and Bert had husked much of the 140 acres of corn. It had been a long and hard fall. "Now, young man," Tom said at bedtime the night they finished, "I'm not gonna call you 'til breakfast's ready in the morning. Just have yourself a good sleep."

Bert scarcely believed that he would be able to sleep until breakfast. What would the others think? And what would they say? Who would milk his cows? Even if they didn't call him, he knew that he would waken when the rest got up. And once awake, he would get up with them. It was a surprise, therefore, when the first sound he heard the next morning was his being roused just in time for breakfast. It was seven o'clock. The milking was done. He could hardly believe it.

Winter Activities

WINTER PASTURE

FOLLOWING cornhusking the cattle and horses were turned into the cornfields to forage on the dead grass, corn leaves, and dried husks as well as on some corn missed in the husking. This roughage relieved the need for feeding hay during the winter. As soon as the cattle had cleaned up one cornfield they were transferred to another.

When Christmas vacation began, the boys started to drive some thirty cows and calves daily to pasture; when school reopened after Christmas this task was assigned to Bert. At this time Eddie and Bill were riding horseback to school in Westover while Bert, Ernie, and Jane were attending rural school one and a half miles east of the farm. The pasture to which the cattle were taken was one and a half miles west.

"How's Bert gonna take the cows down there an' still get to school?" asked Ernie. "Last year we went to school right there by that pasture, so we took 'em when we went to school and brought 'em home at night. But we're goin' to the other school now."

"Yow, it's gonna make more walkin'," agreed Tom. "Bert'll take them down there an' then go to school after that."

"That'll be one an' a half mile to take them down there an' then more than two mile to school," concluded Bert.

"Well, I hadn't stopped to add it up."

"And at night I'll come home an' then walk a mile across the field to get 'em an' one an' a half mile home again. That's about seven mile every day," summarized Bert.

"Well, I guess you'll get your exercise."

At about seven thirty in the moring, in the early dawn, Bert began to move the cattle down the lane and thence onto the road. Some forty-five minutes was required for the drive, after which he walked and jogged to school. Since school began at eight thirty he was always late.

"Don't you want to come in an' get warm?" asked a neighbor who came from his house and intercepted Bert one morning as he hurried along. "It's down to zero this mornin'; you must be cold."

This was an unexpected windfall. It had not occurred to him to seek shelter. After walking and jogging more than three miles thus far, he was really not cold. But he accepted the invitation. After all, it might get down to ten below or he might be making this trek in a blizzard some morning and this respite would be welcome.

"You must get awfully cold takin' those cows an' then walkin' all the way to school," the mistress of the house consoled him. "I got some cocoa an' a cookie for you." Leisurely he partook of this refreshment.

"Now you stop here every mornin'," insisted the lady as she followed him to the door. "I'll have cocoa for you. You stop an' get warm."

Daily he followed this routine until early March when the drive was discontinued.

SHOEING HORSES

Each day as the children walked home from school they picked up the mail from the mailbox a half mile from home. One afternoon in early December they found a large package by the mailbox. Bert and Ernie carried it home between them.

"Whatever in the world's in this package?" asked Ernie as they wrestled it through the door. "Pop, what'd you order from Sears an' Roebuck, anyway? It's heavy as everything."

"By doggies, that's my horseshoein' stuff. Go ahead an' open it up."

Sorting through the excelsior they lifted out the contents. There were several pairs of horseshoes, a box of horseshoe nails, a farrier's knife, a horseshoer's rasp, a hammer, pincers, and a cardboard box containing chunks of steel that looked like setscrews. "What are these things, anyhow?"

157

asked Bert, holding up one of the small pointed pieces of steel.

"Hey! That's a funny lookin' horseshoe," commented Ernie. "Looks like a horse would slip all over the ice with that on. An' they've got holes in 'em."

"Well, you go to the shop an' get that horseshoe layin' on the workbench," said Tom, "an' I'll show you the difference between that one an' this." Ernie soon returned with the type of shoe a blacksmith would make.

"Now you see these sharp calks on the heel at each side an' the big one in the center at the front? Well, a blacksmith makes these on there by poundin' 'em out sharp like chisels when the iron's red hot. But I ain't got a forge an' I don't know how to do all that, so Sears sells this kind without the points on 'em. You just take them little round calks an' screw them into the holes, one at the back on each side an' two in front."

After breakfast on Saturday morning, while the boys gathered to watch, Tom set about to shoe a team. Tying a horse to a post in the barn he took a position behind the animal's front leg, facing toward its tail. As he grasped the long hair of the fetlock and pulled, the horse lifted its front foot. In a bent-over position, Tom stepped astraddle of the lifted foreleg, holding it between his legs just above his knees. The horse's foot was turned with the sole upward.

Using the farrier's knife he trimmed off the excess tough tissue from the sole of the foot. With the pincers he then nipped away the irregular circumference of the hoof, reducing it to the proper size and shape. From time to time he placed a shoe upon it to guide his progress. When the hoof was the right size, he took the rasp and smoothed it around the edge until it fit the shoe.

The horseshoe nail resembles the old wrought-iron nail in that it is flat, tapering from the base of the rectangular head to near the tip where it ends in a very sharp point. The shoe has rectangular holes cut into it to receive the nails and nailheads. Tom placed three or four nails in his mouth and laid the shoe upon the horse's upturned foot. Setting the point of a nail into one of the holes in the shoe, he drove it down. The point of the nail, being straight on the outward side and tapered on the inward side, drew itself slightly outward as it penetrated the hoof. It emerged about an inch above the edge of the hoof. Promptly he bent the nail down toward the edge of the hoof. Failure to do this might find him impaled on the nail if the horse withdrew his foot from between his legs. When the nails had been driven and bent, he set the foot on the floor and with the pincers clipped off the projecting ends. Then he again took the foot between his legs; pressing the sharp corner of a small, heavy iron bar against the clipped nail and the hoof, he struck the nailhead, driving it tightly up into the shoe. At the same time, the clipped end of the nail was clenched by the bar. Thus clenched, the nail would remain tight.

Shoes on the forefeet prevented a horse from falling on the ice. Shoes on the hind feet were desirable for winter hauling, but a horse with its hind feet shod had to be kept in the barn, for if allowed to be with other animals he might kick and injure them. This Tom learned to his sorrow. He had shod one team on all four feet, and not liking to keep horses tied up in the stall all winter, he had turned them out with the rest. At feeding time one day he missed Prince, a rangy bay he had brought from Indiana. He found him in the grove, hobbling toward the barn, half dragging one hind leg. A hole in the skin of his hip, from which blood oozed, was evidence that he had been kicked by a shod horse. The veterinarian guessed that the bone was cracked. He disinfected the puncture but doubted that this would do much good. If the bone was not cracked, the horse might improve within a few days. If not, they had tried, anyhow.

For several weeks Prince limped about the yard or stood sleeping. Occasionally he would get down but then was unable to get up. When this happened Tom placed three poles, teepeelike, above him, passed a heavy rope around his ribs just behind the front legs, and ran it through a pulley overhead. With a team on the rope he could hoist Prince into a standing position.

Finally, one Sunday when the family came home from church Prince was down. Tom decided that the horse would never be able to get up by himself again and that he might as well put him out of his misery. Walking up alongside Prince, he lifted the ax and brought its blunt end down on the animal's head. Twice more he struck to make sure, then walked away. There were tears in his eyes.

"He was a good horse," he said. "Me an' him's been through a lot of hard work together."

SHELLING CORN

When Tom was ready to shell corn in February he contacted a neighbor who owned a sheller that he powered with a Fordson tractor. If a farmer had but a few hundred bushels to shell, he would set the starting time for one in the afternoon and request neighbors to each haul a load to town. They would be finished by nightfall. But if he had a thousand or more bushels, the operation would begin at about eight in the morning and run all day or longer. Since Tom lived six and a half miles from the nearest town, a man could haul but two loads in a day. This required ten to twelve haulers.

During the afternoon on the day before shelling, the rig pulled briskly up the lane, the lugs on the rear wheels of the tractor throwing off chunks of frozen earth as it towed the equipment. The Fordson tractor was some four and a half feet high and about twice as long. The driver sat between the rear wheels, with the steering wheel in front of him. Behind the tractor trailed the sheller. It was about ten feet long, four or five feet wide, and six feet high and was mounted on steel wheels. Behind it was attached a wagon containing the drags, drive belt, cans of oil, and a barrel of kerosene.

The usual type of corncrib consisted of two bins, each some ten to fourteen feet wide, set up off of the ground on cement foundations, and far enough apart so that a grain wagon could easily be driven between them. The two bins were roofed over to form one building. In the space between, wagons and the family car were usually kept. Bins for oats were often built in the space over this driveway. The floor of the corncrib was twelve to fifteen inches above the ground, and along the bottom of the bins were long horizontal doors, perhaps two feet high, hinged at the top. When these were opened the corn would roll out. With the rear end of the sheller set at the end of the driveway, the men unloaded the drags.

These were horizontal conveyors having chains that traveled inside along the bottom. Metal crossbars were riveted to these chains to move the corn. Each section of the drag was a dozen or so feet long and could easily be connected to the next. When the chains were coupled, the whole long unit was pushed against the concrete footing beneath the doors. The end nearest to the sheller was attached to the machine. The tractor was lined up at right angles to the sheller, some twenty-five feet from it, and the drive belt was placed on the sheller and tractor pulleys. Then with a heavy block of wood as a chock in front of the rear wheel to hold the tractor in place, all was ready to go.

The drive pulley of the sheller was mounted on a shaft that passed through the machine longitudinally. Mounted on this shaft was the cylinder, which was eight or nine inches in diameter and about five feet long. Made of heavy, smooth steel, it was studded with cast-iron lugs about one inch square that removed the kernels from the cobs. The cylinder was housed in a heavy metal tube, having at its bottom a sievelike opening that allowed the corn kernels to pass through, but not the cobs. When the kernels had been shelled off, they passed over an air blast that removed the debris. This was discharged out through a blower pipe along with the husks and trash. The clean kernels fell into a small hopper below the cylinder and were delivered to the bottom of the elevator. Here cups on a moving chain carried them up a tube to the top of the sheller where they slid down a spout into the wagon. The cobs were discharged at the end of the cylinder where the chain of the cob conveyor carried them up an incline and dropped them onto a pile.

"Well, I guess this is where we have to go to work," joked Tom with Eddie when all was ready. He took a shovel and began dislodging the ears in the open door. The corn tumbled into the drag and moved toward the sheller. The machine shuddered as the cylinder, seizing the ears, shelled off the corn and spit out the cobs. The husk pipe rattled as the debris slithered up the sheet-iron tube and floated away to cover a nearby bed of dry weeds with a billowing coat of whitish yellow corn shucks.

For a time Tom and Eddie dug the corn loose and allowed it to tumble out. When it would no longer roll out from the door by itself, Tom prepared to crawl inside.

"I'll knock it down for a while longer so that you can get at it from out here. When there's room for both of us in there I'll call you."

After a bit he signaled Eddie to crawl in with him and they began the hard part of the day's task. Shovelful after shovelful, with no time to stop, they went at it. One worked near the drag, knocking the corn down and scooping it out. The other worked toward the far side, throwing one shovelful after another out through the open door. The tractor snorted, the husk pipe rattled, and the cob pile grew. The wagons were filled and driven away.

Some corncribs had an opening from one end to the other along the center of the floor. Before filling the crib this was covered with short boards. At shelling time the drags were pulled under the crib below this opening. The short boards were then removed one at a time, allowing the corn to roll down from both sides into the drags beneath the floor. This required very little scooping.

There was a fifteen-minute stop for lunch at midmorning and again in midafternoon. Since few haulers were on the site at any one time, they went into the house for this refreshment. As others returned from town, they were directed to the house for their lunch. Dinner would be served from about half past eleven until two. A man loading late in the morning could eat before he set out, for if it was a long haul he might not be back until toward three o'clock. Likewise, those loading and leaving at about ten in the morning could expect a hot meal when they returned, though it might be after one o'clock.

Corn is about twice as heavy as oats. Therefore, while one would fill a triple-box wagon if he was hauling oats, a wagon loaded with corn would not be filled above the top of the second box. Hauling corn was usually a colder job than hauling oats because corn was often shelled in cold weather. In addition, corn kernels are hard and smooth, absorbing considerable heat from one's body if he sat or stood in it on a cold day. Winter underwear, four-buckle overshoes, a heavy coat with a good collar, warm mittens, and a cap with ear coverings were essentials for hauling corn in the winter.

One day during Christmas vacation Bert, then eleven, went to haul corn for a neighbor who lived six miles from the elevator. Though he was on his way before the sun rose, he

162

found several teams ahead of him when he arrived at the shelling site. It was about ten degrees above zero. While waiting for his turn he went to the barn where others talked as they waited. Near the corncrib, sheltered from the wind, still another group gathered about a small fire. It was a cold pastime.

When at last he was loaded he set out for town. Because there was little snow on the roads, wagons were the order of the day. When he reached the elevator, ten or a dozen teams were ahead of him waiting to unload. Each drove his wagon onto the scales and was weighed, after which he drove into the elevator building. This was a large structure, fifty or more feet high, built beside a railroad spur. On the dump inside he stopped so that the wheels rested on two long timbers that pivoted so the rear of the wagon could be dropped down and the front raised upward. The operator opened a trapdoor in the floor behind the wagon, removed the bottom endgate, and elevated the wagon so that the grain slid out into a hopper under the floor. From there, metal panlike cups mounted on a belt carried the grain vertically to the top of the building, where it was directed into a bin.

The operator then swept the bed clean, lowered the wagon, and replaced the endgate. The driver drove out of the elevator and back to the scales to have his empty wagon weighed. This weight was deducted from the weight of the load to give the net.

Bert had left the shelling site at ten o'clock. He spent two hours on the road and forty-five minutes waiting to unload. He found himself ready to start back to the sheller at a little before one. By trotting the team all the way he was at the farmhouse ready for dinner at about two in the afternoon.

By the time he was again loaded it was half past three. It had clouded up since morning and had begun to snow and to drift. By half past four, when it began to get dusk, he was still an hour away from the elevator. Because the day had turned cold it was necessary to walk to keep warm. With the lines tied together and passed around his back he trudged along the edge of the road in the lea of the wagon. The wheels raised swirls of snow as they cut through the drifts. With his head pulled down into his coat collar and his eyes half-closed against the gusting elements he pushed on.

Reaching home at about seven o'clock, he gratefully surrendered the horses to Eddie, who came out from the house to put the team away. Tom inquired how he had gotten along while Jean brought his supper, hot from the stove. He had been away from home for eleven hours, most of this time standing outdoors in the wind, riding in the wagon, or walking beside it in temperatures ten to twenty degrees below freezing. A man could put in a disagreeable day at hauling shelled corn in winter.

PLANS FOR A NEW CHURCH

The alarm clock jangled for a moment and then was still. Jean turned over and collected her thoughts. Tom did not move until she touched him.

"Yow, I heard it," he said drowsily. "Is that ha' pas' five?"

"Yes, an' it's Sunday, so you'd better get the fire started if we're gonna get to Sunday school by ten o'clock."

The children slept until breakfast on Sunday mornings. Dressed in a warm coat and overshoes Tom went to the barn, his shadow cast by a bright moon on the snow bobbing along beside him. Standing at the gate of the feedlot he whistled, repeating a tuneful blast three or four times. Then he called, "Here, Rolly! Here Jake! Cope, cope, cope!"

Two or three horses appeared from around the corner of the strawstack. Others rose from their beds on the straw and after shaking themselves ambled toward the gate, their feet squeaking on the hard-packed snow and their breath making puffs of frost. He let Rolly and Jake through the gate and closed it upon the others. Maude whinnied softly as she nudged him with her nose. "Ho, you want some breakfast, too, do you? I don't see why, you ain't done no work for a week." Still Maude persisted. "Well, all right, but that means I'll have to let the rest of these dead beats in an' feed 'em, too."

Reopening the gate he patted Maude affectionately on the hip as she passed through. The others followed. Inside the barn he tied them and threw corn into each feedbox. "Now, you rascals," he said in parting, "you don't get no hay. After breakfast you'll all go back to the straw pile for dessert."

Jean and Jane washed the dishes and straightened up the house while Tom and the boys did the chores.

"Put on clean underwear, now," called Jean as the boys went upstairs to dress. "An' throw the dirty clothes in the box in the corner so I won't miss 'em when I wash in the mornin'."

At about half past eight they set out in the bobsled. The boys and Jane raced each other behind or rode on the runners. The horses, fresh from several days without the harness, trotted briskly. They arrived at the church in Westover a full twenty minutes before Sunday school time. Tom and Eddie tied the team to the hitching rack and blanketed them. Rolly had an icicle two inches long hanging from his nose and Jake had frost all over his chest. "Sure glad I'm not a horse on a day like this," commented Bill.

The Sunday school superintendent was the only one in church. The family gathered around the grating in the floor, holding their hands over the upsurging heat from the furnace in the basement. They kept their coats and overshoes on.

"Why don't you open the doors so's it'll get warm in the Sunday school room?" inquired Ernie. "It's always cold in there."

"I think we'll have all the classes in here," advised the superintendent. "We'll likely not have very many people today."

Ernie looked at him in disbelief. "You mean not very many will come on account of it's so cold?"

"We generally have about half a crowd on a day like this."

"Well, gee whiz! You'd think that if we could come six an' a half mile and be here early, the kids in town could come two or three blocks to Sunday school."

The superintendent smiled. "It's pretty cold today."

"Let me remind you that our church board president has called a short meeting of the board for right after church," stated the minister at the close of the sermon. "I know it's a bad day to ask you to stay, but we need to have a short meeting. I guess you'd rather take a little more time for this today than to come back some night when it might be even colder. Let's gather here near the front after the benediction."

"The thing we have to decide," began the board president, "is whether we want the architect to go ahead with plans for a new church. We've been talking about it for a year and we have a halfway agreement with him. Now he tells me that since the end of the war, prices of building materials and labor are going up. He thinks that if we want to build within the next few years we ought to get about it right away."

"I know we've talked about building," put in E. J. Hanson, a local merchant, "but I don't think this is the time to begin. We hear that things are improving and I guess in some places that's happening, but in my business I don't see any improvement. And from what I hear, it's that way with other businesspeople in town, too."

"Well, prices of corn an' hogs an' stuff has been good the last three years. I think it's a good time to get squared away on this problem." Tom spoke with confidence. "You said it'll take six months or a year before plans can be ready. I think we should get 'em made. Then if it don't look good we can wait. But if it seems all right, we can go to it." He looked about at the group as he spoke. Some members made no response. Others agreed as he made his point.

E. J. was on his feet as soon as Tom had finished. "I was converted in this church. It has served the town well, along with the other churches here. We own the land and the church is paid for. If we need to add to the building to get more room for Sunday school, we have plenty of ground for doing that. I don't think we need to buy land somewhere else and build a big brick church in this little town."

Claude Mulhaney, a well-to-do farmer, then took the floor. "I probably wouldn't have come this morning on account of its being so cold, but I wanted to hear what you've learned from the architect. So I brought the kids in the sled, like Tom, and came. Now most of us have got children in Sunday school. I've got five, Tom's got seven, E. J., you've got two. And when you stop to think about it, there's a lot of us that's got more than a passing interest in what happens here. We want a good place for us and our children to go to Sunday school and church. I'm with Tom. Le's make a contract with the architect and get a blueprint. Then we'll know what it'll cost and we can go from there."

So the debate went. They could jack up the building and put a full basement under it or there were other things they could do to avoid mortgaging their church's future for the next ten years.

"I must say that it's discouragin' to teach Sunday school when the classes are crowded together like they are in that little Sunday school room," put in Jean. "We have the adult class in this big room out here with the high school boys and girls an' the seventh an' eighth graders, an' you know how noisy it gets in here. But we have just as many little ones in that small room yonder, an' today it ain't even warm enough so we can meet in there. When they're all here, like they will be along towards Easter, it's a real madhouse. We certainly have to do somethin'. They tell me this building is about twenty-five years old. We'll probably have to replace it in another ten years, no matter what we do now. So, I say le's investigate the cost of building."

After a half hour of discussion the minister suggested they take a straw vote, which would not bind anyone, but it would give them a consensus. The chairman put the question, and the result was seven for and five against making a contract with the architect.

The minister further suggested that they take a recess to talk it over. Though the vote was favorable, it was so close that he did not think it best to proceed unless more were fully committed. When the motion was again put it carried with a good majority. They would proceed with plans.

"I'm glad we're goin' to do somethin' about a new church," commented Jean as they sat down to Sunday dinner at a quarter to three. "With all of the good-lookin' farms you see all around here, you'd think we could afford a church that's big enough an' good enough for us an' our children."

Misfortune

APPENDICITIS

BEGINNING in 1919 and continuing over the next two years, there occurred a series of incidents that badly cramped Tom financially and brought sorrow and concern to the family. The first involved Tom.

He complained to Jean of severe indigestion one day in February, and she insisted that he see the doctor. Because the roads were too bad for driving the car, he set out after dinner in the buggy, and it was dark when he returned. He climbed carefully down from the seat as the boys began to unhitch. "Mom said you had a stomachache," prodded Bill. "Does it still hurt?"

"Doctor said I have a bad case of appendicitis. You boys put the team away; I'm goin' to the house." There he reported the doctor's verdict and went to lie down.

"What'll you do if it ain't better in the mornin'?" asked Jane, who had little understanding of appendicitis.

"Well, le's hope it is better," said Tom bravely. "Doc may be wrong. It may not be appendicitis."

"Appendicitis can act awfully fast sometimes," replied Jean. "I just hope that it's not any worse in the morning. Then Eddie an' Bill are gonna take the buggy to school an' you're gonna go with 'em an' take the train an' go to the hospital."

That settled it. Tom had almost never been sick and he stood pain well. But he knew that this was not a passing spell of indigestion and that he would have to go to the hospital.

"I want you to drive the buggy to school tomorrow," Jean said to Eddie the following Sunday night. "I'm gonna take the train to Humston to see your dad. He's only been gone three days, but it seems like a month to me."

The countryside slid slowly by. The combination freight and passenger train that served the small towns along this branch railroad line made one round trip daily, going as far as Humston in the morning as it collected freight cars of grain, pigs, cattle, and sugar beets and dispensed empty cars. It arrived at Humston at about noon.

"How're you gettin' along at home?" asked Tom, after initial greetings.

"Things are just fine. We get up a little earlier so's the boys can get the work done. Then everybody but the little ones goes off to school. I feed the chickens and gather the eggs and keep things goin'."

"Well, I worried about how you'd make out. Never dreamt I'd be laid up like this."

"I'm so thankful that if it had to happen it came just when it did. Corn shellin's finished an' there's really nothin' that has to be done 'til you come back. It's just the right time for it — if it had to be."

At this point the doctor entered. "Well, Mr. Harper, I see you have company."

"Best medicine a man can have," bantered Tom.

"You folks are lucky the train runs up here in the morning and back at night." The doctor looked at Tom's chart. "We had a man about fifteen miles from here last winter who had appendicitis and they had to operate on him on the dining room table at his home at one o'clock in the morning. Snow was so deep the doctor rode out to the man's house in a bobsled. Just no way they could get him here in time."

A week or so later Tom arrived in Westover on the afternoon train. Eddie and Bill were waiting at the depot. The cold damp wind cut through their coats as they paced up and down to keep warm.

"Here's your coat," said Bill, holding Tom's Alaskan dogskin over his arm. "Mom told us to bring it for you."

Tom's eyes were brimming as he took it. He remembered the pride with which the family had presented it to him four years before. He considered the devotion with which they must have garnered every nickel in order to buy it. It was a measure of their love for him. The coat was frayed and the hair worn from it about the corners of the collar and at the buttonholes. It was a warm coat. He put it on.

Day by day his strength returned so that when the time for sowing oats arrived he had recovered.

For a year or two a red spot on Bill's chest had slowly grown larger. At length he called it to Jean's attention. When she asked how long he had had it, Bill could not remember. Upon observing the spot Tom was not much concerned, but he thought the doctor should look at it. This consultation resulted in Bill's going to the hospital, where the tumor was removed. He lost some time from school, but after a few weeks he appeared to be all right.

"I've been intendin' to ask you what arrangements you made with the hospital for payin' for Bill's operation," said Jean a few days after Bill had returned home.

"Well, I told them that my operation last spring took all the cash I had. I could sell some hogs or cattle, but we'll need that money for new machinery an' cash rent to pay the landlord an' for reg'lar livin' costs. So I signed a note with them 'til I could figure out what to do."

"Have you talked to people at the bank about borrowin'?"

"Yeh, Berg said he'd loan it to me. But he said land was the highest he'd ever seen an' he thought this might be a good time to sell the place back home." Then with a smile he added, "It don't look now as if we'd ever move back there to live." So they sold the Indiana farm, thereby severing the remnants of old ties and committing the family to find success in their adopted environment.

THE PASSING OF BILL

Threshing at Tom's farm had been completed and the machine had been moved to the next job. Bill, aged fifteen, had gone to haul grain and Eddie, seventeen, to haul bundles. Tom was tidying up the barnyard after threshing. He had sent Bert, then eleven, with the mower to cut a small patch of hay that afternoon. They would put it up as soon as the last threshing job was finished.

Bert was well along with the cutting when he saw Ernie coming across the stubble field. Ernie often came to the field to ride on the machine for a few rounds, to visit, or to bring drinking water. But on that day he carried no water bucket. Bert stopped the team at the corner and waited.

"Pop says for you to bring the mower an' come to the house. They phoned from where they're thrashin' an' said that Eddie or Bill has been hurt. I don't know which. Pop an' Mom's gone there in the car."

"What happened? How'd he get hurt?"

"Well, they phoned, an' Mom answered. She just went to the door an' called Pop an' said, 'We have to go. One of the boys is hurt.' As they was drivin' off, Pop told me to come an' get you. That's all I know."

As the boys came from the barn after putting the team away, the car drove up the lane. Tom and Jean went into the house, quickly changed to their best clothes, and reappeared. Tom carried his necktie in his hand, and Jean's high-topped shoes were not yet laced. Bert and Ernie stood observing Bill, who sat in the rear seat looking pale. He said nothing. They did not speak to him. Jean got into the back seat with Bill.

"Bill's got his foot hurt," said Tom. "We have to take him to the hospital at Empire. You boys do the chores. We may be back tonight or we may not, I don't know. Eddie'll be here in a little bit, an' he can tell you what happened." Then they were gone, driving eighteen miles to the nearest hospital over rough dirt and graveled roads with a boy who needed ambulance care. It would be an hour before they would get there.

Eddie knew, in a general way, what had happened. Bill had taken a load to the elevator at the corncrib. The oats were running heavy, so he had to get unloaded promptly and get back to the machine. He placed the cables on the front wheels and set the hopper in place behind the wagon. When no one came to assist him, he started to unload by himself.

Tom's elevator had a square end on the tumbling rods that fit into the knuckles to turn them. However, this elevator had a hole through the rod and the knuckle and through this a steel pin had been placed. When Bill stepped near the knuckle to engage the jack, a projecting end of this pin caught in the cuff of his turned-up overalls and began to wind up his pant leg. This pulled his foot under the rotating rod, and the end of the pin dug into his foot as it turned. Some of the men heard Bill hollering and came running. Taking his pocketknife, one of them cut away some of the overall leg, but it was so twisted and wound up that they could not remove him.

"How'll we ever get him out?" asked one man hopelessly as others approached.

"Take the power out of the stakes," responded one of them as he knelt by the power and motioned for another to take the opposite end.

The power unit weighed at least two hundred pounds. Two men would not try to unload it from a wagon alone. It was held in pace by four stakes, with a chain over the top to stabilize it. Seizing the unit the two lifted it from the stakes and set it to one side, freeing the tumbling rod and knuckles. The men commented later, and others agreed, that it seemed impossible that two men had lifted this heavy piece of machinery, staked down as it was. How they had done it they did not know.

In 1920 there were few ambulances, even in the cities, and none was available in rural areas. Also, there were no antibiotics, and blood transfusions were unknown. Even the best hospitals at that time were primitive by current standards, and the one to which they took Bill, while good for a small city like Empire, was by present standards lacking in equipment and know-how.

"We'll have to cut the foot off," said the doctor. "There's nothing else we can do. Ankle's all torn up 'til we never could piece it together again. It's full of dirt. He'll have the blood poisoning by morning. The only thing to do is to amputate."

The accident had occurred on Wednesday. Friends arranged for Tom and Jean to stay with relatives in Empire, and they brought Jean home on Thursday and Friday to be with the children briefly. A neighbor lady came daily and helped thirteen-year-old Jane prepare meals. The boys did the chores. They waited. By Saturday the children began to understand that Bill probably would not live.

At about one o'clock on Sunday morning they were aroused by the sound of the car driving into the barnyard. Tom and Jean entered the house to give the sad report, first to the family, then to their friends. Carrying a kerosene lamp they went from room to room, rousing the children who were already awake, quietly waiting. They stopped at each bed to

172

repeat the short story and to weep momentarily. Then Tom telephoned friends and asked them to tell others. The funeral would be that day, Sunday. The infection was, the doctor said, so virulent that no time should be lost before the interment.

The next morning friends arrived to be with the family. At one in the afternoon they set out to meet the hearse. There were about a dozen cars that began the sad cavalcade. The funeral was short. The casket was open for viewing the body, and following Tom and Jean, friends shepherded the children to it. As in a dream they went to the cemetery and then home. Then it was over. Time healed their sorrow and life gradually readjusted into normal patterns again.

During World War I, Tom had bought twenty-five-dollar war bonds from time to time until he had what for him was a little nest egg. To pay the hospital after Bill's death, he endorsed these bonds to the doctor and paid him the last of the cash from the sale of the Indiana farm. This did not cover the total amount, but having been bereft of his boy and his savings at one stroke, he felt that he had paid all he could. He needed money to run the farm and to care for his family. He could not consign all of his assets to the doctor.

Statements continued to arrive with polite requests for payment. These Tom disregarded, but they were a source of concern to Jean. Tom had at one time talked of suing the farmer where the accident had occurred for enough to pay the hospital bills. But Jean refused to consider this. It would not bring back their boy and it would only make hard feelings within the neighborhood.

"We must do something about the bill from the hospital," said Jean one day more than a year after the accident. "Whatever we may think about it, we took our boy there for help and they did the best they could. We ought to pay it as fast as we can."

But Tom could see no way for paying the bill. However, from time to time Jean sent five or ten dollars gleaned from the sale of eggs or poultry. Finally, some eight years later, she had paid the bill.

The Utilities

SOME FARMS had a cistern that stored rainwater caught from the roof of the house. This was used for washing clothes, bathing, and household cleaning. A drilled well was usually the source of drinking water, and at that time a good supply of water could usually be found about fifty feet or less below the surface of the ground. Since there were few large rocks in the soil, a well-drilling rig that lifted and dropped a pointed heavy steel bit could stab a hole into the soil to the water level with relative ease. A steel casing four or five inches in diameter was lowered into the hole. This provided a shielded space into which the water pipe was lowered and could be raised again for repairing. Water stood a few feet deep in the bottom of this casing.

A galvanized iron pipe about one and a half to two inches in diameter was lowered into the casing. Attached to the pipe near its bottom was the cylinder. A quarter-inch steel wayrod was passed down the pipe and attached to a piston in the cylinder. When lifted by the wayrod the piston raised the water in the pipe. Valves in the cylinder held the water stationary while the piston passed down through it for another lift.

Screwed onto the top of the water pipe was a round, cast-iron hollow pump some four feet high. Mounted near the top of the pump was a curved handle for moving the wayrod up and down. After several strokes of the handle, water was lifted in the pipe until it ran out from the pump spout. Usually a cement or wood platform was built around the pump as a place to stand.

In Iowa the frost line during winter was about four feet below the surface. Water standing in a pipe closer than this to the surface would freeze and burst the pipe. To prevent the well pipe from feezing, a vent was usually filed in the pipe six or eight feet below the ground level. This hole was small enough so that when water was pumped, the amount that drained out was not noticeable, but when pumping was finished, the water drained down to below the frost line and would not freeze in the pipe.

The well was often centrally located in the barnyard. If the stock tank was but a few feet away, a pipe from the pump carried water to the tank aboveground. If the tank was at a distance, then a wooden barrel or small steel or cement tank was set adjacent to the pump, partially submerged. From this, water flowed through a pipe below the frost line to the stock tank. The tank was usually made of wood staves about an inch and a quarter thick set around a heavy wooden circular bottom and held together by steel hoops. It was about thirty inches deep. Some tanks were of steel or cement, but if made of cement there was danger of the sides cracking when ice froze in them.

Many farmers built covers over their stock tanks to keep out the dirt and to retard freezing. Livestock did not like to drink very cold water, and since temperatures fell to twenty or more below zero each winter, the tank heater was developed to warm the water.

A popular type of heater was composed of three sections of sheet-metal tubing, rectangular in cross section and about ten inches high by fifteen wide. One section rested on the bottom of the tank below the water. At one end of this, toward the center of the tank, a vertical section rose above the water and to this a smoke pipe was attached. On the other end of the horizontal section a tube slanted upward to end also above water level near the side of the tank. This had a removable cover where fuel was introduced. A stone was placed on the tank heater to prevent it from floating.

A small fire was kindled in the bottom of the heater, and when it was burning well, more fuel, usually cobs, was added and the cover kept on. A few pieces of coal might be used to hold fire overnight. The water in the tank would still freeze slightly, but a slow fire in the tank heater kept the water at a temperature more suitable for the animals.

A common landmark on the Iowa prairie was the windmill. This was erected over the pump and generally used only for pumping water. It was usually about fifty feet high so as to catch the wind above the treetops. Towers for the older mills had legs of five-by-six-inch timbers. The towers tapered toward the top and were braced diagonally with one-by-six-inch lumber. Most towers built after about 1920 were of galvanized steel. The mill's source of power was the wheel at its top. This was composed of wooden slats or sheet-iron blades radiating from its center. Each slat was set at an angle and the pressure of the wind against the slats turned the wheel.

One type of wheel was assembled as a rigid unit that faced the wind when operating, held thus by a large weather vane. The mill was stopped by turning a crank or pulling a lever at the base of one of the posts. This turned the wheel edgewise to the wind and applied a brake. Another type of wheel was built from sections of slats, each connected to the next section by a pivoting joint. When the mill was shut off, this wheel folded somewhat like an umbrella folded. It still faced the wind, but in the folded position the vanes did not catch the wind and did not turn except, sometimes, in a high wind. A few feet below the apex of the tower was a platform on which one stood when working on the wheel. When the wheel of the windmill turned, an offset on the end of its shaft lifted a steel rod up and down. Attached to this was a two-by-two-inch wooden wayrod that hung down and could be connected to the wayrod of the pump. Thus when the wheel turned it lifted and lowered the wayrod and pumped the water.

If there was no windmill, the farmer often used a one-and-a-half horsepower gasoline engine for pumping. A machine called a pump jack, which bolted onto the pump, could be operated by the engine to lift and lower the wayrod. But whether the farmer depended on the windmill or the gasoline engine, there were times when mechanical power was unavailable. Then he mounted the well platform and taking the pump handle in his two hands he supplied the power.

To insure water for livestock grazing far from the farmhouse, a well was sometimes drilled in the pasture. When the water became low in the tank there, a small barrel floating in the tank turned the mill on, and when the tank became full the rising float shut it off. With this device the water supply was self-maintained. Also, on some farms the pump serving the farmhouse might be at some distance from the buildings. In this case the well would have a force pump, which lifted the water to the surface and forced it through pipes to the water tank. To stop or start a windmill that was a short distance from the farm buildings a chain was run along a fence to the windmill. From a post near the barnyard, the farmer could operate a lever or a crank to control the mill.

Very few farms prior to 1930 had well water piped into the house. Usually the well was within fifty yards of the house and water was pumped by hand at the well and carried in a pail to the kitchen.

When the windmill was in position over the pump, its four legs were bolted at their bottoms to heavy posts set in the ground ten or twelve feet apart. The tower was assembled lying on the ground, with two legs secured to their respective posts by one large bolt each. Then a rope was tied around the top of the tower near the platform and laid over the frame to the base, extending along the ground forty or fifty feet beyond. A second long rope was also tied near the platform and laid in the opposite direction to the first. Near the base of the tower a timber sixteen or eighteen feet long was stood on the ground and the first rope passed over its top.

When a team attached to this rope began to pull, the lift of the rope over the top of the timber raised the small end of the tower upward toward a standing position. As the tower vaulted upright the second rope was snubbed around a post or tree to halt it in a vertical stand. Blocks were then placed under the free legs to stabilize the tower until all legs could be secured to their posts with two bolts each. When connected to the wayrod of the pump, the windmill was ready to use. Heavy wires were generally run from the top of the tower to posts, trees, or buildings to stabilize the windmill so that it would not blow down in a storm.

Many older farm homes had a cellar underneath with a dirt floor and rock or brick walls. Newer ones usually had basements with cement floors and walls of cement blocks, and occasionally one had a storm cave, which was located near the house. Each of these was cool in summer and warm in winter. They were suitable places for storing vegetables and canned fruit as well as dairy products.

The pump house was a small structure usually built around the pump beneath the windmill, with the wayrod passing down through a hole in the roof. If there was a gasoline engine in the pump house the exhaust pipe was passed through the wall to carry the fumes outside. In the pump house was a wooden or cement tank through which the cold water from the well passed. Shelves inside this tank were so located that containers placed on them would be partially submerged. Here containers of dairy products and other food were placed for prompt cooling. Water from the well was often the only cooling medium because home refrigerators were then unknown and virtually no farmers had iceboxes.

THE LAUNDRY

Washing for a large family on the farm during the decade following 1910 was a toilsome task. Because most families washed on Monday, this day for decades was referred to as blue Monday. The washer used by Tom and Jean at Deep Creek was known as the rocker type. The tub consisted of two boards cut like half-moons, with the round edges facing down. It was made water tight by nailing a piece of sheet metal around the bottom. It stood on four legs. The two sides were about eighteen inches apart. The agitator fit inside the semicircular tub and was of the same shape. Slats were nailed around the curved edge of the agitator. When the tub had been filled with hot soapy water and the clothes dumped into it, the agitator was thrust in on top and rocked back and forth by the handle until the clothes were clean.

To wring the clothes, one took each piece and twisted it

to squeeze out the water. Long articles such as sheets and overalls required two people to wring, each holding one end. So difficult was the business of washing that Tom or one of the boys always took half a day from the field to assist Jean with it.

In 1916 Tom bought a new washer. The wood tub was about two feet in diameter, fifteen inches deep, and stood on four legs. The cover was hinged and had a clasp to seal it when closed.

Inside the cover was the dolly, a block of wood about eight inches in diameter and probably one and a quarter inches thick into which were set four round pegs about four inches long. The dolly turned back and forth, creating turbulence in the water to wash the clothes. The machine could be powered by a gasoline engine or by hand. A flywheel helped to keep it running steadily.

Wringing the clothes also had been refined. A device called the wringer was clamped to a board at one side of the tub. It consisted of two rubber rolls fifteen or so inches long and about two inches in diameter set in a wood and steel frame. When a crank attached to one roll was turned, the clothes passed between the rolls, which squeezed out the water.

Bert, then nine years old, often assisted on washdays. During warm weather they placed the washing machine in the shade of the house where the twenty-gallon iron kettle had been hung. Taking two milk pails, Bert filled this with water from the well. Then he kindled a fire beneath it, cut a bar of laundry soap into the water, and waited for it to boil. A tablespoon or two of lye was then added to separate out the minerals, which rose to the top in a brown scum and could be skimmed off.

The white clothes, mostly sheets and Sunday wear, went into the boiling kettle first. After a period they were dipped out with a broomstick and placed into the washer. Hot water was dipped from the kettle into the machine, the lid closed, and the machine operated by pushing and pulling an oscillating handle. Then the machine was opened and the clothes were fed through the wringer into a basket or tub.

Meanwhile, the kettle was refilled and the men's work shirts, women's aprons, and other colored clothes were boiled. A device sometimes called a stomper was often used to agitate the clothes during boiling. It was a funnel-like cup mounted on a stick that was thrust up and down in the clothes, with the open end down. Clothes having dirty spots were often wet with hot soapy water and rubbed on a corrugated metal–covered washboard to remove the soil. When the colored clothes were through boiling they were washed and wrung while the overalls boiled. The overalls in turn were washed and wrung. After all the clothes were washed, the machine was emptied and filled with cold water. The clothes were agitated in it and wrung. Following this, more cold water was put in the machine and bluing was added. A few clothes at a time were put into this, sloshed around by hand or agitated with the stomper, and then wrung out. Bluing, usually added as a liquid, helped to make white clothes look bright and clean.

During cold or rainy weather, water was heated on the kitchen stove and the washing was done indoors.

When that washing machine wore out in 1925, Tom bought one having two tubs and powered entirely by a gasoline engine. The farmer was becoming more dependent upon the internal combustion engine.

A few years later he bought still another washing machine that had its own gasoline engine beneath the tub. He also put a small stove in the basement for heating water. The old iron kettle was no longer used. Instead, on washday a copper clothes boiler was placed on the stove, filled with water from the cistern, and heated. Then the machine, which was mounted on castors, was rolled alongside the stove and filled with hot water. When the clothes had been put into the machine, one had only to step on a pedal to start the engine. The wash would be finished in a couple of hours. Blue Monday had ceased to be!

After washing, the clothes were hung on lines outdoors to dry, after which they were brought into the house and sorted before ironing. Most clothing then was made of cotton, and ironing was necessary to remove wrinkles from all but the rough work clothes. The irons were boat-shaped hollow pieces of steel having a detachable handle. The person ironing generally used one iron while one or two more heated on the stove.

Ironing was not very effective unless the cloth had first been sprinkled. To do this, one laid the cloth on the table, and dipping the fingers into a bowl of water shook water droplets over the cloth. This was then tightly rolled up and left for an hour or so, by which time the moisture would have evenly permeated the cloth, leaving it slightly damp. Picking up the iron from the stove, one tested it by wetting the forefinger with the tongue and quickly swiping the wet finger across the bottom of the iron. If it hissed, it was said to be siss hot, ready for ironing.

Cloth to be ironed was laid on a flat, padded ironing board and the iron passed briskly over it. It was necessary to work fast at first and perhaps lift the very hot iron a little. As it cooled, the tempo could be slowed, and finally the iron was exchanged for a hot one.

Some irons then on the market were heated by pressurized gasoline, but they caused a number of explosions that resulted in fires and deaths. Consequently they were not widely used.

HOUSEHOLD FUEL

The farmstead to which the family moved in 1918 had a large grove of willow trees that grew fast but did not live long. As a result, after several years a willow would begin to die, while a maple or an ash tree of the same age would be in its prime. If it was cut down, shoots would grow from the trunk and within a few years these would again make a good windbreak.

As soon as cornhusking was finished, Tom cut down these dying trees. Then one day during Christmas vacation the boys took a team, dragged the trees into the barnyard, and piled them up. A neighbor who had a circular saw for cutting up logs and a tractor for power loaned Tom this equipment to saw the trees into stove lengths.

The blade of the saw was perhaps two feet in diameter and had large triangle-shaped teeth filed on the sides and set alternately like a crosscut saw. The tractor drove the saw with a belt and a flywheel on the saw helped to stabilize the power. The logs were placed on a movable saw table and pushed toward the saw, which cut off the ends. One of the boys standing beside the saw tossed the cut logs onto the woodpile. Limbs and small top sections of the trees were cut into short lengths for the cookstove. Large chunks would later be split for the heater. Thus a day of sawing produced a supply of wood that lasted well into the next summer.

During the first several years in Iowa, Tom had used little coal for fuel because of its cost. Coal was required for the steam engine at threshing time, and lumps left over were hoarded for use in the heating stove in severe weather. Later he bought coal regularly for winter fuel, but for the most part, wood and corncobs represented the main fuel supply, especially for the kitchen range.

Soon after the corn was shelled, a day was set aside for putting the cobs into a dry storage place near the house. A day or two after the shelling, a wagon was driven up beside the cob pile and scooped full. Then the load was driven to the storage place and scooped off. If the cob pile was the result of a full day of shelling, it might require two men a day or so to get the cobs into a dry place.

Because cobs were used in quantity in the cookstove, it was not practical to bring them into the house in a small container. A one-bushel peach basket or old washtub was often used for this purpose. If there was a shortage of fuel for the kitchen range, cobs could be gleaned from the horses' feedboxes and mangers and from the feedlot where corn had been fed to the pigs, though cobs from the hog lot were usually loaded with dirt, which made them less desirable to use.

Because there was no natural or bottled gas on the farms or in the small towns in Iowa at that time, heating depended on these solid fuels. Some kerosene-burning stoves were then in use, mostly as an auxiliary to the kitchen range, but furnaces burning fuel oil did not appear on the market until the mid-1930s.

Kerosene lamps, for decades the main source of light on the farm, were being improved during the 1920s, and some families had types that gave a bright white light. Also, the gasoline pressure lamp, then commonly used to light large buildings, was miniaturized for family use.

A few farms located adjacent to incorporated areas secured electricity from a power company. A very few others had their own small power plants, which were of two types. The first had storage batteries that supplied direct current. A gasoline-powered generator operated automatically to keep the batteries charged. The second type had no batteries but received its current from a generator powered by a gasoline motor. When a light or an appliance was turned on, the motor started and operated the generator until the switch was turned off. In almost no instance was electricity produced by wind power in Iowa at that time. It was not until the coming of rural electrification sometime after 1935 that electricity became widely used on the farm.

A New Perspective

TIME TO MOVE AGAIN

IT was the middle of April in 1920. Tom had finished sowing oats in the forenoon and was working about the barnyard when Jean called him to the phone.

"Hello," said Tom, taking up the receiver.

"Are you Tom Harper?"

"Yow."

"Are you interested in renting another farm?"

Tom removed the receiver from his ear and looked in surprise at the end of it from whence the voice had come. He turned and looked questioningly at Jean.

"Hello, Mr. Harper," said the voice.

"Yeh, yeh, I'm here. Where are you?"

"I'm at the First State Bank in Westover. I've been talking to Mr. Berg here and he tells me —"

"If you can wait for an hour, I'll meet you there," replied Tom.

"Yes, I'll wait here for you. I'll be at the bank."

"Gotta go to town," said Tom. "An' the boys has got the car at school. Hafta ride a horse, I guess."

"Who was it, an' for pity sakes, what did he say to you?" asked Jean.

"Somebody who asked if I wanted to rent a farm. Ain't no horse in the barn, but I guess Toots is in the grove. Better change my pants."

"Why don't you see if Mabel Anderson will take you in their car? I'll call her while you change your clothes."

As Tom entered the bank Frank Berg greeted him and ushered him into his office. Here he introduced Tom to a slight blond man named Ralph Dolan. Together they went to a conference room.

"I'm glad you were able to get into town today," began

Mr. Dolan. "Mr. Berg thought you might be interested in renting a better farm."

"I prob'ly am, but I don't appreciate your callin' me up on the party line an' talkin' about it."

"Well, I don't have a party line at home, so I didn't think about that. I own the farm two miles south and a mile west of town. It's for rent."

Tom thought for a moment. "That's where Norman Chrysler lives. Did he buy a place?"

"Yes, Norman's bought a place of his own. He's going to move in the spring. I have talked to the men here at the bank and to several others who know you and your family. They recommended you."

"That's a half section, I think," responded Tom. "I'm runnin' five hundred acre this year. The boys an' I can handle a half section all right. Le's see the lease." Tom suggested a few changes in the wording of the lease, after which they both signed it.

"How are you gonna go over there to plow?" asked Eddie as they were discussing the prospects of the new place.

"Doggies, I hadn't thought about that yet. But I managed it when we was eighteen mile away from here at Deep Creek, so I oughta be able to figure out a way to go three mile to plow, I guess."

"Lots of people are gettin' Fordson tractors now," suggested Eddie. "Why don't you get one of 'em?"

Tom considered this. "I think you got a good idea there, but I'm not sure your mother would go for it. She sure hung back about buyin' the car."

"But you bought it, didn't you? She learned to drive, an' now she wouldn't be without it."

"Yeh, Pop, how about that?" added Ernie. "Tell her you'll teach her to drive the tractor if she'll let you get one."

PLOWING WITH THE TRACTOR

Soon after threshing, Tom outlined his plan for the fall. They were to haul Magnussen's oats as well as some of their own to the elevator at Westover. Bert would stay home from school to do that. When he took the first load, he would carry an empty kerosene barrel on top of the oats. After unloading he would go the Standard Oil bulk station and have the barrel filled with kerosene. He was also to get a thirty-gallon barrel of cylinder oil, and upon returning from town he would leave the oil and kerosene at the field where Tom was working at the new farm.

Tom left home in the car at six thirty as soon as the milking and breakfast were finished. Often he did not return until after eight in the evening. By current thinking, this three-and-a-half-mile drive to work would be nothing, but at that time it was an innovation.

When Tom became tired of facing forward on the tractor seat he sat crosswise, sometimes leaning back against the fender. From this position he could see both behind and ahead. If he became bored with this he sat up on the fender with one hand against the steering wheel or perhaps with his foot against a spoke of the wheel to steer. After some experimenting the boys attached one end of a strong screen-door spring to the left steering arm and secured the other end beneath the motor. The spring held the right wheel against the furrow bank, and the driver then did not need to steer at all except to turn. This was indeed a great change from struggling with five horses, the heat, and flies while using the horse-drawn gangplow.

With feelings of satisfaction Tom considered his state of affairs. First he had needed the car in order to have the horses for full-time field work. Then he needed the tractor to release the horses from the problem of working far from home and to relieve him from the slow pace of the horse-drawn plow. He would see this pace quicken as the years went by. Just now he savored the rewards of the machine. In 1914 he had been at the edge of poverty, wondering whether he could successfully make a living for his family. Six years later he found himself a tenant on one of the better half sections of land in the area, with twelve horses, forty cattle, a car and a tractor, a fine family, and a good name at the bank. Life looked good.

For many years the disc used in Iowa had been a horse-drawn type that was eight feet long. About 1920 there appeared on the market a ten-foot disc made for use with horses or to be pulled behind tractors such as the Fordson, Samson, John Deere, or Titan—all in common use then. About this time also the tandem disc appeared. This was two discs built together. The front one threw the dirt outward and the second, immediately behind it, threw it inward. The tandem disc could be pulled only by the tractor, and it had no trucks. Thus after one pass across the field with a tandem disc, and a harrow behind it, the soil was disced twice and harrowed— ready for the seed.

Tom had two good conventional discs. All through early spring he discussed with the boys the need for pulling both at once with the tractor. As the children walked home from school across the fields one afternoon in April, they saw that he had solved the problem. They waited as he approached across the field. He had cut down a small tree and placed it between the trucks of the discs to hold them the proper distance apart. Then he attached a cable to the ends of the timber and passed the cable through a clevis on the drawbar of the tractor.

"Get on here an' see if you can manage it," he invited Bert.

Bert smiled in anticipation. He had driven the tractor a few times while Tom had been plowing, but he had not expected that he would operate it alone in the field until he was older. He shifted into second gear, advanced the throttle, released the clutch, and the tractor moved off, bouncing over the corn hills. Mounted on the fender Tom rode along to observe. He was proud of his solution. In order to be heard above the noise of the tractor he shouted into Bert's ear.

"Now at the end you have to turn wide, so begin at a safe distance. The disc will swing away out there, but don't let it get into the fence or you'll have yourself a time gettin' out."

What might have been a serious accident occurred later that spring when Eddie was discing with the tractor and Bert was using a disc with four horses. Eddie had stopped the tractor and could not get it started again. When Bert came to the end of the field, he drove his horses to one side and went to assist. The tractor finally started with a roar, and a cloud of water vapor and smoke obscured everything. This burst from the tractor startled the team and they began to run. The disc to which they were hitched had no trucks, the weight being carried by the tongue, which was held up by the neck yoke. Both Eddie and Bert dashed to stop the team, which was running across the nearby hayfield. The opposite sides of the disc pushed against each other so that they thrust the center up out of the ground, resulting in a bucking action that caused the ends to leap out of the sod again and again. Soon the tongue fell out from the ring of the neck yoke, ran into the ground, and broke off. By this time the horses had decided that to run with a disc was next to impossible and they soon stopped. Eddie continued discing with the tractor, and it was Bert's unpleasant job to take the team to the house in the middle of the morning and report the mishap to Tom.

HARVESTING WITH THE TRACTOR

At harvesttime in 1923 Tom bought a hitch for pulling the binder with the tractor. Proudly he showed the boys how it would work. But while the hitch would pull the binder, there was no method for steering the tractor from the binder seat.

Jane, who had been in eleventh grade the previous year, had plowed corn with them that spring, and Tom now drafted her to drive the tractor during harvest. These were the only instances when he asked her to assist in the field.

"Now you just keep the front wheel runnin' right along the side of the standin' oats," instructed Tom. "It'll be hard to manage at the corners at first, but you'll soon get onto it."

Jane was confident, but apprehensive. "How will I know when you want to stop?" she asked.

"Well, I've got the bamboo pole here an' when I want you to stop I'll hit the fender with it."

However, this plan did not work well. When Tom saw trouble approaching, it took too long to grab the bamboo, hit the fender of the tractor, and wait for Jane to step on the clutch. The boys solved this by devising a vertical steel arm, which they bolted to the clutch. To this they attached a rope that was anchored to a lever on the binder near the seat. When Tom wanted to stop the tractor he turned this lever down, where it locked in a safe position. He released it when he was ready to go. He was then in full command of the driving except for the steering. A year later he bought a steering device by which he could drive the tractor from the binder seat with two ropes. The power age was coming up fast.

The Fordson was a good small tractor and it had shown that there was a market for such a power source on the farm. But, good as it had been, it was too light for some work required of it, and it was hard to start in cold weather. Competitive companies began to move into this market. Among these were John Deere, Hart Parr, Oliver, Case, International Harvester, and Moline.

The Moline tractor was unique in that it had but two wheels, the engine being mounted on the axles of the drive wheels. The engine burned gasoline and it was one of the first tractors to use spade lugs. Because the operator drove the machine from the seat of the implement, special field equipment was built for this tractor. For doing common hauling about the farmyard, a two-wheeled trailer with a seat for the driver came with the tractor.

Tom had been somewhat concerned because his horses were becoming old and he had considered the need to produce more colts. However, new makes of tractors in a variety of designs represented a dependable source of power. They were sturdy, strong, and safe and were already replacing the horses. As a result, he did not again produce many young horses. He kept horses for hauling, cultivating corn, and light fieldwork, but the tractor took most of the heavy assignments. With it he could do more work in the same time and with less human energy than before, and the sun set no limits on the hours he could work. He could trade off time on the tractor with one of the boys and it could go until the job was finished. It never got tired.

THE BEGINNING OF AGRIBUSINESS

In the mid-1920s a corporation bought a quarter section in the neighborhood. No one lived in the house on the land again. The corporation tore out the fences and plowed the entire piece of land. When spring came, workers returned with a tractor and with a tandem disc and four-row corn planter, both built to be used with the tractor. Empty white sacks soon lay along the ends of the fields, evidence of the commercial fertilizer that had been deposited in every hill of corn.

With added mechanization on the farm the number of horses began to decline. This was followed by fewer dairy cows, pigs, and even chickens as the farmer gave more time to grain production. The newborn moth of agribusiness was flexing its wings.

JOE

One day during the first fall that Tom plowed with his tractor he heard a strange noise in it and had trouble shifting the gears. Leaving the machine in the field he walked to the farmhouse where Norman Chrysler lived.

"Somethin's the matter," reported Tom when Norman came out from the barn. "I'll have to phone to town an' ask someone to come an' see what's wrong."

"Why don't you go up the road and see whether Joe Voss is at home. If he is, like as not he'll take a look at it for you an' maybe he can fix it. He's got a Fordson, too. He does all of his own work an' he's helped me a time or two when I had trouble."

Joe Voss was at home. After Tom had introduced himself and stated his problem, Joe thought about it for a moment. "Sounds like you burnt out the bearing for the plow gear. I'll go an' take a look at it, if you'd like."

He put some tools into his car. In the field Tom started the motor and attempted to shift gears; after observing the problem Joe concluded that the bearing for the plow gear had burned out.

"I suppose I'll have to drive it to town in high gear or in low so they can fix it. Wonder how long that will take."

"Well, maybe not. Quite a few of these bearings give out. I expect you can get a new one at the garage and we can put it in."

"You think we can fix it right here in the field? How long will it take?"

Joe glanced at the sun. "It's about eleven now. If you'll get the bearing an' eat your dinner, I'll start takin' it apart if you want me to. Then I'll go to dinner an' be back about one. We should have it runnin' before night."

When Tom tried to pay him for his work, Joe declined the money. "I know how it is," he said. "A man's got work to do an' it takes forever to take a tractor to town or to bring a man out here to work on it. Once you see how, you can take care of it yourself the next time."

When Bert was plowing with the tractor a year or two later he heard a sharp cracking sound. He shut off the motor and walked to the house to explain to Tom what had happened.

"Well, go see if Joe's at home. Tell him how it sounded. Maybe he can tell you what's wrong."

Bert cut across the field to where Joe was plowing. "Somethin's wrong with the tractor. It's makin' a crackin' noise; sounds like it's right under the seat. I can feel it with my feet."

Joe thought a moment. "There's a big bearing right in front of the drawbar here." He indicated the rear of his tractor. "That burns out sometimes. I expect that's what's wrong. Don't drive it any more this afternoon an' I'll come and look at it after supper."

Early next morning Tom drove to town and secured a new bearing, stopping at Joe's house on the way back to pick him up, and drove to the tractor. In a half hour the repairs were completed and Bert was again plowing.

"I got a new timer and roller for the tractor," Tom told Bert at noon a few days later. "Maybe we'd better put them on before you go back to the field." So they set about to do this small repair job. From each of the four terminals on the coil box a wire ran to a corresponding terminal on the timer. Carefully they removed each wire and connected it to the new timer. Loosening the nut they lifted off the timer roller and placed the new one on the shaft. "All right, now, see if it'll go. Be careful, it might kick you," cautioned Tom.

Bert took the crank; after a few quarter turns he took hold of the right front wheel with his left hand and spreading his feet well apart began to spin it. It fired, jerking the crank out from his hand, and the motor raced backward for several turns. "Well, it's got fire in it, anyhow," said Bert.

"I'll retard the spark." Tom turned the spark-adjusting lever. "Now try it again."

"Wow!" chortled Bert as the motor kicked again, lifting him entirely off the ground.

"Well, I'll have to set the roller back a little." Tom removed the timer. Loosening the nut he moved the roller and tightened it again. Then it did not fire at all.

"Must have moved it the wrong way," advised Bert.

Again Tom removed the timer. "Now turn the crank so I can see which way it goes."

Bert complied.

"I'll be dogged. Moved it the wrong way, sure as the world." He adjusted it in the opposite direction, but to no avail. After a few more adjustments it was clear that they had lost the point of reference. They did not know which way to adjust the timing nor how far.

"I wonder if Joe's at home," questioned Bert.

"Might as well go an' see. We ain't gonna get it at all, I guess, unless we're lucky."

When Joe arrived he first examined the wiring. "Red, green, brown, blue," he said, touching each wire in turn. "Well, it's wired right."

"Oh, it's wired, all right," assured Bert. "It kicked like a mule an' then it run backwards for several turns."

Joe smiled. "If you could have got it to run forward like that it would have been all right, huh?"

"It had plenty of spunk goin' backwards."

Joe removed the front spark plug and inserted the blade of a screwdriver. "Now you turn it, an' when it comes to the easy part of the turn, go real slow." Presently the crank came up with no compression. "Slow now. Stop — right there." The screwdriver had risen in the spark plug hole until it was at the top. This meant that the piston was at the top and that if the spark plug had been in place it would have fired.

Joe's eyes followed the cord from the plug to the coil box and from there back to the same color on the timer. With a pencil he made a mark under that terminal on the timer shell. He set the roller at that point.

"Now before you crank," he said to Bert, "put your thumb on top of the crank alongside your first finger instead of takin' hold around the crank with your thumb. Then if it kicks it may knock the crank out of your hand, but it won't break your arm." After a few turns and a few adjustments they had it running.

Tom and Bert marveled that though they had struggled with the problem for over an hour with no success, Joe had it running in less than ten minutes.

Joe was an unusually competent mechanic, though all he knew about the skill he had learned from working on his own car and tractor. He helped them many times when they were having trouble but never charged them a cent.

A MODERN FARM KITCHEN

The house on the place to which they had moved in 1921 was a dream come true for Jean.

"My, but it's nice to have such a big kitchen!" She stood in the doorway between the kitchen and dining room surveying these rooms that ran across the east side of the house.

"Are we gonna eat in the kitchen?" asked Jane as she spread fresh paper on the cupboard shelves.

"Oh, land no! With this big beautiful dinin' room, I wouldn't think of eatin' in the kitchen. We'll eat in the dinin' room. I just can't get over havin' all this room."

The house was spacious and less than ten years old. It was fresh and clean. The walls were well painted, the floors and trim cleanly varnished, and every room had cross ventilation. From the living room a stairway went to the four bedrooms upstairs. Those over the kitchen and the living room had registers in the floor for winter heating. Each upstairs bedroom had a closet.

From the kitchen a short stair went down to a grade entrance. There it turned and went on down to the full basement, which had a cement floor. In the floor near the foot of the stairs was a drain. In the corner stood a porcelain sink and beside this a suction pump that brought soft water from the cistern outside. Gutters carried rainwater from the roof into the cistern.

All of these features were excellent when compared with the houses in which the family had previously lived. But the kitchen was almost beyond Jean's fondest hope. It was probably twelve by fourteen feet, with three windows side by side looking east and one toward the north. The north exit door led onto the wide back porch. From the kitchen she could survey most of the barnyard and eastward as far as she could see.

Under the east windows was a built-in L-shaped cabinet standing thirty-four inches high, twenty inches from front to back, and ten feet long. The top was covered with wood flooring over which cream-colored oilcloth had been laid. Beneath the counter were two tiers of drawers reaching to the floor and a large cupboard for pans. A special feature was a V-shaped bin that held a forty-nine-pound sack of flour. Above the counter were cupboards for dishes. In all of her longings for ample space to work in and conveniences to work with, Jean had not imagined anything better than this, unless it would be to have electricity.

Another special feature of the kitchen was a sink like the one in the basement, with a pump that supplied soft water. "Looks like washdays will be a cinch from now on," concluded Jane. "All we'll have to do will be to pump the water and pour it into the boiler on the stove. Not more than four steps. Sure beats carryin' it from the well."

As Tom moved away from the sink to dry his hands when they had washed up at noon, Ernie and Bert took his place. Pouring the used water down the drain, Ernie set the pan under the spout of the pump and with a few strokes of the handle filled it again. "Hey! How about that!" he exclaimed. Four strokes of the pump handle an' I got all the water I want for washin'. An' soft water to boot."

They wiped their hands on the roller towel. This was a continuous loop of toweling that was sold by the yard. It hung on a wooden roller set in a frame mounted on the wall.

A year or two before, Tom had bought a new kitchen range. Eventually it devoured numerous loads of corncobs, many cords of wood, and occasionally a few lumps of coal. The firebox was at the left side, and directly over it were two round removable cast-iron lids, one near the front and one toward the back. Fuel was fed through these into the firebox.

This area was the hottest part of the stove top. Parallel and toward the right were four more lids. Food was cooked over this whole area. Directly beneath the grates in the bottom of the firebox was the ash pan, which could be pulled out through a lower door at the front for emptying.

When lighting the fire a damper was opened to let the smoke go directly up the chimney. This gave a good draft to a new fire. Later the damper was reversed so that the smoke and heat passed across the top of the oven, down the right side, and under it. From there it passed up the smoke pipe. This speeded the heating of the oven by passing the heat around three sides of it.

Some fifteen or twenty inches above the cooking deck of the range, with the smoke pipe passing through it, was the warming oven. This ran the full length of the stove, and as long as there was heat passing up the smoke pipe, this small oven would be warm. Food that had been cooked was often placed there until served.

One of the stove's most attractive features was the reservoir or resavoy, as it was commonly called. This was a rectangular-shaped copper tank holding several gallons of water. It was attached to the right end of the range, its top on a level with the top of the stove. A cover flush with the stove top could be raised for filling or for dipping out water. Heat passing between the reservoir and the right side of the oven heated the water.

There were seven children then in the family — growing fast, working hard, and eating large amounts of food. Morning activities before breakfast in summer went something like this:

"Now you set the table, sister," Jean instructed Jane. "I'll go out an' feed the little chickens, then I'll be right back. I'm goin' to make biscuits, so don't slice bread for toast."

"Are we gonna have milk or cocoa? Shall I put out glasses or cups?"

"Well, if you want to make cocoa, you can. Dip out about twice as many cups of milk as there are of you. The boys'll want more than one cup."

Returning in about ten minutes, Jean got out a pan and

dipped from the bin the flour needed for biscuits. To this she added lard, milk, and seasoning and mixed them with her hands. Then pulling the bread board from the cabinet under the counter, she poured the dough onto it and rolled it out with a rolling pin.

At this point Tom and Eddie approached the house with pails of milk for separating. They went down to the basement and one of them took the crank of the cream separator and began to turn it. The bell on the crank rang with each turn until the machine was up to speed, then it began to click. When the milk pan on the separator had been poured full and the machine was at the proper speed, the faucet was opened and the separation of the milk from the cream proceeded. Upstairs Jean and Jane made note of these operations and gauged their tempo accordingly.

"The oven's hot now, sister. Take a glass an' cut the biscuits, then grease the pan an' put 'em in. The rice is about done. I'll put the sausage in the warmin' oven. Better go to the basement an' bring up the butter when you get the biscuits in the oven."

"Shall I feed the calves before breakfast?" asked Eddie, thrusting his head in at the door of the grade entrance. "How long will it be?"

"Yeh, go ahead an' feed 'em; I'm makin' biscuits so it'll take a little longer."

With the oven hot and the biscuits in it, things settled into a rapid routine. When the boys returned from the barn and washed up, operations in the kitchen began to culminate. Mother and daughter took up the fried potatoes, put the rice into a serving dish and set it on the table, and poured cocoa into cups.

Placing the skillet on the stove with the grease from the sausage in it, Jean took a heaping tablespoon of flour from the bin, dumped it into the hot grease, and stirred out the lumps. Then she poured in a dish of milk and stirred it briskly. When it came to a boil and thickened she poured the gravy into a serving dish.

"The gravy's done an' the biscuits are ready. You can get to the table now. Jane, take up the biscuits an' I'll put on the gravy an' get some cream for the rice."

The family gathered about the table. Tom asked the blessing and all set to with good appetites to fortify themselves against the day's demands.

Mealtime was not the only occasion when the kitchen was busy. For a number of years the family consumed a forty-nine-pound sack of flour weekly. Jean baked from eight to ten loaves of bread twice weekly besides light bread biscuits and baking powder biscuits as well as some pastry. She prepared her own yeast. For this she used the water from boiled potatoes, which she poured into a quart jar with yeast added. This grew to proper strength within a few days. The cover to the jar was always set loosely, for if sealed tightly the pressure from the growing yeast would explode the jar.

On Saturday the kitchen was especially busy as food was also prepared for Sunday. Two chickens would be caught and their necks wrung off; then they would be plucked, drawn, and cut up. There would be at least one cake to bake and two or more pies. Jean usually expected to cook as little as possible on Sunday.

EDDIE'S GRADUATION

Activities preceding Eddie's graduation opened new horizons for him. He had a part in the class play, which he survived without stage fright. The class banquet was, he thought, a memorable event. It presented undreamed-of experiences, with tasty food prepared in ways he had not imagined but delightful to his palate. But it was, he thought, a wasteful exercise of serving courses and, he presumed, of washing dishes.

The banquet was followed by the final week of classes, baccalaureate, final exams, and graduation. Each of the younger children observed these activities with deep interest as they visualized themselves in that role a few years hence.

Jean anticipated the events happily. She had hoped that all her children would be high school graduates. Now it was about to begin. Tom took it more as a matter of fact. It had been a struggle for him to keep Eddie in school, for it had often meant that he worked longer and harder than many of his neighbors. In fact, some of them had asked him why he wasted money to keep the boys in high school when he needed them for working at home.

All of the night before graduation it rained hard and it continued the next morning.

"Better ride a horse this mornin'," advised Tom at breakfast. "An' you'll need to take your cap an' gown wrapped up under your raincoat. If it rains all day, we may not be able to get to graduation an' you may not be able to get home, so you'd better plan to stay in town after school. I expect the water in the ditch'll be up to the bridge if it keeps on, an' if the bridge ain't safe we can't go. But take your stuff so you can be there, anyhow."

"Why don't you walk down to the bridge an' see whether it looks safe," said Jean at noon. "I sure hope we can go!"

Dressed in leather jacket and overalls Tom set out to examine conditions at the dredge ditch. The water was over the road on both sides of the bridge but the bridge was safe. He was soaked when he returned. Kicking off his mud-coated shoes on the back porch he entered the kitchen, where he stood dripping. They could not drive the car and they had no buggy, but he supposed they could go in the wagon.

"I don't care how we go. I'd be glad to walk, an' I'd not care if I got wet. I've waited twelve years for this night. So I say let's go in the wagon or walk or however we can. It's only three mile. We can get there somehow."

In the theater where graduation ceremonies were held, they sat near the front in seats reserved for families. The rain drummed on the roof. A trickle of water ran down the aisle and disappeared into the orchestra pit. Proudly, though wet, they waited until the curtain was opened to reveal Eddie along with fifteen fellow graduates sitting on the stage, self-conscious but pleased.

Both Jean and Tom had misty eyes as the diplomas were handed out. Eddie was the first high school graduate in the Harper family—there would be six more to follow. It was another landmark for the family.

Some Close Calls

FIRE

O NE day in the fall of 1915 Jean ran from the house into the yard screaming that the house was on fire. From the barnyard a young man who was visiting them heard her and raced to the house followed by Bert and Ernie. A spark had apparently popped out from the woodburning stove into the woodbox and set it on fire, and when Jean went into the kitchen from washing on the porch she found the woodbox aflame. Upon reaching the house the young man seized a dishpan, scooped water from a washtub, doused the fire, and sluiced down the smoking wall and ceiling.

When Tom asked the blessing at supper that night he expressed thanks for the safety of his family and requested that this might continue. He realized that for this to happen he must alert the family to the problem and provide safety measures. The woodbox was moved to a safe place, and an evening or two later he explained the problem of fire to the older children. In addition to fire from the stoves and lamps there was also the possibility that fire might start from a faulty chimney.

He outlined an escape plan. In case of fire downstairs in the night, Eddie or Bill was to reconnoiter from their second-floor bedroom down the stairs to see whether they could escape in that direction. If not, they would proceed as follows: collecting the six sheets from the three beds, the older boys, then aged eleven and thirteen, were to tie a corner of one sheet around eight-year-old Jane and let her down from the window as far as they could reach. She would then be near the ground and they could drop her. Next they would tie a sheet around Ernie, then five, and Bert, who was six, letting each down so that Jane could shepherd them away from the house. After tying two of the remaining sheets together and anchoring them to the bedpost they were to throw this rope out the window and each of them would go down it hand over hand. Then they were to go to Romier's place nearby. These neighbors had a telephone and could contact Tom and Jean, since most of the places where they might be had phones. In addition, there were two rules to which the children must rigidly adhere: they must not run in the house; they must not throw anything in the house.

Another brush with fire occurred several years later when Tom and Jean were away one evening. One of the children was chasing another trying to recover a stocking cap when the one having the cap threw it. It miscarried, striking a lighted kerosene lamp. The lamp chimney shattered and the lamp fell to the floor where it lay on its side, still lighted. The bowl containing the fuel did not break, but kerosene dribbled out through the burner onto the floor where it burned in a puddle.

Immediately there flashed through Bert's mind a precedent for the action needed. One night when Tom had lighted the pressure gasoline lamp, it flared with a large yellow plume of flame. Thinking that it might explode, he seized the lamp and strode to the front porch where he held it at arm's length, ready to throw it into the yard. However, the flame subsided to the normal glow and the danger passed. It was emblazoned on Bert's mind that Tom had been ready to throw it out of harm's way rather than risk a conflagration. Seizing the flame-free stem of the kerosene lamp, he rushed through the kitchen, opened the door, and threw the blazing torch into a snowbank. When he returned to the living room, the other children had stamped out the burning kerosene on the floor. The parents commended the children for their decisive action. The loss of the lamp was immaterial so long as all were safe.

HAZARDS OF USING THE TRACTOR

"I want you to take a look at my shoulder, Eddie," said Tom one night in the fall of 1921. He removed his shirt. "Is it cut at all?"

"Well, you've got a big red welt there, but it's not cut. What hit you there, anyhow?"

"I turned sideways on the tractor seat so I could look ahead an' back without twistin' my neck all the time. I guess I relaxed a little too much, an' the next thing I knew a lug of the tractor wheel hit me an' turned me the rest of the way around. I thought for a minute it was gonna knock me off the seat."

"Sounds like you forgot that you'd taken the fenders off," said Eddie. Maybe you should've left 'em on."

"Yeh, I expect I should've. I guess I'd better take 'em to town an' see if I can get 'em welded. The irons broke, an' the fenders was so loose it didn't seem safe to have 'em on. But maybe it's not safe to work without 'em either."

Continuous jolting of the Fordsons caused the supporting fender irons on early models to fail. Even when the supports were welded back together, they soon broke again. Because of this the owners of the earlier models often removed the fenders entirely. The Ford Motor Company corrected this by installing safe fenders on later models.

This brush with danger by Tom was the first of several in which others in the family were also involved. When Bert was driving the tractor on the loose gravel along the edge of the road, the soft soil drew the tractor into the edge of the ditch. Because he was unable to return it to the roadway, he turned down into the shallow ditch and traveled there. As soon as he came to a place where the bank was less steep he attempted to drive up onto the road again. But when the front wheels were up on the edge of the road and the rear wheels seemed about to climb out, the wheels began to spin. He tried again at another spot with the same results. After considering the options he backed the tractor onto the bank behind. Then he put it into high gear and the tractor lunged forward up the incline onto the road. Fortunately, he managed all this without the tractor turning over. From that time on, when he was on the road with the tractor he avoided the soft shoulder at the risk of being a traffic hazard.

On another occasion Tom had taken the tractor to town for overhaul. When he brought it home it was early in the afternoon and he decided to go to the field to see how it worked. To replenish the radiator they filled a small steel drum with water twice each day and hauled this to the field on a wooden sled behind the tractor. However, instead of using the sled that afternoon, Bert placed the eight-gallon water drum on the tractor seat and held it as he stood on the drawbar, his arms around the barrel to steer. Again, they were using the tractor without fenders, and with the machine in high gear and at a slow throttle, he set out.

What happened next was not clear. When he came to himself, he was wedged between the water drum and the exhaust manifold on the side of the tractor engine, which was four feet ahead of the seat, and the tractor was standing still. His seat was blazing hot. He wrenched himself free and stood appraising the situation as Tom, who had been following, came hurriedly to the scene. The motor was running, the transmission was still in gear, and the tractor stood with the water drum depressing the clutch. The drum was crushed where the wheel had forced it through the ten- or twelve-inch space between the rear wheel and the dash.

Bert must have fallen against the unguarded rear wheel, for while he was being thrust forward he visualized himself falling in front of the rear wheel, which would run over him unless he evaded it. In a flash he saw that he should turn himself toward the body of the tractor, allowing it to pass above him as he lay inside the path of the rear wheel. He was not able to do this, but the drum saved his life by falling on the clutch. He could never understand why there was not one cut, bruise, or abrasion on his body. His only discomfort was a burn the size of an egg on his seat, but that didn't matter. He was unhurt. A little burn would soon heal. The next day he located some irons and installed the fenders again. Never after that was the tractor used without them.

PERILS OF AUTOMOBILE TRAVEL

One Saturday night during the summer of 1923 Ernie, Jane, and Bert set out for town. About a mile from home they picked up a neighbor's hired man. It was dark when they turned the corner and started along the graveled road toward town, two miles away. Suddenly Bert saw a team of horses in front of the car, the bright spots on their harness shining like moons. He had heard of a man who was driving a car in a snowstorm one night and had run into a team of horses; that episode ended with one of the horses occupying the front seat of the car. It had been a messy accident.

While the roads were thought wide enough for the traffic of that day, they were narrow by current standards. One generally drove down the center, turning toward the right side when meeting another vehicle. There were no painted stripes on the graveled roads, and at night the only clue by which to steer was to watch the strip of soft gravel and vegetation along the roadside. Night driving with the Model-T was precarious because the car had magneto-powered lights, which illuminated the roadway poorly at slow speeds.

When Bert saw the team directly in his path he instantly turned the car toward the right ditch. There was a clash of metal, and a storm of dust engulfed them. Then the car lay in the ditch with him somewhere under it. He immediately thought of the others. The motor raced for an instant and then stopped. All was quiet.

"I'm not hurt," Bert called. "Any of you kids hurt?"

"We're not hurt."

He was able to crawl out through the space between the fender and the hood. Ernie stood holding his shoulder and Jane was limping about. The man riding with them had been thrown clear and except for a sprained wrist was unhurt. Cars stopped and several men turned the Ford onto its wheels. The young people and the hired man got in and drove into town. Jane had a cut on her thigh and Ernie suffered a broken collarbone. With a new windshield the car seemed little worse for the episode.

At about this same spot sometime later Bert, driving a Model-T pickup, turned out toward the left side of the road to pass a horse and buggy. When he brought the car into the center of the road again it swerved sharply toward the right. He corrected this only to have the steering wheel cramp violently to the left, whereupon the car skidded completely around on its wheels to face in the opposite direction. This momentum caused it to turn slowly over onto its right side along the edge of the road. The top of the car had been turned down and Bert fell out onto the opposite bank of the shallow ditch, landing on his back as the car slowly rolled down toward him. With his foot he could just reach the back of the front seat. He gave this a thrust to retard its fall, then leaped out of the way as with a horrible crash of windshield glass the car rolled into the ditch where he had been. There it lay upside down, the wheels whirling as the motor roared, the transmission still in high gear. He pulled the choke wire to stop it. It was apparent that the car was badly damaged, but, strangely, this did not matter. He felt about the happiest he could remember—he had had a close call and was unhurt. After supper Tom and he took a team and rope, righted the car, made temporary repairs, and drove it home.

Model-T Fords had a Y-shaped rod, called the wishbone, that held the front axle in position. The nut that secured one end of this to the axle had come loose and dropped off. This allowed the steering to become uncontrollable. The Ford Company corrected this problem on later models.

One Saturday night when the family was in town, Tom met Ernie and Bert on the street and invited them to go with him to the doctor's office. Sitting in a chair was a middle-aged woman with her face bandaged. In a consulting room the doctor worked over a man whose face was badly cut. A boy of about twelve entered and also stood observing. His arm was in a sling and he had a bandage or two about his face.

"Who was that, anyhow, an' whatever happened to 'em?" asked Ernie when they were again on the street.

"They had a wreck on the way into town tonight," replied Tom. "It must have been pretty bad."

"It sure didn't look very good," concluded Bert. "Why'd you take us up there to see 'em, anyhow?"

"I just thought you should know that with so many cars on the roads now, some pretty bad things can happen."

"Was there anyone else in the wreck?"

"You heard the lady saying, 'Poor Edith'? That's her daughter. Somebody said she was still unconscious. Neighbors comin' by in a truck brought 'em all in to the doctor."

On the way to church the next morning they drove to the scene of the mishap. The cars were still there, smashed together, each a total wreck. It was reported that the crash was heard in town, some two and a quarter miles away.

This was the first serious auto accident in the community. It bore witness to several points of concern: that the dusty, narrow, unmarked graveled roads were not safe for busy night travel; that as more cars and drivers found their places on the roads, better highways and traffic laws would be needed; and, finally, that Iowa had reached the point when more such accidents could be expected.

The Growing Importance of Gasoline

GASOLINE CAN BE DANGEROUS

THE lamp that supplied heat for the incubator had to be filled with kerosene daily. Tom kept kerosene in a fifty-five-gallon barrel painted black and gasoline in a similar red barrel. One evening Jean sent one of the children to the barrel to get a gallon of kerosene so that she could fill the incubator lamp. The next morning Tom placed cobs in the kitchen range and poured kerosene from the can over them. When he tossed the match into the firebox, there was a whoosh as the fire leaped from the opening and the firebox glowed full of bright, clear flames.

"What in the world was in that can!" he exclaimed in an amazed tone that could be heard throughout the house. "Mom, what's in this kerosene can, anyhow?"

"Well, it's kerosene." Jean hurried down the stairs. "It's kerosene. I filled the incubator lamp with it last night."

"You got gasoline in it from somewheres. You say you filled the incubator lamp with it?" Together they went to inspect. Tom lifted the damper and looked into the burning chamber above the lamp.

"Oh, that's too bright a flame for kerosene," said Jean. "I thought it was awfully bright when I looked at it at bedtime. Well, how do you suppose we got gasoline into it?"

Then she recalled that she had sent someone to refill the can. It had been toward dusk so that the colors on the barrels were probably not distinguishable and the can had been filled from the wrong barrel.

"Could have exploded an' burned the house down," commented Tom.

A few years later a neighbor was involved in a gasoline

fire. He had had to go on an errand late one night in summer but found that the car needed fuel. He drew a five-gallon can of gasoline from the barrel and when he picked it up to pour the gasoline into the car he apparently struck a spark with the steel can on the cement floor.

There was a flash of fire as a spot of spilled gasoline burst into flame. The fire leaped up the side of the can and began to burn from the top openings. In order not to burn his hand he thrust a stick through the handle of the flaming can and carried it outside, but in doing this he spilled burning gasoline. To save the car he pushed it out of the garage.

By this time the fire had spread. Realizing he could not control it alone he phoned neighbors and the fire department in town three and a half miles away. Fortunately, no other structures stood near the burning garage and there was no wind. By the time a fire truck arrived, it was too late to save the garage. When the fire died down they doused it with water from the stock tank. It was another incident suggesting that as people faced the approaching age of power they encountered dangers of which they were not fully aware, and they had insufficient information for dealing with them.

STARTING THE TRACTOR AND CAR IN WINTER

Grinding feed was a task performed periodically during the winter, and the tractor supplied the power for this job. The Fordson, like the Model-T, had a magneto that powered the ignition, and in cold weather a person cranking could not turn the motor fast enough to supply the necessary spark. To facilitate starting the tractor in winter, some farmers used a package of dry cells called the HOT SHOT battery to assist the ignition. Another option was to use the six-volt wet battery that powered their radio receivers.

One can now get attachments for preheating the motor, but these aids were unknown years ago. To preheat the tractor Tom spread corncobs on the ground under the crankcase. Over these he poured some kerosene and lighted it. From time to time he added a little used crankcase oil onto the fire to keep it going.

One could hear the oil in the crankcase sizzle as the heat

penetrated the heavy metal. After half an hour it was time to heat the fuel lines before cranking the tractor. To accomplish this he dipped two or three long corncobs into a can of kerosene and lighted them. These torches were held under the gasoline-filled carburetor as well as under the adjoining tubes through which the motor sucked fuel.

With the oil in the crankcase warm and the gasoline lines hot, the time to crank finally came. Sometimes the motor started promptly, but often they cranked for half an hour to get it going. Once started, the radiator was filled with water and a blanket was thrown over it to prevent cold air from passing through it and freezing the water until the motor and radiator became warm. Thermostats in motors were then unknown as were water pumps, pressure radiator caps, special coolants, and the like. Automobile owners often used a solution of alcohol and water in the radiator to prevent freezing during the winter, but alcohol was not generally used in the tractor radiator.

Problems in starting the car were also common during the winter. If alcohol was not used in the cooling system, a very good method for preparing the automobile for starting was to pour the radiator full of hot water. Another good trick was to pour a teakettleful of hot water over the carburetor and vapor tubes.

Another procedure that helped in starting the Model-T was to jack up a rear wheel and put the transmission into high gear. After these preparations, one pulled the choke wire with one hand and turned the crank as fast as possible with the other. Often the reward would be a burst from the motor that sent the rear wheel spinning while clouds of exhaust and water vapor engulfed the car, filling the garage with an impenetrable fog.

Prior to the use of alcohol as an antifreeze, the radiator was covered with a blanket after the car was started until the water in the radiator and motor became hot. If the radiator did not freeze when traveling on the road, it might freeze while standing at the destination. Accordingly, if the car was to stand for two or three hours in cold weather, a lighted kerosene lantern was placed under the radiator. With a blanket thrown over the front of the car to protect the lantern from the wind, freezing could be prevented. If alcohol was not used, radiators were drained in cold weather.

A neighbor had an unusual method for starting his tractor. He was shelling corn with a Titan tractor in cold weather. To prime the engine, ether was used. This was carried on the tractor in a pint-size can and squirted into the fuel line through a small hole.

Eight or ten men were waiting for the operations to begin, and after half an hour of futile cranking they considered some other method to start the engine. The upshot was that they wound a long rope onto the drive pulley of the tractor. Then with a fresh shot of ether in the manifold, several men took the free end of the rope and ran away from the tractor, rotating the motor at a good clip as the rope unwound. After repeating this maneuver several times the Titan started. Necessity often generated surprising examples of ingenuity.

Delivering the Rural Mail

MUDDY ROADS WERE A PROBLEM

THE rural mail route during the 1920s covered some twenty-five miles of country road. The route did not pass every farm, but usually the mailbox was within a mile of the farmhouse.

When Eddie began to carry the mail in the fall of 1921 he was delighted with his new job, but when rain set in during the fall he had problems.

"You're late tonight," remarked Jean when he arrived home for supper. "Did you have trouble?"

"No, I really didn't have trouble. It's just that most of the roads aren't graveled an' they're muddy. I drove in low about halfway around the route today."

"Are the other carriers having bad roads, too?"

"Well, Ham's route has more gravel than mine, so he was in an hour ahead of me. But Jess was still out when I came home. I was out for eight hours. That's an average of about three mile per hour, an' I used nearly a tank of gas."

"Well, I'm glad you've got a good car."

"Yow, the Model-Ts are good for carryin' the mail. Oscar's havin' trouble gettin' through the mud because his car is heavier than a Ford an' it's built closer to the ground. He got stuck twice yesterday. He would be there yet but a farmer came along each time an' pulled him out."

"Well," continued Jean, "it'll freeze up pretty soon an' then it'll be better."

"I hope the freeze comes soon an' that it doesn't snow 'til Christmas," replied Eddie. "Ham said he wore out the rear end of his Ford every year for the last three years from drivin' in the mud an' snow. That costs money, to say nothin' of what you spend for gasoline."

Though the fall and spring represented tough problems

for the mailmen, the winter was apt to be one long struggle. Covering the twenty-five miles during a snowstorm was no snap. Rural carriers then received $150 per month, with no mileage allowance. During some months surprisingly little of this would be left after paying bills for repairs and gasoline.

BUCKING THE SNOWDRIFTS

Cars of that day had either no heaters or very poor ones. Instead of comfortable sedans, the touring car was the usual model, and the best protection from the cold that one could expect was to have oilcloth side curtains with celluloid windows.

Early one morning during Christmas vacation in 1925 Eddie, who then was married and lived in town, phoned. Because of the storm the night before, he would need help to get around the route and he asked whether Bert or Ernie could ride with him. Bert walked a mile to the graveled road and met him there.

"Don't look like you'll have much trouble if the roads are all like this," suggested Bert.

"Oh, this road is beautiful. The farmers coming to town keep the first two or three miles open well enough so I can get through most of the time." He brought the Ford to a sliding stop at a mailbox, thrust his hand out through the side curtain, tipped open the front of the mailbox, and shoved the mail into it. Then as he stepped on the low pedal he slammed the mailbox door, thrust the car into the center of the road, and dropped it into high gear. "I can make the first few miles in no time at all, but when we get out into the boondocks you'll see why I need you today."

"Wow," said Bert after they had turned onto a narrow dirt road. "Nobody's been along here today an' it's drifted full."

Eddie kicked the car into low gear as they struck a drift that ran completely across the road. The car lurched through, the axles dragging. Then, stopping on a bare spot, they got out and put on the chains. With the car in high gear they plowed into the drifts as fast as they could go. When the car lost momentum Eddie thrust it into low and jerked the throt tle to the bottom. The car plunged and bucked as it lurched through. At last, after much snorting, it stopped. He put it into reverse, backed out of the drift, and making another run at it gained a few more feet. Again he backed up and attacked. Again it stalled. This time, however, when he tried to reverse, the rear wheels spun, digging down until the frame of the car rested on the crust. There it sat, the radiator boiling.

They shoveled the crusted snow from under the axles and running boards until the weight of the car again rested on the wheels. After scooping a fresh track ahead of the front wheels through the rest of the drift, they prepared to move the car.

"You drive an' I'll push," directed Eddie.

With the first attempt, the car traveled but a few inches. Then putting it quickly into reverse, Bert moved it backward a foot or so. Again thrusting it into low he moved forward for another gain; then he reversed it again, never forcing the rear wheels to spin. With Eddie alternately pushing and pulling, Bert continued through the drifted section and they were again on clean roadway. This experience was repeated several times in the next six or eight miles. Often they parked the car while they scooped ahead of it for 100 feet or more.

Twelve or fifteen miles out from town they came to a road on which there was but one house, and it was nearly two miles away. This road was drifted deep as far as they could see.

"You don't mean to tell me you're gonna try to go down that road?" asked Bert as Eddie placed the mail into the box at the corner.

"Not on your life. I prob'ly won't go down that road 'til April or May. Certainly not 'til the snow's all gone an' it's dried up. When it thaws, there'll be a couple of ponds down there you could row a boat on. The water'll stand over the road 'til the middle of April, maybe even into May. So we'll turn an' go four miles around to get to that farmhouse; then we got pretty good sailin'."

As they approached the farm Eddie turned into the barnyard. "We've got a package for these people an' I could put it in the mailbox, but we'd better see whether we need water in the radiator. After the way it boiled a ways back, there's prob'ly no alcohol left in it an' not much water."

"That's my late Christmas package," said the lady when Eddie approached the door. "My, but you look cold. Come in and have a cup of hot coffee, both of you."

"Four o'clock," said Bert as they were leaving the house after a brief respite over a cup of coffee beside a warm stove.

"Yep. Be dark by the time we get to town. There's a couple of drifts ahead for us yet, but it's likely cars have been through them before now."

Mail carriers through the previous dozen years had used various means of transportation. One carrier during World War I carried the mail in a one-horse cart. When the roads were too difficult he rode the horse. Carriers commonly used a buggy chassis onto which an enclosed cab was built, and one even installed a small coal-burning stove for warmth. At their own expense some would hire a farmer to drive them about the route in a bobsled when snow prevented the use of a car.

The carrier spent about an hour in the post office preparing the mail. Once he was out on the route he could complete the twenty-five-mile circuit in about four hours if the roads were good. Traveling over muddy or drifted roads presented serious problems until during the late 1920s and 30s when most mail roads were graded to a good highway standard and graveled.

Leisure Time

WHEN THERE WASN'T ANYTHING TO DO

THE children found unending ways for passing their leisure time. When living on the big Magnussen farm a favorite Sunday afternoon pastime during summer was to ride the horses through the grove bareback and without bridles. The rider directed his mount with a stick. The more fractious horses would run among the trees, through narrow passages, and under low boughs in attempts to dislodge the rider. One had to be alert to lift up his legs so as not to be crushed against a tree and to duck under approaching limbs. Tom chided the children for pestering the horses, for they had worked all week and should be allowed to rest on Sunday. But it was good fun and they continued. One Sunday afternoon Ernie, mounted on an uncooperative mare, found her running through a narrow opening between a tree and the corner post of the yard. He lifted his leg to prevent it from being rammed against the post, when in an instant he found himself lying on the ground and the horse trotting away. He had not seen a wire that ran from the top of the high corner post to the nearby tree; this had struck him across the chest and held him while the horse ran from under him. He fell to the ground unhurt, whereupon he decided that Tom was right; the horses should rest on Sunday.

On rainy days the children often played in the cattle barn. Heavy timbers were built across the haymow and spiked in pairs to opposite sides of posts. These were spaced perhaps twenty feet apart about eight feet above the ground. A favorite prank, when playing chase, was for the pursued to climb up and run across these timbers or to slide down the center post in the middle of the empty haymow.

In an adventurous mood one day, Bert crossed out to the center of the timbers to go down the center post, but instead of sliding feet first he lay down on the timbers and lowered his head and shoulders. With his knees hooked over the top he clasped his arms tightly around the post below, transferred his legs down, and slid down head first.

It was a good trick, which he practiced for several weeks. But one afternoon as he lowered his legs into position he forgot to keep the tension on the post with his arms. In an instant he found himself at the bottom, his head painfully twisted to one side as it struck the hay beneath him. For a moment he lay in a heap, trying to understand what had happened. Gingerly he got up, tested his arms and legs, and then went about some other activity. That ended his sliding down the pole head first.

HOME BREW

On their excursions about the farm one fall, Bert and Ernie found a lush crop of currantlike berries, which when ripe were of excellent flavor. After cautiously tasting them, they ate their fill. When there were no unsatisfactory results they decided to crush enough to fill a half-gallon fruit jar, added some sugar, and set it aside to see what would develop.

They hid the jar in the orchard until after dark and then buried it in the landlord's oats bin, which was over the driveway of the corncrib. The following Sunday they tasted it. It was excellent. It would have been fine to have consumed it just as it was, but they decided to let their original plan run its course. They would sample it again later.

The landlord visited the farm the following spring, and while there he sold his oats. They got out the teams and began to haul. To fill the wagon they drove into the driveway of the corncrib and opened the chutes in the floor of the overhead bins, allowing the oats to run out into the wagon. After removing a few loads, Tom, the landlord, and both boys all happened to be up in the bin at the same time. In the corner of the bin where the oats had been drained was a lump of blue, matted, discolored oats intermixed with broken glass. Tom dug cautiously into it, looking questioningly at the boys but saying nothing. The boys kept straight faces. They realized that they had buried their jar of berries in that corner and then had forgotten all about it. During the winter the fruit had frozen and burst the jar, saturating the grain nearby with a bluish tinge and spoiling perhaps a bushel of oats.

It had seemed like such an interesting experiment. They speculated later how they could have completely forgotten to follow it up. They wondered also what the consequences might have been if it had fermented and they had drunk it and become intoxicated. Perhaps the fates had decreed that since the family was known for its total abstinence, they were not even to be tempted.

SATURDAY NIGHT

It was a Saturday night in the summer of 1924 and Ernie, Jane, and Bert went off to town. While still a half mile from the main road to Westover they could see the dust rising along the graveled road. Down this road on Saturday night farm families went to do the week's shopping, sell their produce, and visit with friends whom they seldom saw at any other time during the busy summer.

As they parked the car Jane handed the grocery list to Bert. Since he would take the eggs to the store she suggested that he get the groceries. "An' here's fifty cents Mom gave me to get Sunday school collection. Get ten nickels with it."

"Where are you goin'?" inquired Bert.

"I have to meet Lorraine by the post office. I'll see you again about ten o'clock," replied Jane, and she was gone.

"Well, I have to get a haircut," Bert said to Ernie. "I'll help you carry the eggs to the store. Then why don't you stay an' get the groceries? If I don't get to the barbershop soon, it may be an hour before I can get into the chair. There's a line waitin' already."

Jane and Lorraine set out to stroll up and down the two-block business district. A favorite pastime of the older boys was to drive their cars along the street, alert for friends to whom they called as they passed. Careful jockeying by the driver and the young ladies on foot would sometimes bring them to the crosswalk simultaneously, where a few words were exchanged. This often ended with the young ladies being invited to get in and go for a ride. Jane and Lorraine walked the circuit, stopping now and then to get a bag of popcorn or an ice cream cone and keeping an eye on what was going on.

At the grocery store Ernie, munching peanuts, presented the eggs and waited for the credit slip. When it was ready he gave his list to the grocer, who put up the order. The grocer also took the fifty cents and returned ten nickels. After taking the groceries to the car Ernie went to the barbershop. "How much longer will you be?" he asked Bert.

"Well, Ole's gotta have a shave tonight, so that'll take another ten minutes. I figured to be out in an hour, but I guess I won't. You'd think a grown man like him could shave at home, wouldn't you?"

Back on the street Ernie, now a seventh grader, encountered a friend and they decided to go to the school grounds and play on the recreation equipment. Here they climbed up the ladder and went down the slide. Hurrying back up the ladder they were about to go down again when two couples approached from across the street. The boys seated themselves in the swings and with the girls on their laps began to swing as they whispered and giggled.

"Who is it?" asked Ernie in a hushed voice.

"I can't tell. But le's slide down with a big yell an' beat it. That'll scare 'em good." Accordingly, with a boisterous "YEEOOUEEE!" they slid down and ran.

Back at the barbershop Ernie found Bert still waiting. Bert pointed to a chair that had just been vacated. The occupant now sat on a stool with his head bent over the sink. "You mean Herman's gonna have the barber wash his hair?" Ernie was incensed.

"Reckon so. Looks like that'll take another ten minutes. I could have been in the chair by now if he'd just had his hair cut. Never saw a guy come in here before an' have someone else wash his hair."

"Yow, what kind of a sissy is he, anyhow, I wonder."

By this time others were also losing patience. "I got some things to do yet," announced one farmer. "If you get around to where you got time to cut my hair, I may come back."

"Only be about ten minutes, now, I think," said the barber, somewhat embarrassed.

"Yow, well, I waited an hour, already. Maybe it'll have

to grow for another week," the farmer said as he departed.

To avoid the problem of waiting, barbers later installed a numbering system. In using this plan a client took a ticket and went about his business until his number appeared on a lighted panel visible from the street. Then he went to the shop, knowing that he would be next in the chair.

On cement blocks in front of several stores merchants had placed long boards for benches where men in clean overalls sat talking.

"Well, maybe you'll not believe it, but with that new Oliver tractor of mine I cut thirty acres of oats yesterday. Wasn't sure I could do it. But we was out there before six in the mornin' an' I said to the boys, I said, 'Now boys, if you've ever put in a day's work at shockin' you're gonna put in one today, 'cause I aim to keep you steppin'. An' Ole, he said to me, he said, 'Paw, you cut 'er down an' we'll set 'er up.' Well, sir, at eight in the evenin' we was all through."

"Yeh, you can cut oats with 'em all right. Now that Hart Parr I bought this spring—"

The women gathered around the counters in the stores, holding small children while older youngsters held to their skirts or raced about.

"Now Susan, you quit hangin' on my dress. How you think I can hold Jessie in my arms all night here with you pullin' on my skirt. Run along an' play with Jossie. Go on now. Honestly, Pearl, kids make me tired. Don't know why I always come an' bring 'em ever' Saturday night, anyhow."

"Prob'ly for the same reason I do, Tillie. It's tiresome to bring 'em an' come, but it's tiresomer to stay home after you been there all week already."

In the middle of the block a man and his son ran a produce business. They bought cream and poultry for cash, and on Saturday night farmers brought their produce here and waited to get the checks.

"You buy chickens?" asked a stranger who entered through the rear door at about nine o'clock.

"Yeh, we buy chickens," responded the owner as he surveyed the stranger.

"Got a couple coops in the pickup. We'll bring 'em in."

"Can we have the money in cash?" asked one of the men. "I have to get a casting for my binder an' I have to buy some groceries. I don't know anybody here an' I might not be able to get a check cashed."

"Every merchant in town knows my checks," replied the owner of the shop. "My checks is my bookkeepin' record. I can't pay cash." Looking knowingly at his son he pointed casually with his thumb toward the street. The two men were obviously nervous. No one in the room knew them. It was the time of year for chicken thieves, and some farmers had reported poultry stolen.

Leaving the office the son walked across the street to the business place of the mayor. The two exchanged a few words and then both went out. The mayor crossed the street to the produce office. As he entered he greeted several of those who waited. He knew all of them but the two strangers.

"Where are you men from?" he asked. "I don't think I ever saw either of you before."

"No," one of them replied. "We don't come to Westover often. But I had to get a part for my binder at the implement store, so we thought we'd bring our chickens here while we was at it."

"Are these your chicken crates?" asked the mayor, examining the coops.

"Yow, they're ours."

"Well, those have the name of a poultry dealer in Hysop. That's fifteen mile from here. How do you happen to have his coops?"

"We live near Hysop. We sell chickens to him all the time so we borrow his coops now an' then."

"Well, you know what I'd do if I was you? I'd load them back onto the pickup an' take them back to Hysop."

"Well, we got rid of 'em," said the dealer when they had gone. "I don't intend to be caught buyin' stolen chickens."

"We really had nothing on them," replied the mayor. "But we don't want every chicken thief bringing his loot here to sell. If they come back again, let me know."

"How much money you got left?" inquired Bert as they sauntered along the street.

"I just got ten cents, I spent a nickel for peanuts while you was in the barbershop. How much you got?"

"It took most of mine for the haircut, but I got a dime. Le's go to the Sweet Shop an' get a candy bar."

The Sweet Shop was crowded with teenagers. On the wall three large oscillating fans droned steadily. Behind the counter the owner and two high school girls dispensed malted milks, ice cream cones, and sundaes to the milling throng. The air was blue with cigarette smoke and humid from the press of people. At the counter the boys paid for candy bars and went back out into the street.

"Wonder where Jane is. Have you seen her?" inquired Ernie.

"She and Lorraine walked past the barbershop once, but I didn't see them again. It's nearly time for us to go home. Wonder where she is anyhow?"

At the corner cafe they spent their last nickels for ice cream cones and stood outside on the sidewalk eating them. At this point Jane and Lorraine appeared out of the shadows from the direction of the school grounds.

"Where you been?" asked Bert. "We been waitin' for you. You know Mom said for us to start for home by ten o'clock."

UNWANTED VISITORS

Neither Tom nor Jean, as a rule, went to town on Saturday night. While there was no evidence that any of their poultry or livestock had ever been stolen, there were occasions every year when it appeared that someone had been on the premises at night. Besides this, there was always the possibility that the cattle might get out. For these reasons someone usually stayed at home.

One hot Saturday at twilight when Jean was alone she went to the front porch to sit in the breeze. As she relaxed there, the dog came around the house with his head up, making little questioning growls down in his throat. Then with threatening barks he ran down along the tomato patch at the end of the sweet corn rows. Soon Jean heard the leaves of the corn rustling, and this sound crept toward the end of the corn patch where the house stood. The dog continued threatening as he paced back and forth.

"Go get him, Bob," she urged. "Get him; take him out of there. Go get him, Boy!"

The dog ran a few paces into the corn, growling and barking furiously. The rustling stopped, then began to move away toward the far end of the corn patch. The fence at the end squeaked. It was about dark. Nothing was visible. They always kept a good watchdog, and Jean was especially glad that Bob was alert to what was going on that night.

Dairying as an Auxiliary Industry

THE GUERNSEY HERD

IN the spring of 1922 Tom bought ten Guernsey heifer calves, some of which had not yet been taught to drink milk from a pail. Ernie set about to teach one of them to do this. Straddling the calf's neck, and with a pail of warm milk on the ground in front of her, he dipped his fingers into the milk and inserted them into the calf's mouth. When the calf tasted the milk she turned her nose upward as she had done when nursing her mother and sucked hungrily at Ernie's fingers. Ernie pushed his hand slowly into the pail to lead the calf's nose down toward the milk. But before she reached the milk the calf thrust her nose skyward again, and Ernie's fingers slipped out. Dipping his fingers, Ernie tried again, and after several balks he brought the calf's nose into the milk.

The half-starved young bovine buried her nose in the fluid as she awkwardly opened and closed her mouth in an effort to drink. But because her tongue was tightly wrapped about Ernie's fingers she got little more than a taste. Frustrated, the animal thrust her nose at the bottom of the pail, chewed on Ernie's fingers, and when out of breath, yanked her head from the pail, exhaling milk from her nose and mouth all over Ernie's pants and smearing his arm up to the elbow.

With his hand again in the calf's mouth Ernie twisted his hand sidewise and spread his fingers apart to let the milk flow through. After several false starts the calf got the hang of it and began to gulp the milk haltingly. In a few days, after additional training, she learned to drink by herself.

When grown, the Guernseys proved to be gentle and their milk was rich. It was one of Tom's better investments.

The small dairyman like Tom milked by hand, and during the hot summer it was sometimes an unpleasant chore.

Flies pestered the cows constantly. To combat this the cows were sprayed with a fly repellant. Even then they switched their tails, often hitting the milker about the head or wrapping their tails about his neck. If the spray was not effective or if the cow could not dislodge the flies by switching, she often stamped her feet. To do this she brought her hind foot forward in a stiff-legged kick that sometimes upset the pail. Or sometimes she would thrust her foot into the pail so that the milk had to be thrown out. The milker sat on a low stool, and to guard against kicking he held the pail up between his knees. The cow shifted her weight toward the left as she prepared to kick with her right leg. The milker could detect this and to thwart her he would thrust his left arm in front of her right leg, seizing the hamstring of her left leg. When she brought her right leg forward, his arm stopped it. Another way of preventing kicking was to tie the cow's legs with a rope crossed above the hocks. One of the best safeguards against kicking was a chain that was hooked onto the hamstring of the left hind leg, passed around outside of each leg, and attached to the hamstring of the right leg.

Milk is manufactured within the cow's udder and dispensed through four teats. At the top of each teat is a looplike muscle that remains closed most of the time to prevent milk in the udder from passing down into the teat. When a calf nurses or someone milks the cow, this sphincter muscle opens, releasing milk down into the teat. The bottom of the teat is closed by another such muscle, which prevents milk in the teat from dripping out.

With the thumb and forefinger encircling the teat near its top, the milker squeezes to close the top of the teat, preventing the milk from surging back up into the udder. Then closing the next finger and the next, and finally the little finger, he squeezes the milk from the teat. With practice he performs this rapidly, and the cow lets down milk as fast as he extracts it.

When milking is finished, each teat is stripped. To do this the milker continues until he is certain that no more milk is available. Repeated failure to thoroughly strip the cow leaves some milk in the udder and causes her to give less and less until she dries up prematurely.

The boys one time counted the number of squirts of milk

and found that it took about twenty-five hundred to fill a three-gallon pail. This was about fifty squirts of milk for each eight ounces, a fact probably never considered by one hungrily consuming a glass of milk.

At about this time Tom began to sell cream to a restaurant, and soon two families in town asked him to deliver milk daily. Ernie and Bert, who were going to school in town, delivered it. Milk then retailed for seven cents per quart. The customers put the money into the empty bottles daily, and the boys were permitted to have this income for their own use. At that time a nickel would buy a package of theme paper, two pencils, an ice cream cone, a candy bar, or a pack of gum containing five sticks.

Tom and the boys were milking fifteen to eighteen cows, and a five-gallon can of cream would be ready for the creamery at least twice each week. There were several years when this income netted the family more than enough to cover their grocery costs. Later, when several other families also asked to buy milk and cream, the boys had a small milk route to service daily before school. A little later a local grocery store asked to handle Tom's milk for retail; as a result most of their customers then went to the store for their milk.

THE CREAMERY

All through this period Westover had a cooperative creamery. It stood on the corner of Main Street, across from the school grounds, and here the farmers delivered bulk cream. Because the creamery depended upon a constant daily supply for regular operation, it employed men driving a fleet of trucks to go about the countryside collecting cream. Each driver had two routes that he covered twice weekly.

In 1929, when Bert was teaching rural school, he had finished his day's work and was about to leave the building when the door burst open and two men came in, asking if they could get warm.

"Well, there's not much fire left in the stove, but it's twelve below outside, so it's a lot warmer in here than out there. Go ahead and get warm," he replied.

They opened the stove door and spread their hands toward the dying fire as they stamped and absorbed the warmth of the room.

"How do you happen to be out on the road freezin' to death?" Bert inquired.

"I haul for the creamery in Westover, an' I can't drive the truck because of the snow, so we had to take the bobsled. We've been on the road since six this mornin' an' it's still eight miles to the creamery. We saw your flag still up so we figured maybe you'd let us get warm."

It was now approaching four thirty and beginning to be dusk. "I'd say you two will be a little late for supper," jested Bert. "I expect you've got mostly ice cream in those cans by this time."

"You can say that again. Some of it was froze when we picked it up at ten this morning. But we'll set it into the creamery an' they'll turn a steam hose onto it. By churnin' time in the mornin' it'll be thawed out."

When a can of cream was presented at the creamery, the contents were weighed and a sample was taken for testing the butterfat. Twice a month a check was issued to each farmer. When the cream had been weighed and sampled, the contents were poured into a vat for pasteurizing. After the can was emptied it was cleaned with a steam jet and set out on a platform for the owner to reclaim it. Cans collected by truck were returned to the drivers, who returned them to the farmers on the next trip. A familiar sound on Main Street each morning was the cream trucks jolting along the street, the empty cans rattling and banging together as the drivers took off for the day's run.

The churn in the creamery was a drum perhaps four feet in diameter and eight or so feet long. The cream was piped into it, the openings closed, and the churn rotated. When the churning was finished the buttermilk was removed. Then water was introduced into the churn to wash the butter, after which salt and coloring were added and the churn opened. The butter was removed and placed into tubs. Some of this was sold locally, the rest being shipped to other cities.

The buttermilk from churning was piped into a storage tank, which had to be emptied daily. Most of it went for pig swill. Churning began early in the morning, and by four or five o'clock farmers with pickup trucks or with trailers behind

225

their cars could be seen going to get their day's supply of buttermilk for the pigs. For this they paid one cent per gallon. However, not all of the buttermilk ended up as pig swill. On the floor of the churning room there was usually a five-gallon can of it and anyone wanting a drink of buttermilk could have as much as he could drink. It was free.

Time to Slow Down

THESE were good years for Tom and his family, but by 1928 it was apparent that changes in his future were in the making. One by one the older children left home. His supply of home-grown help was coming to an end. After almost twenty years of strenuous activity he realized that he could not continue the pace indefinitely. He used the tractor a great deal, he hired help more often, and, excepting for the busiest seasons, he and the boys did not work in the fields on Saturday afternoons. He began to talk about semiretirement. The years had been good to him and it was not an easy decision. He held on until 1935, when he bought a small farm and began to decelerate.

Epilogue

DRIVING through the Midwest some seventy years after the inception of this saga, one finds a checkerboard of paved highways with connecting well-graveled roads where narrow dirt roads had prevailed in 1913. Along these traffic arteries behemoths of trucks now roll where the buggy, the wagon, and the bobsled had prevailed prior to 1920. In the fields tractors of new and strange design, some huge in comparison with earlier models, pull machines the size, shape, and purpose of which seem strange to one gone from the farm for fifty years.

At the site of the farmstead where Tom's sister had lived and where the family had stayed briefly on arrival in Iowa, only the broken-down walls of the cellar, the remnants of some other buildings, and a few trees remain. The house where the family had first lived by themselves in the new land has been gone since 1920. At the farm where they next lived, their first independent venture after arriving, completely new buildings stand today.

At their next location, where once a thirty-acre grove enclosing all of the feedlots, barns, and other buildings necessary for operating a five-hundred-acre farm proudly reposed in 1920, now only the corncrib and windmill, without its wheel, remain. Not one tree, rock, or other familiar object can be seen. A visit to the location of that farmyard by one who had spent several strenuous years working, eating, and sleeping there proved indeed to be a futile venture into nostalgia.

In instance after instance, one finds a set of buildings from which several surrounding farms are operated, the original structures of the latter falling to pieces or torn down. If the house is livable it may be occupied by a retired couple, a widow still enjoying the security of the land where she had spent her prime years, or a young family who earn their income in a nearby town or city.

In the towns and small cities, retired farmers now collect daily at the cafes for morning and afternoon coffee, some to discuss with friends their winter residences in Florida, Arizona, or California. But to them home is where their land is.

ABOUT THE AUTHOR

FLOYD A. ROBINSON was born in Indiana in 1909 but moved to north central Iowa as a child and was raised on farms and educated in the rural school system.

He learned to ride a horse bareback at the age of six. Also, when he was six he used a team and cultivator in the field, working a full day with his father and older brothers. By the time he was in the sixth grade he could harness a four-horse team, hitch them to an implement, and work all day alone. In the seventh grade he could service the Fordson tractor and with it disc or plow all day by himself.

He graduated from Iowa State Teachers College, now University of Northern Iowa, and received the M.S. degree from the University of Minnesota. For twelve years he taught in rural schools and small cities in Iowa. He retired after thirty-nine years, teaching also in Michigan and California.